Practical Conformal Prediction with Python

Build Reliable and Trustworthy AI with Uncertainty Quantification, Prediction Intervals, Model Calibration, and Conformal Prediction in Python

Ravindra Sharma

www.orangeava.com

First Published: August 2026

Published By: Orange Education Pvt Ltd, AVA®

Address: 9, Daryaganj, Delhi, 110002, India

275 New North Road Islington Suite 1314 London,
N1 7AA, United Kingdom

ISBN (PBK): 978-81-69646-41-3
ISBN (E-BOOK): 978-81-69646-42-0

Scan the QR code to explore our entire catalogue

www.orangeava.com

Get a Free eBook

We hope you're enjoying your recent book purchase! Your feedback is incredibly valuable to us and helps other readers discover books that truly make a difference.

If you found this book useful or enjoyable, we'd greatly appreciate it if you could leave a short review with a 5-star rating on Amazon. Your review supports our work and allows us to reach more learners worldwide.

As a thank-you, we're happy to offer you a **free digital copy of this book** plus a **30% discount code** for your next purchase on our official websites:

www.orangeava.com

www.orangeava.in (For the Indian Subcontinent).

☑ **How it works:**

Leave your review on Amazon, take a screenshot of the confirmation or use the following link to submit the claim and email it to **info@orangeava.com.** Once received the required detail, we will send your rewards within 24 hours, **along with one month free subcription to the book on AVA SkillShelf!**

Claim Form

https://rebrand.ly/4d2477

Thank you for your support—it truly means a lot to us.

Downloading the code bundles and colored images

Please follow the links or scan the QR codes to download the ***Code Bundles and Images*** of the book:

https://github.com/ava-orange-education/Practical-Conformal-Prediction-with-Python

The code bundles and images of the book are also hosted on ***https://rebrand.ly/68pqkgj***

In case there's an update to the code, it will be updated on the existing GitHub repository.

Errata

We take immense pride in our work at **Orange Education Pvt Ltd,** and follow the best practices to ensure the accuracy of our content to provide an indulging reading experience to our subscribers. Our readers are our mirrors, and we use their inputs to reflect and improve upon human errors, if any, that may have occurred during the publishing processes involved. To let us maintain the quality and help us reach out to any readers who might be having difficulties due to any unforeseen errors, please write to us at:

errata@orangeava.com

Your support, suggestions, and feedback are highly appreciated.

Dedicated to

My Beloved Family:
Geeta Sharma, Anil Sharma,
Radha Sharma, Saurabh Sharma, and
My Nephew, Vivaan Sharma.

About the Author

Ravindra Sharma is a Senior Data Scientist with over seven years of experience developing and deploying machine learning solutions across a wide range of industries and business domains. Throughout his career, he has worked in diverse environments, from fast-paced startups to multinational consulting organizations, gaining experience in both product-driven and client-focused roles. This breadth of experience has enabled him to bridge the gap between technology and practical, business-oriented solutions.

Ravindra holds a Bachelor's degree in Electronics and Communication Engineering from the Indian Institute of Information Technology, Design and Manufacturing (IIITDM), Jabalpur. His professional expertise encompasses stakeholder management, data-driven decision-making, AI strategy, machine learning solution delivery, and translating business challenges into scalable, data-driven solutions.

Driven by the belief that a data scientist is first and foremost, a problem solver, Ravindra is passionate about making advanced machine learning concepts accessible to practitioners and learners alike. He regularly shares technical insights through articles and tutorials published on platforms such as GeeksforGeeks, Medium, and Towards Data Science, and has also authored research work presented at academic conferences.

Through this book, Ravindra aims to make the rapidly growing field of uncertainty-aware machine learning approachable for students, researchers, and industry practitioners by combining intuitive explanations with practical, hands-on Python implementations. His goal is to help readers build AI systems that are not only accurate but also reliable, transparent, and trustworthy.

About the Technical Reviewer

Shashank Gollapudi is a Staff Software Engineer with more than 16 years of experience building large-scale distributed systems across the social media/ads and financial services industries. He specializes in real-time data platforms processing 10M+ events per second, privacy-preserving advertising infrastructure, and audience targeting systems that drive billions in revenue.

His work spans privacy-enhancing cryptographic frameworks, dynamic auto-scaling architectures, and experimentation platforms. Previously, Shashank led cloud migrations and data governance initiatives in commercial banking. He holds a Master's degree in Management Information Systems, and is proficient in Python, Java, and C++.

Acknowledgments

There are several individuals to whom I owe my sincere gratitude for their unwavering support and encouragement throughout the writing of this book. First and foremost, I would like to express my deepest gratitude to my parents for their constant encouragement, patience, and belief in me. Their steadfast support has been invaluable in the successful completion of this book.

I would like to thank my friends, Megha, Bhupi and Kushal, for their valuable insights, constructive feedback, and encouragement throughout the writing process. Their expertise and support are sincerely appreciated.

I would also like to express my sincere gratitude to the editorial team at Orange Education Pvt Ltd for their encouragement, understanding, and constant support throughout the writing of this book. Their flexibility and confidence in this work provided me with the time and opportunity needed to bring this book to completion.

Preface

This book is an ultimate practical guide to understanding and implementing conformal prediction for building trustworthy, uncertainty-aware machine learning systems. The book introduces the fundamental concepts of conformal prediction, a model-agnostic, distribution-free framework for quantifying predictive uncertainty and demonstrates their practical application through clear explanations and hands-on Python examples based on real-world problems using illustrative datasets. Covering both the theoretical foundations and practical implementation, it enables readers to bridge the gap between predictive accuracy and reliability.

Hence, whether you are a data scientist, machine learning engineer, researcher, or student, this book provides the knowledge and tools to develop AI systems that are not only accurate but also transparent, robust, and dependable. By fostering a deeper understanding of predictive uncertainty and model reliability, the concepts presented in this book are applicable across a wide range of machine learning tasks, from simple predictive models to complex, large-scale AI systems, making conformal prediction an essential component of every machine learning practitioner's toolkit.

This book is organized into seven chapters, beginning with the Python environment and code setup required for all experiments. It then introduces the application of conformal prediction across major machine learning tasks, including regression, classification, and forecasting, before exploring techniques for scaling these methods, and deploying them in real-world scenarios across diverse domains such as finance and retail. Throughout the book, all the concepts are explained in a clear and intuitive manner using visualizations, real-world examples, hands-on Python exercises, and chapter-end quizzes to reinforce learning, and keep readers engaged. The following is a brief chapter-wise summary:

Chapter 1 introduces the motivation behind Conformal Prediction (CP) by addressing the fundamental issue of uncertainty in machine learning. It explains why traditional models, while accurate, fail to express confidence in their predictions, and how this limitation undermines decision reliability. Readers will learn the concept of distribution-free, model-agnostic uncertainty estimation, and understand why Conformal Prediction offers a critical step toward building trustworthy AI systems.

Chapter 2 builds the theoretical base for Conformal Prediction, covering its statistical principles, calibration methods, and key assumptions. It introduces conformity scores, exchangeability, and coverage concepts - the mathematical building blocks that make CP both valid and model-independent. Readers also set up their Python environment and get familiar with the essential CP libraries.

Chapter 3 explores how Conformal Prediction extends to classification problems, transforming single-label outputs into calibrated prediction sets. It walks through Inductive, Mondrian, and Adaptive CP methods with detailed Python implementations, helping readers handle imbalanced data and evolving distributions.

Chapter 4 introduces Conformal Prediction for continuous targets, focusing on constructing prediction intervals that maintain statistical validity. It explains Split, Cross, Jackknife+, and Quantile-based approaches, with exercises using real datasets. Readers learn how to balance interval width with coverage to create interpretable and efficient models.

Chapter 5 adapts Conformal Prediction to time-series forecasting, where the exchangeability assumption breaks due to temporal order. It covers sliding-window, weighted and adaptive approaches to maintain valid uncertainty estimates over time, with applications in energy and demand forecasting.

Chapter 6 focuses on computational scalability in Conformal Prediction, detailing techniques to handle large, high-dimensional, or streaming datasets. Readers learn methods like batch calibration, approximate quantile estimation, and distributed computation for real-world deployment.

Chapter 7, the final chapter wraps everything together, and connects Conformal Prediction to modern AI applications, showcasing its role in different domains like finance, retail, and so on through end to end case studies.

DID YOU KNOW

Did you know that Orange Education Pvt Ltd offers eBook versions of every book published, with PDF and ePub files available? You can upgrade to the eBook version at **www.orangeava.com** and as a print book customer, you are entitled to a discount on the eBook copy. Get in touch with us at: **info@orangeava.com** for more details.

At **www.orangeava.com**, you can also read a collection of free technical articles, sign up for a range of free newsletters, and receive exclusive discounts and offers on Print Books and eBooks.

PIRACY

If you come across any illegal copies of our works in any form on the internet, we would be grateful if you would provide us with the location address or website name. Please contact us at **info@orangeava.com** with a link to the material.

ARE YOU INTERESTED IN AUTHORING WITH US?

If there is a topic that you have expertise in, and you are interested in either writing or contributing to a book, please write to us at **business@orangeava.com**. We are on a journey to help developers and tech professionals to gain insights on the present technological advancements and innovations happening across the globe and build a community that believes Knowledge is best acquired by sharing and learning with others. Please reach out to us to learn what our audience demands and how you can be part of this educational reform. We also welcome ideas from tech experts and help them build learning and development content for their domains.

REVIEWS

Please leave a review. Once you have read and used this book, why not leave a review on the site that you purchased it from? Potential readers can then see and use your unbiased opinion to make purchase decisions. We at Orange Education would love to know what you think about our products, and our authors can learn from your feedback. Thank you!

For more information about Orange Education, please visit **www.orangeava.com**.

Table of Contents

Chapter 1
The Illusion of Certainty

Introduction

Before we can learn *how* to quantify uncertainty in Machine Learning (ML), we need to understand *why* it matters. Machine learning models are often celebrated for their ability to uncover patterns, and make accurate predictions. Yet, despite all their power, most models return just a **single prediction:** a house price, a sentiment label, a demand forecast without telling us **how confident they are** in that prediction.

In the real world, that missing piece is not just a detail, it can be the difference between a safe decision and a risky one.

Thus, whether you are setting a medical dose, deciding loan eligibility, or forecasting the next week's demand in a supply chain, uncertainty is always present. Sometimes it comes from the **randomness in the world itself**. Other times, it arises because the **model simply does not know enough**. In either case, the cost of ignoring that uncertainty can be high leading to flawed decisions, broken trust, and even real-world harm.

This chapter lays the foundation for the key ideas we will build upon throughout the book. We will explore what uncertainty means in machine learning, why it happens, and why it is dangerous to ignore. Therefore, by the end, you will be ready to appreciate the true value of the framework this book is all about such as: **conformal prediction,** a principled way to produce predictions you can trust.

Structure

This chapter is organized into five sections, each building toward a complete understanding of the confidence problem in machine learning:

- The Confidence Gap in Machine Learning
- Understanding and Quantifying Uncertainty
- Types of Uncertainty

- Foundations of Conformal Prediction
- Python Setup

The Confidence Gap in Machine Learning

When we build machine learning models, we often focus on getting accurate predictions. But in most real-world applications, accuracy alone is not enough — what truly matters is how confident we can be in those predictions. Decisions like approving a loan, diagnosing a disease, or forecasting demand all depend not just on *what* the model predicts, but *how uncertain* that prediction might be. Ignoring uncertainty can lead to overconfident models and high-risk decisions. To see why this matters, let us forget all the technicalities for a moment, and try to understand this with some intuition.

Picture this: It is late at night, and you are driving on a quiet highway. Your dashboard tells you there is 50 kilometers of fuel left, and the nearest gas station is 40 kilometers away. You do not just blindly believe the number, because you know it could be off, maybe, you have been driving uphill, or there is a headwind, or the car is consuming more fuel than usual. Should you trust the estimate and keep going, or slow down, or turn off at the next exit? At that moment, you are not just reading a prediction — you are *reasoning about the uncertainty* behind it. In real life, we instinctively account for uncertainty when making decisions, even if the prediction itself looks precise. This example, perhaps, gives us a starting point to appreciate the role of identifying uncertainty, and shows why it is essential to understand and address it - not just in everyday decisions, but in machine learning as well.

Now, let us get back to our original discussion, when we talk about machine learning models, they often provide just a single number whether it is the probability that a person will default on a loan or an estimate of how many units of a product will sell in the coming weeks but they do not express how reliable that number is by accounting for the uncertainty introduced by external factors just like in our car example. Unlike humans who instinctively build in a buffer for uncertainty, models rarely indicate how much their predictions might be off, inherently they solely focus on minimizing the optimization objective to make the predictions as close to real outcome as possible, and they do not focus on quantifying the uncertainty. Their outputs may look precise, but they are still shaped by underlying assumptions, changing data patterns, and hidden variables — all of which can affect accuracy.

In machine learning, ignoring uncertainty can quietly turn a smart prediction into a dangerous one.

- **Loan Approval Example:** A loan approval model predicts a borrower has a **98% chance** of repaying. Looks reliable, but the model does not mention it has very little training data for people with similar financial profiles. The loan gets approved, and the borrower defaults — not because the model was wrong, but because it did not communicate its uncertainty.

- **Medical Diagnosis:** A medical diagnosis tool says a patient is *unlikely* to have a stroke, and does not flag any concern. What is left unsaid is that the model is unsure about patients with rare symptoms or mixed risk factors. A serious condition goes unnoticed — not due to bad modeling, but because the model did not express its doubt.
- **Demand Forecasting:** A retail forecasting model predicts demand which will be **200 units** for a product next week. The team relies on this single number and orders accordingly. The model does not reveal that past demand swung between 150 and 300. When demand spikes, shelves go empty and revenue is lost.
- **Fraud Detection:** A fraud detection model passes a transaction as *low risk*. But that transaction falls into a category where the model has always been uncertain — new users making foreign purchases. A fraudulent charge goes through, not because the model failed to spot it, but because it never indicated how unsure it was.

In high-stakes decisions like these, **overconfident predictions give us a false sense of safety**, and the consequences can be irreversible. That is why addressing uncertainty is not optional, it is essential for making machine learning systems safe, reliable, and worthy of trust. The question is: how do we make machine learning predictions not only accurate but also honest about their uncertainty?

Understanding and Quantifying Uncertainty

In the previous section, we explored overall how uncertainty is, and how it can turn even accurate machine learning predictions into risky decisions when it is left unexpressed and build the foundation on *why* uncertainty matters. In fact, it is time to dig into the *what* and *how* behind it: where does uncertainty come from in machine learning, and how can we measure it? Unlike humans, models do not pause to reconsider or express doubt — their outputs look precise, even when the data or model is far from certain. In this section, we will break down the core sources of uncertainty in machine learning, and introduce the tools we use to quantify them, laying the foundation for uncertainty-aware methods like Conformal Prediction.

Now, let us understand the origin of uncertainty in Machine Learning (ML), and its impact through a dummy dataset of housing prices.

Imagine we are building a machine learning model to predict housing prices based on the size of a house (in square feet). Our initial hypothesis is the bigger homes cost more. We collect data, fit a regression model and begin predicting. But what we do not see at first is: **some houses with the same size can sell for wildly different prices** due to external factors like neighborhood, build quality, or timing in the market and our traditional regressor does not include this uncertainty in its estimates, it simply gives a price against the area based on historical patterns learnt (refer to *Figure 1.1*).

```
import numpy as np
import matplotlib.pyplot as plt
from sklearn.linear_model import LinearRegression
from sklearn.model_selection import train_test_split
import pandas as pd

# Generate 200 synthetic house listings for simulation
n_samples = 200

# Feature: house size in square feet (ranges from 500 to 3500)
sizes = np.random.uniform(500, 3500, n_samples)

# True price follows a linear trend: $50k base + $200 per sqft
base_prices = 50_000 + 200 * sizes

# We add random noise scaled by the size of the house to simulate real-
world variability
noise = np.random.normal(loc=0.0, scale=sizes * 50, size=n_samples)
prices = base_prices + noise
```

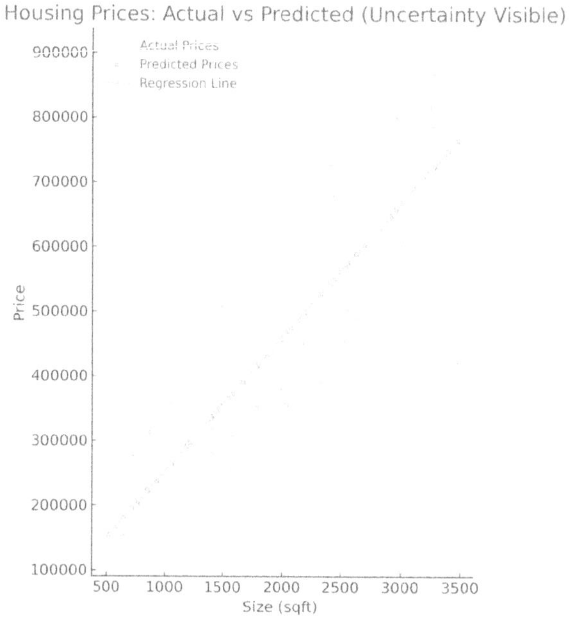

Figure 1.1: *Uncertainty in Real Data*

Let us try to uncover the maths behind this to understand in detail why a machine learning model (in this case the regressor fails) to capture uncertainty.

In a typical linear regression task, the model assumes a linear relationship between input x and target y, and tries to find the line that best fits all the actuals keeping the errors minimal, as shown in the following *Figure* 1.2. It is a zoomed view for a smaller set (10 points) of how this fit process looks like.

```
# Focus on houses with size between 1000 and 1500 sqft for a zoomed-in
view and select
mask = (sizes >= 1000) & (sizes <= 1500)
z_sizes_all = sizes[mask]       # Filtered house sizes
z_prices_all = prices[mask]     # Corresponding observed prices

# Select up to 10 random samples from this zoomed-in range to visualize clearly
k = min(10, z_sizes_all.shape[0])

# if values within the size range are itself less than 10 then select
all of them else choose random 10 values
if k < z_sizes_all.shape[0]:
    idx = np.random.choice(np.arange(z_sizes_all.shape[0]), size=k,
replace=False)
    z_sizes = z_sizes_all[idx]
    z_prices = z_prices_all[idx]
else:
    z_sizes, z_prices = z_sizes_all, z_prices_all

# Predict prices using the trained regression model
z_pred = model.predict(z_sizes.reshape(-1, 1))

# Plot the observed and predicted values
plt.figure()
plt.scatter(z_sizes, z_prices, s=30, label="Actual prices (zoomed)")
plt.show()
```

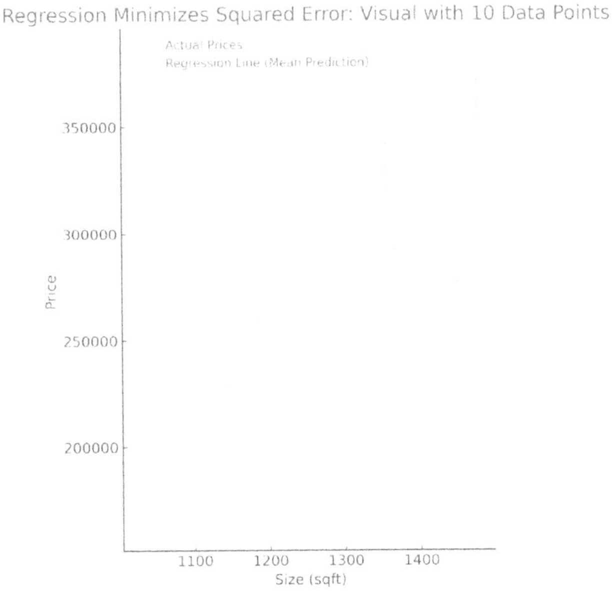

Figure 1.2: *Error Visualization in Regression*

This example reveals a fundamental challenge in **machine learning models**: they typically focus on learning to predict the **most likely outcome or the expected value** *(in this case mean)* by optimizing a loss function like a mean squared error or a cross entropy loss, without capturing the full range of possibilities that might exist in the real world. When the **data is volatile, a single point prediction fails to tell the whole story**.

In a business context, relying only on such point estimates can lead to risky decisions. For example, in our scenario *a real estate investor basing offers solely on predicted housing prices may significantly underbid or overpay, because the model did not convey how uncertain those prices really are*. In other words, even accurate models can mislead if they fail to **express uncertainty**.

We saw how machine learning models often make confident predictions even when the data they are trained on contains a lot of hidden variability. Now that we understand *why* this uncertainty arises, the natural next question is: **how do we express it?**

The answer to the above question lies in the title of the book itself **CONFORMAL PREDICTION**, and we will talk about it in great detail in subsequent chapters. For now, let us take a simple high-level view of how we can build an interval around a model's prediction rather than relying on just a single number. **The basic idea is to use the model's past mistakes to decide how wide that interval should be**. If the model has often been very wrong, especially on similar kinds of data, then its prediction deserves less trust and the interval should be wider. On the other hand, if the model's errors have been consistently small, we can feel more confident and keep the interval narrower.

In our housing prices example, after fitting a regression line to the data, if we simply look at the **absolute residuals (errors)** on a holdout set which is often called as a calibration set, then let us pick the *90th error percentile value which simply means 90% of times the actuals are within this range*. Later, we add and subtract this value from the model's prediction across the input space to create the interval. The following is a simplified logic to compute these intervals.

```
# Compute absolute residuals (errors) on the training data
train_pred = model.predict(X_train)

# Absolute difference between actual and predicted prices
abs_resid = np.abs(y_train - train_pred)

# Use the 90th percentile of the absolute residuals to define a simple
error band, this band captures 90% of prediction errors--acts like an
approximate confidence interval
q = np.quantile(abs_resid, 0.90)

# Create a smooth range of house sizes (grid) to plot the model and
error band
```

```
x_grid = np.linspace(500, 3500, 250).reshape(-1, 1)
y_hat = model.predict(x_grid)   # Model predictions for the grid
lower = y_hat - q               # Lower bound of interval
upper = y_hat + q               # Upper bound of interval

# Plotting the results
plt.figure()
plt.scatter(X_train, y_train, s=12, label="Training data")

# Plot mean prediction line (best model estimate at each size)
plt.plot(x_grid, y_hat, linewidth=2, label="Mean prediction")

# Plot the simple interval as a shaded area above and below the mean line
plt.fill_between(x_grid.ravel(), lower, upper, alpha=0.2, label="Interval
(± q90 |residual|)")
plt.title("Mean Line with Simple Error-Based Interval")
plt.xlabel("Size (sqft)")
plt.ylabel("Price")
plt.legend()
plt.tight_layout()
plt.show()
```

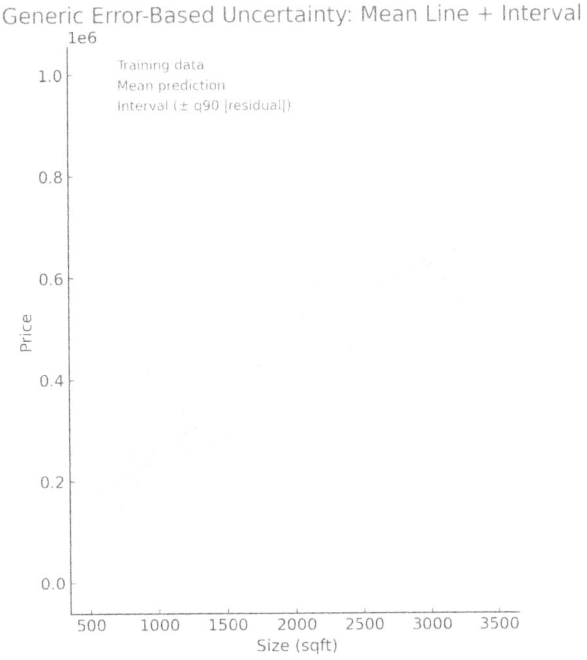

Figure 1.3: *Uncertainty Bands around Prediction*

In the *Figure* 1.3, we can see that by simply utilizing historical errors we create a band which captures the actual prices with a high certainty. Hence, this allows us to make more informed decisions.

Types of Uncertainty

So far, we have seen two things very clearly:

- Machine learning models *usually* give us just *a point estimate*.
- That prediction often *hides a lot of uncertainty*, which can lead to risky decisions in real world scenarios.

But uncertainty itself can come from different places. Sometimes, the data is naturally noisy like housing prices or stock markets where even with perfect knowledge, the outcome would still vary. Other times, the uncertainty does not come from randomness in the data, but from the **model's lack of knowledge**. This can happen when the model is too simple to capture the true complexity of the real-world relationships, or when it is asked to make predictions in parts of the input space that were never included in its training data, leaving it to **extrapolate into unfamiliar territory**.

These are different kinds of uncertainty, and **treating them the same can be a mistake**. One reflects *unpredictable randomness* in the real world, the other reflects *the limitations of our model*. Understanding the difference between them is essential for the way we **measure**, **communicate**, and **mitigate** uncertainty depending on where it comes from.

In this section, we will break down the two most important types — **aleatoric** and **epistemic uncertainty** — and illustrate how they show up in practice. This will give us the intuition we need before we get to the core of this book, that is, a conformal prediction, which handles these uncertainties in systematic, reliable ways. [1]

Epistemic Uncertainty

Not all uncertainty in machine learning comes from randomness in the data. Sometimes, the uncertainty lies in the **model itself**. This happens when the model does not have enough knowledge to make a confident prediction, *perhaps, because it was trained on limited data, or has never seen anything like the input it's being asked to evaluate. This is called epistemic uncertainty*, and it represents the parts of the world that the model has not learned yet, or cannot express. This kind of uncertainty is especially important because it often shows up in real-world situations where the model is deployed beyond the environment it was trained in.

Let us continue our housing prices example to understand this concept. Imagine you are building a model to predict house prices based on size, number of rooms, and age of the building. You train the model using clean and detailed data — but here is the catch: **all the data comes from houses in city A**.

Now, someone wants to use your model to predict house prices in B.

At first glance, the inputs may look similar such as: house sizes, bedrooms, locations within the city, and so on. But the model has **never seen B houses, pricing patterns, buyer behavior, or economic trends**, so while it will still output a number, **that number is made outside its comfort zone**. The model is **blindly applying what it learned in A to a city it knows nothing about**.

This is epistemic uncertainty:

- It arises not because the data is noisy, but because the model **does not have enough knowledge to make a reliable prediction**.
- It appears when the model is used **Out-of-Distribution (OOD)** or on **data different from its training domain**.
- The danger is that the model still outputs a confident-looking number — giving a false sense of certainty.

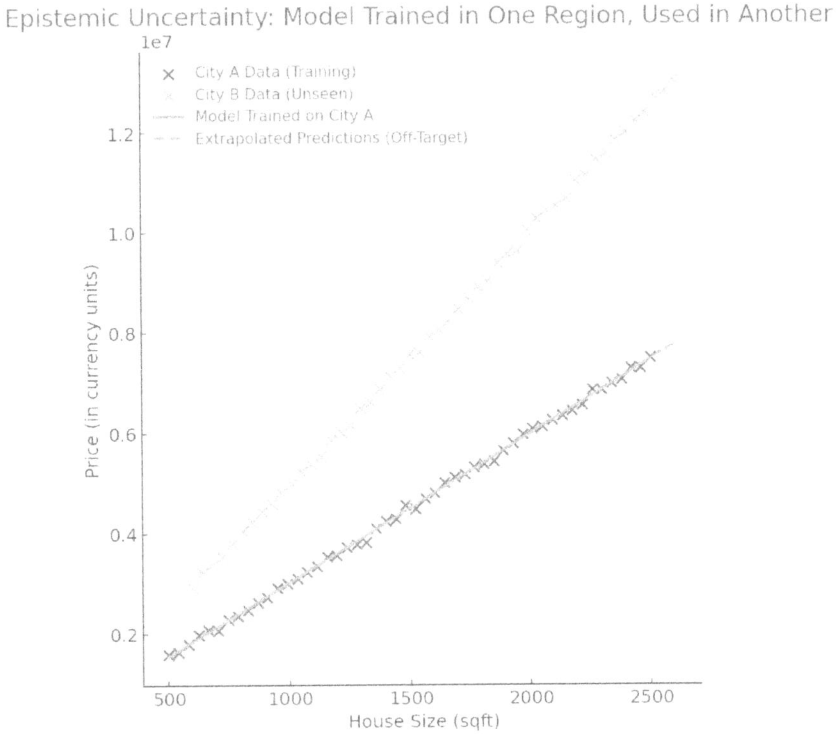

***Figure 1.4**: Epistemic Uncertainty Visualization*

The good news is, **this uncertainty is reducible**. *We can shrink it by collecting more representative data, using more flexible models, or ensuring we don't ask the model to make predictions in regions it wasn't trained for*. This is why it is so important to understand the **different types of uncertainty** before trying to quantify or manage them, each behaves differently and needs a different strategy. Only when we recognize *what kind of uncertainty we are dealing with* can we decide what strategy to use, that is, first reduce the errors through the above-mentioned ideas before quantifying the uncertainty or directly computing prediction intervals for refined outcomes.

Aleatoric Uncertainty

Aleatoric Uncertainty refers to the type of uncertainty that **resides in the data itself, that is the randomness or noise in the data.** This is something that cannot be captured even with the most powerful models since as the name suggests, it is purely random and any machine learning algorithm is inherently built in such a way that it captures patterns from the data. Think of it as irreducible variability which does not have any inherent patterns, such as following are certain examples to make this concept clear.

- **House prices fluctuate due to subjective and unobserved factors:** Even if two houses have the same size, location, and features, *their actual selling prices may differ depending on things like how urgently the seller needs cash, how emotionally attached a buyer is, or even timing and negotiation.* These unpredictable human and market behaviors introduce variability that no model can fully account for. The following is an example to show this data driven fluctuation on dummy data.

- **Sensor readings often include built-in measurement error:** Whether it is a thermometer, a GPS tracker, or a medical device, sensors always have some degree of inaccuracy. *Even when measuring the same object under the same conditions, the readings will slightly vary*, this randomness is not due to the model but inherent in the data collected.

- **Weather forecasts involve natural randomness in atmospheric systems:** Even with the best scientific models and vast data, the weather is influenced by chaotic systems. Slight changes in temperature, pressure, or wind at one point can scale into unpredictable outcomes elsewhere, making it impossible to predict with perfect accuracy.

Across all the examples we explored, from house prices affected by emotional buyer decisions to noisy sensor readings and unpredictable weather — *one truth stood out: some uncertainty is built into the data itself.* Unlike the previous type, this kind of uncertainty *is not something a model can fix by being more accurate or by training on more data.* It reflects real randomness in the world that no model can fully remove, we can only quantify this in our estimates. That is why a model that gives just a single prediction, without indicating the possible range of outcomes around it, is only telling part of the story. **To make responsible use of machine learning in real-world decisions, it is crucial to recognize this noise, communicate it properly, and avoid overstating the certainty of a prediction.** In later chapters, we will see how frameworks like conformal prediction can help us do this, *not by eliminating uncertainty, but by expressing it honestly through reliable prediction intervals.*

Foundations of Conformal Prediction

Up to now, we have uncovered the hard truth about machine learning in detail: even the most sophisticated models tend to deliver **one answer**, while hiding **how unsure they actually are**. We explored the sources of this uncertainty — the noise in the data we cannot avoid, and the gaps in the model's own understanding as well as later saw how both can quietly lead to poor or even costly decisions, if left unaddressed.

This brings us to a natural turning point and our main topic of discussion: Can we build systems that not only predict but also reveal how much trust we can place in those predictions — in a way that works across any model or dataset?

That question leads us straight to *the central idea of this book: conformal prediction. Conformal prediction is a powerful, model-agnostic framework that takes the black box of machine learning and wraps it in valid, measurable confidence.* Instead of a single guess, it gives us a range of likely outcomes — an **interval in regression, a set of classes in classification**, all with a mathematically guaranteed level of reliability. The core idea of CP is simple yet powerful:

"Use model's past errors to quantify how uncertain its next prediction can be."

Conformal Prediction is not a one-size-fits-all solution, it adapts itself to the kind of machine learning problem you are solving. The way it wraps around a model in a **regression task** is different from how it behaves in **classification** or **forecasting**, because each setting has its own way of expressing uncertainty.

For example, in a regression problem like predicting the rental price of an apartment, CP gives you a **prediction interval** around the model's estimate such as, "There's a 90% chance the rent will be between $5,000 and $8,000." The model still predicts a number, but CP adds the *range of possible values* based on real calibration errors.

In classification, things work differently. If you are building a system to detect spam emails, instead of forcing a single label, CP can return a **set of likely labels** such as {spam, promotional} — when the model is not confident enough. This avoids risky, overconfident predictions, especially in ambiguous cases.

In forecasting tasks, such as getting next week's sales for a product, conformal prediction provides **uncertainty bands** around the time-series forecast — for example, "Sales are expected to fall between 600 and 720 units with 95% confidence." Unlike regression, where predictions are made for independent data points, forecasting deals with **sequential patterns and temporal dependencies**, which means the uncertainty can grow or shrink over time depending on recent behavior or seasonality. These bands take into account the temporal dependency, and help planners prepare for both best- and worst-case scenarios over time, instead of relying on a single forecast value that may overlook sudden shifts or trends.

Each of these settings requires conformal prediction to work slightly differently, but the goal is always the same: **to deliver predictions that are both informative and trustworthy using historical errors**. In the chapters ahead, we will explore how CP works in each of these domains in detail, building both the theory and practical Python implementations along the way.

Python Setup

This book includes hands-on exercises using Jupyter Notebooks. To run them reliably, it is important to use an isolated Python environment, and ensure that the required libraries are installed. In this section we will focus on setting up the required dependencies in your local system to run all the hands-on exercises seamlessly.

Need for This Setup

In the early part of my professional journey, I would often try to rush through the setup phase just to jump straight into the exciting bits like `.fit()` and `.predict()`. But over time, I realized that the setup is an equally crucial part of any project because it forms the foundation for everything that follows, such as ensuring consistency, reproducibility, and a clean development workflow. Think of it as laying the groundwork for a stable house: it may not feel glamorous, but without it, the structure cannot stand strong. When you are working with machine learning code (like in this book), it is **very common for projects to need different versions of Python or libraries**. If you install everything into your system Python directly, one project may break another, and your machine can quickly become a mess.

That is why **we always create an isolated environment**, where we install just the required libraries, without affecting other work. This chapter shows you how to set up such an environment using **Conda**, and make it ready to use in Jupyter Notebooks.

Installation

Here, we will discuss through a step-by-step process for setting up the framework required for the subsequent chapters.

Step 1: Install Python

Before we write any code, we need a working Python installation. Now, you could install Python directly from python.org [2], but in real-world data science projects, we often work with different versions of Python and libraries across multiple projects. Managing all of that in a single, system-level Python installation quickly becomes messy.

Think of building a machine learning project like preparing food in a kitchen.

In cooking, you can either dump all ingredients in one big space, and hope for the best or you can **organize** things:

- Different spices in different jars
- Ingredients grouped by cuisine
- Clean prep space for every dish

Python projects are similar, if you dump everything into your "main system" Python (global kitchen), your dependencies can get mixed up. One project may need `numpy==1.21`, another may require `numpy==2.0`. Now, if they are all installed in the same place, things break, just like mixing cumin into your tiramisu would ruin the dessert.

Solution: Create a clean setup where we install Python and libraries *only for this project* using a safe tool, that is where Conda shines.

Conda Description

Conda is **an open-source package manager** and **environment manager**. It lets you:

- Install specific versions of Python and third-party libraries,
- Create **isolated environments** for each project,
- Avoid dependency conflicts altogether.

So, instead of installing Python globally and risking a "version soup," we will install Conda first, and then install python within environments.

We will use Miniconda here, which is the minimal installer for Conda, much lighter than the full Anaconda distribution, and would be more than enough for our experimentations. In the references you can find detailed documentation for both Windows [3] and Mac [4] for the installation of Miniconda.

Step 2: Creating an Isolated Python Environment

Once you have stocked your kitchen and set up your cooking tools, the next thing you need is *a clean cooking station for each dish*. Imagine trying to prepare Italian pasta and Indian curry using the exact same cutting board, same spice rack, same bowls — all at once. Sooner or later, you will end up with cumin in your tomato sauce or basil in your dal.

The same thing happens in Python projects: if we install all libraries, tools, and dependencies into one global space, things will eventually clash — one project's requirements will overwrite another's. That is why we set up **separate environments**: like having separate prep counters for each recipe, ensuring no cross-contamination and easy cleanup. In the next steps, we will create a **dedicated environment** just for our Conformal Prediction project — a clean space where we can install all the libraries we need, without interfering with any other Python project on your system. The following is a snippet of setup of environment creation using conda where we perform the following activities broadly:

- Load conda in the terminal (this also gives us readily available python).
- Create an isolated environment using **conda create** (*we are working with python 3.10 version for these experiments*).
- Activate the newly created environment, and install the required libraries (*it shows as conformal-experiments in the terminal*).

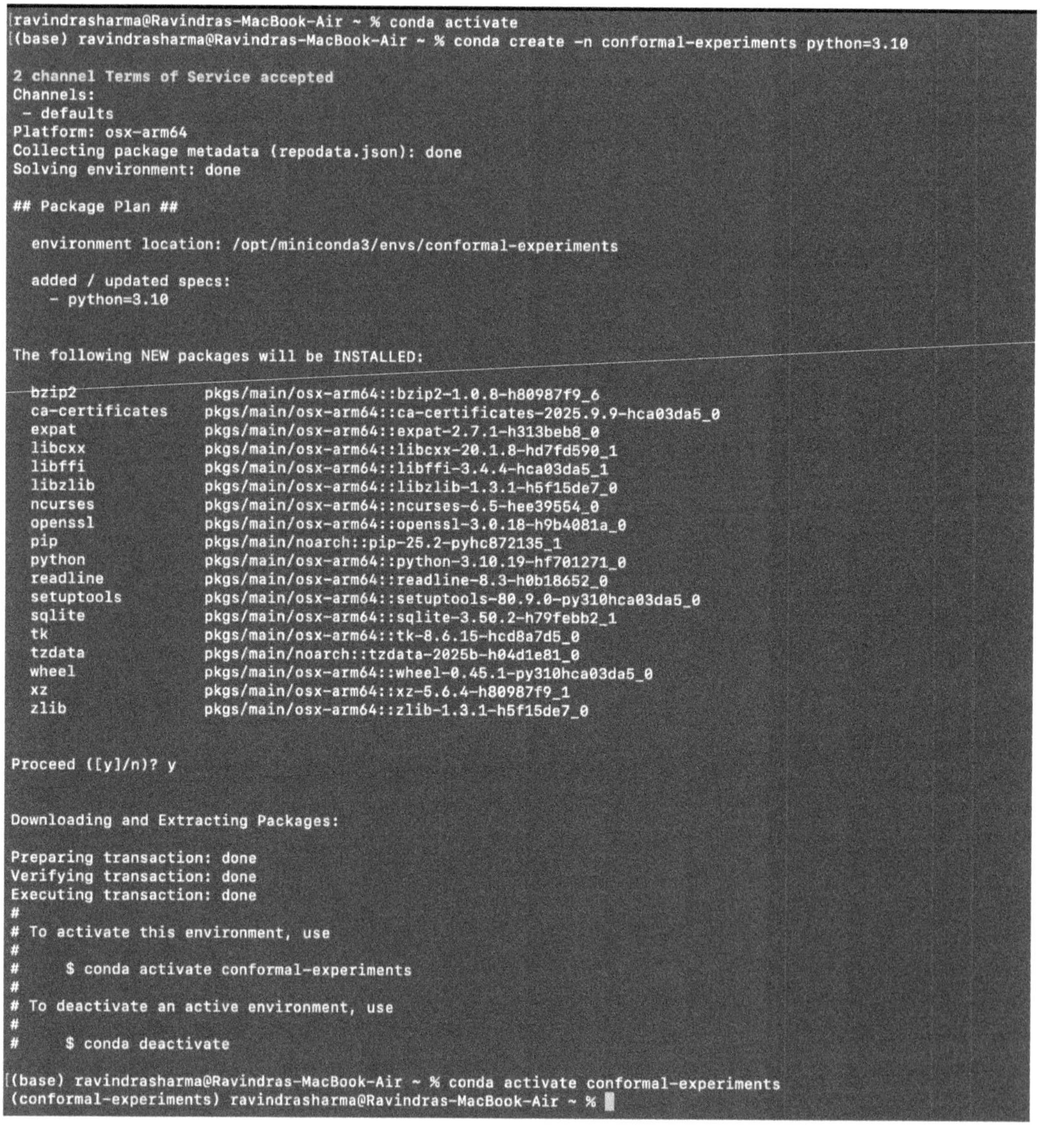

```
ravindrasharma@Ravindras-MacBook-Air ~ % conda activate
(base) ravindrasharma@Ravindras-MacBook-Air ~ % conda create -n conformal-experiments python=3.10

2 channel Terms of Service accepted
Channels:
 - defaults
Platform: osx-arm64
Collecting package metadata (repodata.json): done
Solving environment: done

## Package Plan ##

  environment location: /opt/miniconda3/envs/conformal-experiments

  added / updated specs:
    - python=3.10


The following NEW packages will be INSTALLED:

  bzip2              pkgs/main/osx-arm64::bzip2-1.0.8-h80987f9_6
  ca-certificates    pkgs/main/osx-arm64::ca-certificates-2025.9.9-hca03da5_0
  expat              pkgs/main/osx-arm64::expat-2.7.1-h313beb8_0
  libcxx             pkgs/main/osx-arm64::libcxx-20.1.8-hd7fd590_1
  libffi             pkgs/main/osx-arm64::libffi-3.4.4-hca03da5_1
  libzlib            pkgs/main/osx-arm64::libzlib-1.3.1-h5f15de7_0
  ncurses            pkgs/main/osx-arm64::ncurses-6.5-hee39554_0
  openssl            pkgs/main/osx-arm64::openssl-3.0.18-h9b4081a_0
  pip                pkgs/main/noarch::pip-25.2-pyhc872135_1
  python             pkgs/main/osx-arm64::python-3.10.19-hf701271_0
  readline           pkgs/main/osx-arm64::readline-8.3-h0b18652_0
  setuptools         pkgs/main/osx-arm64::setuptools-80.9.0-py310hca03da5_0
  sqlite             pkgs/main/osx-arm64::sqlite-3.50.2-h79febb2_1
  tk                 pkgs/main/osx-arm64::tk-8.6.15-hcd8a7d5_0
  tzdata             pkgs/main/noarch::tzdata-2025b-h04d1e81_0
  wheel              pkgs/main/osx-arm64::wheel-0.45.1-py310hca03da5_0
  xz                 pkgs/main/osx-arm64::xz-5.6.4-h80987f9_1
  zlib               pkgs/main/osx-arm64::zlib-1.3.1-h5f15de7_0


Proceed ([y]/n)? y


Downloading and Extracting Packages:

Preparing transaction: done
Verifying transaction: done
Executing transaction: done
#
# To activate this environment, use
#
#     $ conda activate conformal-experiments
#
# To deactivate an active environment, use
#
#     $ conda deactivate

(base) ravindrasharma@Ravindras-MacBook-Air ~ % conda activate conformal-experiments
(conformal-experiments) ravindrasharma@Ravindras-MacBook-Air ~ %
```

Figure 1.5: *Python Environment Setup*

Step 3: Installing the Dependencies

We have set up our clean cooking space, and now it is time to gather just the right ingredients for the dishes we will be making. Just like a good chef does not dump *every* spice into *every recipe*, we will only bring in the exact tools we need for this project. That keeps things organized, avoids version clashes, and makes our setup lightweight as well as easy to reproduce later.

In Python terms, these ingredients are **libraries** — reusable packages that help us work with data, build models, visualize results, and even quantify uncertainty through advanced techniques like conformal prediction and forecasting.

Thus, we will install the following libraries for all our experiments:

- **Core stack:** `numpy, pandas, matplotlib, scikit-learn`
- **Notebook tools:** `jupyter, ipykernel`
- **Forecasting:** `mapie, sktime, statsmodels, prophet`
- **Conformal Libraries:** `mapie,sktime`

A requirements.txt file has already been created with compatible versions to avoid any conflicts, and all the mentioned dependencies can be simply installed in our environment by navigating to the directory containing requirements file (base project directly) as well as run the following command in the terminal.

```
pip install -r requirements.txt
```

This file was generated after installing all the required libraries in the project environment using the **command pip freeze**, which records the exact versions of all the installed packages into a single file. The file is placed in the root directory of the project so that it acts as a central list of dependencies for the entire project. So, whenever someone wants to run the code from this book on their own system, they simply need to navigate to the project folder, and run **`pip install -r requirements.txt`**, and Python will automatically install all the required libraries with the correct versions.

Step 4: Register the Environment

At this point, our kitchen is ready: we have set up a clean workspace, and gathered just the right ingredients for the recipes in this book. Now, it is time to **start cooking and tasting** — which, in our case, is running all the experiments around conformal prediction.

That is where the Jupyter Notebook comes in. It gives us a flexible, code-and-text hybrid workspace ideal for learning purposes.

But just like choosing the right stove for the meal you are about to cook, we need to **tell Jupyter which environment** to use, the one with our exact Python version and installed libraries. That is why we register our environment as a **Jupyter Kernel**. It enables Jupyter to use the specific environment enabling running algorithms requiring these dependencies, and all of this can be achieved by running one simple command.

```
python -m ipykernel install --user --name=conformal-experiments
         --display-name "Conformal Prediction"
```

Once we are through with registering the notebook, we can simply launch a jupyter notebook from the terminal directly using command **`jupyter notebook`**, and select our created environment. Then, we can run the experiment notebooks directly, as shown in the following snippet where you can simply go to Kernel, and select the desired kernel from the dropdown once registered.

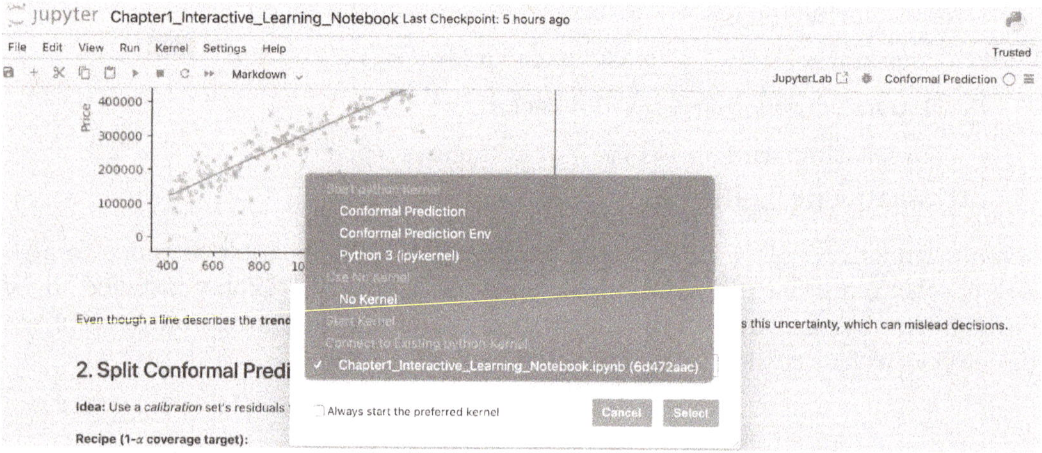

***Figure 1.6**: Environment Selection in Notebook*

With this setup, you have built a clean and complete foundation for all the hands-on work in this book. By installing Python through Conda, creating an isolated environment, installing only the required libraries, and connecting that environment to Jupyter, you have ensured that your code is reproducible, conflict-free, and ready for interactive experimentation. From here onward, you will be writing, running, and visualizing the code in a controlled setup that mirrors the best practices used in real-world machine learning workflows.

To give an overall understanding, the following is an illustration of how the entire framework of conformal prediction looks like.

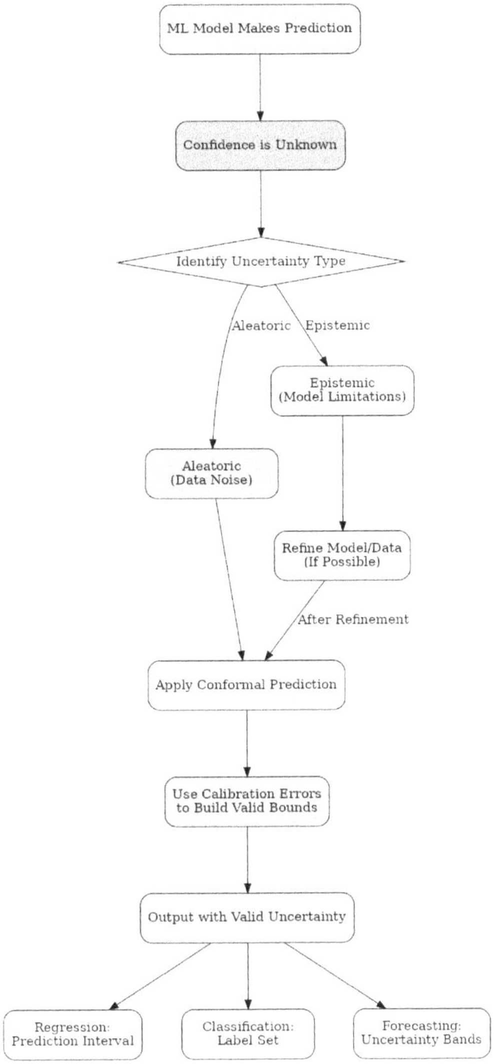

Figure 1.7: *Conformal Prediction Flowchart*

In the next chapter, we will go into the details about the framework of Conformal Prediction focusing around its key ideas along with real world data driven examples.

Conclusion

In this chapter, we uncovered one of the most overlooked weaknesses in modern machine learning: the **gap between a model's prediction and our ability to trust it**. We saw how point predictions no matter how accurate can become fragile and even dangerous when the **uncertainty behind them is ignored**. We explored the **two fundamental types of uncertainties**: aleatoric, which comes from the randomness of the world, and epistemic, which comes from the model's incomplete knowledge. Each behaves differently, each matters in real-world scenarios, and each demands a different approach to handle effectively.

Thus, by understanding these sources of uncertainty through intuitive examples and simple visualizations, we have built the foundation to appreciate what comes next: **conformal prediction**, a framework designed to quantify and communicate uncertainty in a principled, model-agnostic way. With the stage now set, we are ready to move from understanding the problem to learning the solution.

Hence. before closing this chapter, we also set up a clean and reproducible Python environment, ensuring that all the code we will write is executed with the right versions of tools, isolated from system interference. By creating a dedicated Conda environment, installing only the required libraries, and linking it to Jupyter, we have prepared a reliable workspace for the hands-on exploration ahead.

Points to Remember

- Machine learning models often give **single predictions** without expressing how uncertain they are creating a gap between prediction and trust.
- **Aleatoric uncertainty** comes from randomness in the data itself, and **cannot be reduced**, no matter how good the model becomes.
- **Epistemic uncertainty** arises when the model **lacks knowledge** or has not seen similar data before, and **can be reduced** with better data or architecture.
- Ignoring uncertainty can lead to **overconfident and risky decisions**, especially in sensitive areas like healthcare, finance, and forecasting.
- Understanding these types of uncertainty is essential before we learn how **conformal prediction** provides reliable, model-agnostic uncertainty estimates.

Chapter Resources

- Code Exercise

Multiple Choice Questions

1. What is the main issue with typical machine learning point predictions?
    a. They are usually biased.
    b. They do not communicate uncertainty.
    c. They require large datasets.
    d. They only work with linear models.

2. Which of the following is an example of aleatoric uncertainty?
    a. A model being asked to predict on completely new types of data.
    b. A medical image model failing when it has not been trained on rare diseases.
    c. Noise in sensor readings that persists even after retraining.
    d. A model not using enough layers to capture a complex pattern.
3. Which of the following best describes epistemic uncertainty?
    a. Irreducible randomness caused by the world.
    b. Model uncertainty that can be reduced by better data or capacity.
    c. Errors only occurring in high-dimensional spaces.
    d. Uncertainty resulting from model overconfidence.
4. What happens when a model is used to make predictions on an unseen region of input space?
    a. The model detects the error, and recalibrates automatically.
    b. The model produces highly confident but potentially unreliable predictions.
    c. The model stops predicting, and raises an exception.
    d. The model's predictions are always correct if trained on large datasets.
5. Which of the following fields could be harmed by ignoring uncertainty in predictions?
    a. Medical decision-making
    b. Automated credit scoring
    c. Energy demand forecasting
    d. All of the above
6. Why can conformal prediction be applied to any machine learning model?
    a. Because it only works with linear models
    b. Because it wraps around the model without modifying how it learns
    c. Because it requires a predefined probability distribution
    d. Because it needs the model to output uncertainty values
7. Which component of conformal prediction is used to measure how unusual a prediction is compared to the past data?
    a. Calibration score
    b. Nonconformity score

  c. Confidence interval
  d. Prediction margin

8. Why is aleatoric uncertainty considered irreducible?
   a. It arises from lack of training data.
   b. It comes from inherent noise in the data.
   c. It can always be fixed with better models.
   d. It disappears once the model is trained long enough.
9. Which method can be used to reduce epistemic uncertainty before applying for conformal prediction?
   a. Adding more layers to the model
   b. Balancing the dataset
   c. Collecting additional, informative data
   d. All of the above
10. What is a key advantage of conformal prediction in real-world applications?
    a. It guarantees that the model's predictions will always be accurate.
    b. It provides statistically valid uncertainty without assuming data distribution.
    c. It makes machine learning models run faster.
    d. It replaces the need for calibration or testing.

Answers

1. b
2. c
3. b
4. b
5. d
6. b
7. b
8. b
9. d
10. b

Key Terms

- **Point Prediction**: A single value output from a machine learning model, such as predicting a house price or class label, without expressing uncertainty.
- **Confidence Gap**: The disconnect between a model's prediction and its level of certainty, especially when the model does not communicate how unsure it may be.
- **Aleatoric Uncertainty**: Uncertainty that comes from inherent randomness or noise in the data; this type of uncertainty **cannot be reduced** even with more data or better models.
- **Epistemic Uncertainty**: Uncertainty that arises from the model's **lack of knowledge**, such as limited or biased training data; this type **can be reduced** by improving the model or adding more diverse data.
- **Calibration Set**: A portion of data not used for training but used to evaluate the model's prediction errors, often in frameworks like conformal prediction.

References

1. Uncertainty in Machine Learning - Hans Weytjens, Wouter Verbeke
2. https://www.python.org/
3. https://docs.conda.io/projects/conda/en/stable/user-guide/install/windows.html
4. https://docs.conda.io/projects/conda/en/stable/user-guide/install/macos.html

CHAPTER 2
The Foundations of Conformal Prediction

Introduction

In the previous chapter, we explored the limits of traditional machine learning. Models can make accurate point predictions, but they often fail to tell us how uncertain those predictions are. This lack of transparency can make even the best models unreliable in real-world decision making, where it is not enough to know just what the model predicts, but also how confident it is in that prediction.

This is where Conformal Prediction comes into the picture. Conformal Prediction is a flexible, model-agnostic framework that adds a mathematically sound layer of uncertainty to any predictive model. It works with models you already use, such as linear regression, neural networks, or decision trees, and gives you prediction intervals or sets that meet a desired confidence level. These intervals are valid without making strong distributional assumptions about the data.

In this chapter, we discuss the key ideas behind Conformal Prediction. We will see how residuals are converted into reliable measures of uncertainty. We introduce the main concepts like nonconformity scores and calibration, which are the foundation of how Conformal Prediction ensures coverage guarantees. We will also understand how the same principles apply across regression, classification, and much more.

Therefore, by the end of this chapter, you will have a clear understanding of how Conformal Prediction works, and how it transforms a point prediction model into a model you can trust, even when uncertainty is high.

Structure

In this chapter, we will cover the following topics:

- Exchangeability

- Model Agnostic Systems
- Non-Conformity Scores
- Validity and Coverage

Exchangeability

At the heart of conformal prediction lies a simple yet profound idea called **exchangeability**, the assumption that gives conformal methods their remarkable validity without relying on any specific data distribution. Exchangeability means that the order in which data points appear does not matter; every observation, past or future, comes from the same underlying process and is equally representative of that process. In other words, if we were to shuffle all the data points—including the new one we are trying to predict—their joint probability would remain unchanged. This idea is slightly weaker than the common IID (Independent and Identically Distributed) assumption because it does not require independence between points, only that they are drawn symmetrically from the same source. This subtle relaxation makes conformal prediction broadly applicable such as: as long as the data are exchangeable, the relationship between past errors and future uncertainty remains valid. It is this symmetry that allows conformal prediction to make meaningful probabilistic statements about new data, even without knowing the exact form of the underlying distribution—making exchangeability the quiet but essential foundation on which conformal validity stands.

Let us understand this with an example scenario:

- Suppose we are building a model to predict **final exam scores** of students based on their study hours and attendance
- We assume all students are from the **same class**, taught by the same teacher, under the same grading policy meaning each student's performance follows the same underlying pattern and to keep things simple we ignore any uncontrollable factors like test anxiety, seat placement, prior student knowledge, and so on.
- Because of this, the **order in which we observe the students does not matter**; whether we list them alphabetically or by roll number, the dataset still represents the same process.
- This symmetry where every student's data could appear in any order without altering the underlying meaning or likelihood of the dataset is what defines exchangeability.
- Now, when a **new student** takes the exam, we can treat their performance as another draw from this same class distribution, making our conformal prediction intervals valid.

- However, if we included students from a **different course or teacher**, the assumption would break those examples that would not be exchangeable because their underlying conditions differ.

In conformal prediction, this idea of exchangeability ensures that the new student we are predicting for is treated just like the students already in our data, all drawn from the same underlying process. Because of this symmetry, the patterns of errors seen in past students can be used to judge how typical or unusual the new one is, allowing conformal prediction to construct valid, distribution-free confidence intervals for future examples.

Let us now see the above example with actual code examples with dummy data. Assume we have two predictors, **attendance and study hours** to assess performance of a student. Now, we have two classes where Class A has a high correlation with study hours and attendance with some randomness, whereas students of Class B show slightly more erratic patterns and attendance does not have much significance in test performance as compared to in Class A. This is probably due to difference in teaching methods where students are mostly relying on self-studying, and hence, attending classes does not have much impact along with the added noise due to lack of standardized teaching methods.

```
import numpy as np
from sklearn.linear_model import LinearRegression
from sklearn.model_selection import train_test_split

def split_conformal_intervals(X_train, y_train, X_calib, y_calib, X_
test, alpha=0.1):
    model = LinearRegression().fit(X_train, y_train)
    calib_pred = model.predict(X_calib)
    q = np.quantile(np.abs(y_calib - calib_pred), 1 - alpha)
    y_pred = model.predict(X_test)
    return y_pred - q, y_pred + q

def coverage(lower, upper, y_true):
    return np.mean((y_true >= lower) & (y_true <= upper))

# Train / calibration data (exchangeable)
X_train_full, X_test, y_train_full, y_test = train_test_split(X, y,
test_size=0.25)
X_train, X_calib, y_train, y_calib = train_test_split(X_train_full, y_
train_full, test_size=0.33)

# Conformal intervals on exchangeable test set
lower_ex, upper_ex = split_conformal_intervals(
    X_train, y_train, X_calib, y_calib, X_test, alpha=0.1
)
```

```
cov_ex = coverage(lower_ex, upper_ex, y_test)

# Apply same intervals to non-exchangeable test set
lower_b, upper_b = split_conformal_intervals(
    X_train, y_train, X_calib, y_calib, X_test_b, alpha=0.1
)
cov_b = coverage(lower_b, upper_b, y_test_b)
```

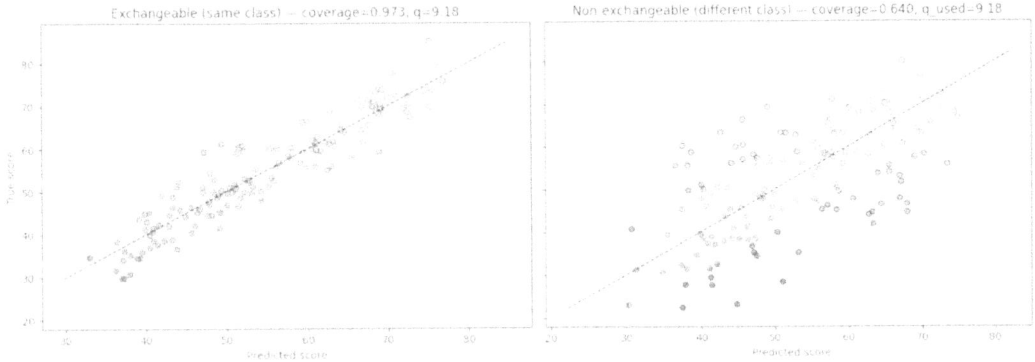

Figure 2.1: *Exchangeability Principle Explained*

We can clearly see from the above plot a model whose intervals were estimated from Class A fail miserably in Class B giving a poor coverage of 64% for a 90% CI intervals, and hence, showing the importance of this key assumption.

Note: *In forecasting, the assumption of exchangeability that past and future observations come from the same underlying process—often becomes fragile because time introduces order, dependence, and change. Unlike cross-sectional data, time series observations are correlated and frequently non-stationary such as: trends, seasonality, and evolving regimes mean that shuffling data would distort their natural structure. This temporal dependence breaks the symmetry that conformal prediction relies on to guarantee validity. However, approximate exchangeability can still be achieved when the process is stable or made stationary—for example, by detrending, deseasonalizing, or using rolling calibration windows that rely on recent observations. In practice, conformal forecasting methods adapt this idea by treating recent residuals as* locally exchangeable, *ensuring that uncertainty intervals remain meaningful even when the data evolve over time, we will discuss the idea of Conformal Prediction in Forecasting in detail as a separate chapter, later on.*

Model Agnostic Systems

We briefly talked about this in the Foundation section, and now, we will elaborate one of the most powerful aspects of CP, it is not a new model. It does not replace your regression algorithm, classifier, or forecaster. Instead, it is a **framework** that wraps around any machine learning model, and turns its raw predictions into something far more valuable such as: **predictions you can trust**. It treats every predictive model as a **black box** that simply maps input features **X** to predictions **y**.

All CP needs are:

- The model's predictions on a **calibration dataset.**
- The corresponding **true outcomes.**

That is it: no gradients, no probabilities, and no parametric forms. In simple words, it works around the principle:

"I don't need to know how you made the prediction, I only care about how wrong you were before."

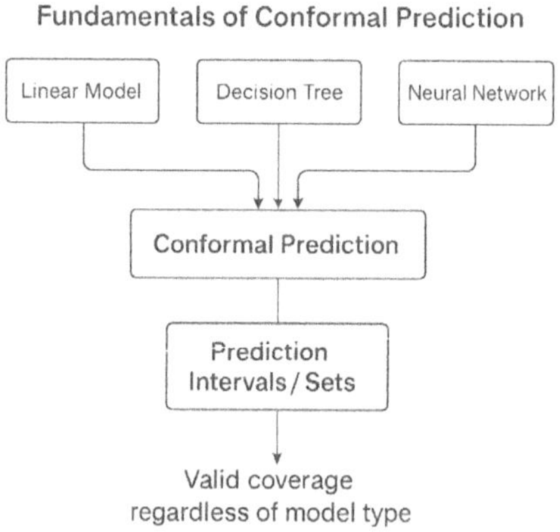

Figure 2.2: *Model Agnostic Visualization*

Imagine your Machine Learning (ML) model takes the following form, where f is essentially your ML model which can be anything: a linear regression, a decision tree, or a complex Deep Neural Network, given the input features **x**, which gives predictions y.

$$\hat{y}_i = f(x_i)$$

To estimate how uncertain these predictions are, Conformal Prediction looks at the model's past performance specifically, such as how far its predictions were from the actual observed values. For each example used to evaluate the model's predictive behavior such as in a calibration or validation step, we compute how far the model's prediction deviates from the true value. A common and simple choice is the absolute residual (in case of regression tasks).

$$r_i = |y_i - \hat{y}_i|$$

Once we have measured how far the model's predictions were from the truth of past data, the next step is to decide **how large an error we are willing to tolerate** in the future. To do this, we choose a confidence level — say, 90% or 95% — which represents how certain we want our prediction intervals to be. For example, a 90% confidence level means we are okay, if roughly 10% of future predictions fall outside our interval. We then look back at all the past errors (the deviations $r_1, r_2,...,r_n$) and find the error value that is larger than about 90% of them. That value — called the **(1 - α)-quantile** — becomes our error threshold $q_{1-\alpha}$.

This approach ensures that the width of the interval adapts to the model's *actual historical performance*, rather than to any theoretical assumption about its errors.

For a new input x_{new}, we construct intervals using the above threshold, one simple way to construct a conformal prediction interval is to expand the model's estimate by a threshold derived from past prediction errors.

$$[\hat{y}(x_{\text{new}}) - q_{1-\alpha},\ \hat{y}(x_{\text{new}}) + q_{1-\alpha}]$$

Thus, it is clear from the above steps that our framework does not make any assumptions on the form of *f*, hence enabling us to run this as a wrapper around any model to provide reliable interval estimates.

```
import numpy as np
from sklearn.linear_model import LinearRegression
from sklearn.ensemble import RandomForestRegressor
from sklearn.model_selection import train_test_split

def conformal_intervals(model, X_train, y_train, X_calib, y_calib, X_
test, alpha=0.1):
    model.fit(X_train, y_train)
    calib_pred = model.predict(X_calib)
    q = np.quantile(np.abs(y_calib - calib_pred), 1 - alpha)
    test_pred = model.predict(X_test)
    return test_pred - q, test_pred + q

# Synthetic nonlinear data
np.random.seed(0)
X = np.linspace(0, 10, 300).reshape(-1, 1)
y = 2.5 * X.squeeze() + 3 * np.sin(1.5 * X.squeeze()) + np.random.
randn(300) * (1 + 0.3 * X.squeeze())

# Train / calibration / test split
X_tr_full, X_te, y_tr_full, y_te = train_test_split(X, y, test_size=0.3)
X_tr, X_cal, y_tr, y_cal = train_test_split(X_tr_full, y_tr_full, test_
size=0.33)

# Two very different models
models = {
    "Linear": LinearRegression(),
    "RandomForest": RandomForestRegressor()
}

alpha = 0.05
for name, model in models.items():
```

```
    lower, upper = conformal_intervals(model, X_tr, y_tr, X_cal, y_cal,
X_te, alpha)
    coverage = np.mean((y_te >= lower) & (y_te <= upper))
    print(f"{name} | empirical coverage = {coverage:.3f}")
```

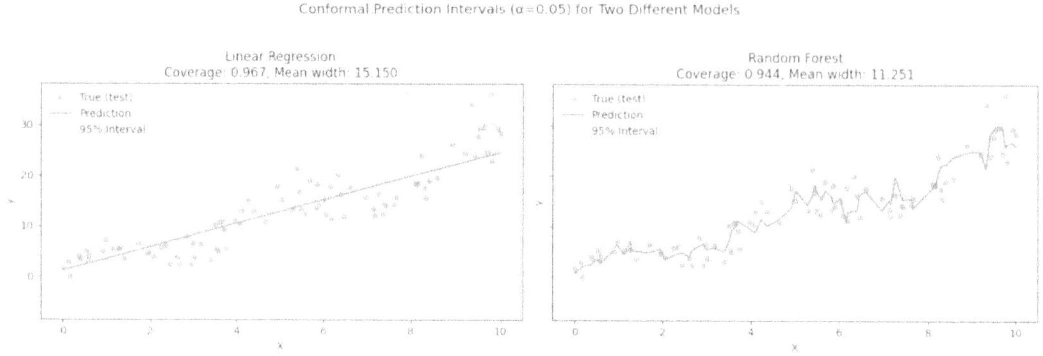

Figure 2.3: *CI Intervals for Different Models*

Here, we have constructed 95% prediction intervals around the outputs of two different models. This example illustrates how conformal prediction not only works seamlessly with any model architecture but also **adapts its interval widths seamlessly** based on the model's performance. In this nonlinear simulated dataset, as expected, the Random Forest captures the pattern more effectively than the Linear Regression model. This difference is reflected in their conformal intervals; **the Random Forest yields narrower, more confident intervals, while the Linear Regression produces wider ones to compensate for its higher residual errors.** Yet, despite these differences, both models maintain approximately 95% coverage on the test set, demonstrating how conformal prediction dynamically adjusts uncertainty, while remaining model-agnostic.

Non-Conformity Scores

At the core of Conformal Prediction lies a simple yet powerful idea:

Each new prediction is like a test of familiarity — the model silently asks, "Have I seen something like this before, or does this feel out of place?"

The non-conformity score captures exactly this notion - *it quantifies how "different" a new example is from the patterns learned by the model.* If a new data point fits well with past data and the model's understanding, its nonconformity score is low. If it behaves unexpectedly or lies in a region the model has rarely seen, the score is high. This score acts as the backbone of the conformal prediction framework. It transforms a model's **past errors** into a measurable scale of **"how unusual"** future predictions are likely to be.

Absolute Error

The simplest and most intuitive way to measure how unusual a prediction is, is to ask a straightforward question:

"How far was I from being right?"

Error-based nonconformity captures this idea directly. It measures the **difference between what the model predicted and what actually happened**. If the prediction closely matches the observed value, the example is *conforming* — it behaves as the model expected. But if the gap between prediction and truth is large, the example is *nonconforming*, signaling that the model was surprised or less certain in that region. This family of nonconformity scores is at the heart of **regression** and **forecasting** conformal prediction methods, where outputs are numeric and deviations can be easily quantified. It gives a natural way to turn model performance into uncertainty: the more error the model historically makes, the wider its future confidence intervals should be.

$$r_i = |y_i - \hat{y}_i|$$

You compute these absolute errors on a held-out calibration set, take a high quantile (for example, 90th for $\alpha = 0.1$), and then expand future predictions by that amount. The result is a simple, distribution-free interval: if the model historically had errors $\leq q$ about 90% of the time, then expanding future predictions by q gives roughly 90% coverage. The following is a code example to explain how prediction intervals are computed using historic absolute errors.

```
import numpy as np
from sklearn.model_selection import train_test_split
from sklearn.ensemble import RandomForestRegressor

def split_conformal_intervals(model, X_train, y_train, X_calib, y_calib,
X_test, alpha=0.1):
    model.fit(X_train, y_train)
    calib_pred = model.predict(X_calib)
    q = np.quantile(np.abs(y_calib - calib_pred), 1 - alpha)
    test_pred = model.predict(X_test)
    return test_pred - q, test_pred + q

# Synthetic regression data
np.random.seed(42)
X = np.linspace(0, 10, 300).reshape(-1, 1)
y = 2*X.squeeze() + 3*np.sin(1.2*X.squeeze()) + np.random.
randn(300)*(0.8 + 0.2*X.squeeze())

# Train / calibration / test split
X_tr_full, X_te, y_tr_full, y_te = train_test_split(X, y, test_size=0.25)
```

```
X_tr, X_cal, y_tr, y_cal = train_test_split(X_tr_full, y_tr_full, test_
size=0.33)

# Any regression model
model = RandomForestRegressor(random_state=0)

alpha = 0.1
lower, upper = split_conformal_intervals(model, X_tr, y_tr, X_cal, y_
cal, X_te, alpha)

coverage = np.mean((y_te >= lower) & (y_te <= upper))
print("Empirical coverage:", coverage)
```

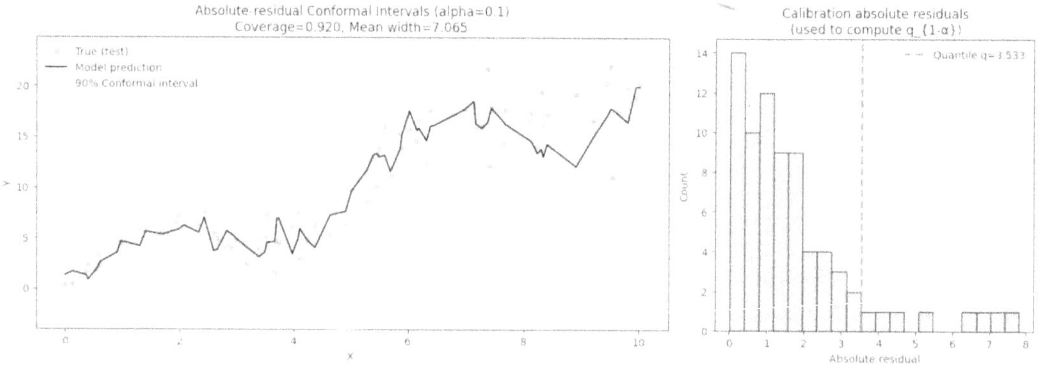

Figure 2.4: *Absolute Non-Conformity Score*

The absolute residual nonconformity score is the simplest yet most powerful way to connect model predictions with real-world reliability. It directly measures how far the model's predictions deviate from observed values, translating raw prediction errors into a meaningful notion of uncertainty. Despite its simplicity, this method captures the true spirit of conformal prediction — learning confidence not from theoretical assumptions or model internals, but from how the model has actually performed in the past.

Normalized Residual Approach

The absolute residual approach assumes that the model's uncertainty - the spread of its prediction errors is roughly the same across all input regions. This means the conformal interval it produces has a *fixed width everywhere*, regardless of how predictable or noisy different parts of the data are. In reality, however, most of the data is **heteroskedastic**, the variance of the target changes with the input. [1]

Some regions of the feature space are stable and easy to predict, while others are inherently volatile, for example:

- In a **sales forecasting** problem, small-volume SKUs show erratic and spiky demand, whereas mature, high-volume products exhibit stable and predictable patterns.

- In a **manufacturing process**, production yield may fluctuate widely under certain machine settings or ambient conditions but remain consistent under optimal configurations.
- In **real estate price prediction**, high-end luxury markets may display large price swings for similar properties, while mid-range housing prices are more tightly clustered.
- In a **medical regression task** predicting patient recovery time, younger or healthier patients may follow predictable recovery curves, while older patients show higher variability due to comorbidities.
- And in a **financial time series**, predictive uncertainty naturally grows as the forecast horizon extends, leading to wider potential outcomes, the further you look ahead.

When such variability exists, conformal prediction based on **absolute residuals** becomes inefficient; it overestimates uncertainty where the model performs well and underestimates it where the data is inherently noisy. The result is uneven coverage — too conservative in simple regions, and too narrow in complex ones. The **normalized residual nonconformity** addresses this imbalance by redefining how we measure the model error.

Instead of treating all deviations equally, it evaluates each prediction error *relative to the model's local level of uncertainty*. In other words, it expresses every residual in standardized, unitless terms — answering the question:

"How large was this prediction error compared to how uncertain the model was expected to be here?"

By dividing each residual by an estimate of local noise, the normalized score removes the effect of heteroskedasticity — making errors from all regions directly comparable. During calibration, conformal prediction then learns a universal tolerance level (for example, the 90th percentile of these normalized deviations), representing how far predictions typically stray from the truth when measured in local uncertainty units. At prediction time, this tolerance is *multiplied back by the model's local uncertainty estimate*, allowing each interval to adapt dynamically, that is, widening in noisy regions, narrowing in stable ones.

This simple normalization-denormalization process transforms conformal prediction from a one-size-fits-all interval generator into an adaptive, context-aware uncertainty estimator, one that faithfully follows the data's changing volatility, while maintaining global coverage validity. The following is a summary flowchart of how the process looks like broadly.

- Compute residuals in the calibration set.
- Normalize it by the local noise to get everything on the same scale and unitless.
- Compute quantiles same as in absolute errors (*q90,q95, and so on*)

- Denormalize at the time of interval computation to bring in the same scale.

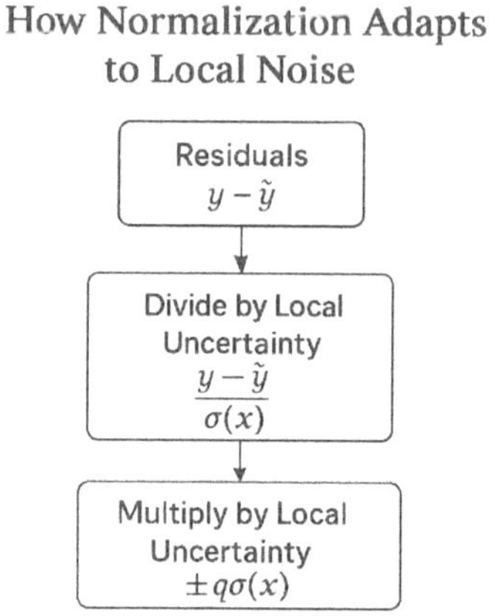

Figure 2.5: *Normalization Score Workflow*

We have mentioned **local noise** multiple times, and it truly sits at the heart of how normalized residual conformal prediction adapts to changing uncertainty. Let us now understand it more clearly. The term $\sigma(x)$ represents how much variability or randomness the model expects around its prediction at a specific input x. It is usually learned from the model's past errors by observing where predictions tend to fluctuate more, and where they remain stable. Mathematically, this can be expressed as $\sigma(x) = g(x)$ where $g(.)$ represents a secondary model between dependent variables x and absolute errors. This local noise can be captured either through a secondary model trained on residuals or by simpler techniques such as local averaging or nearest-neighbor smoothing. By dividing each residual by this estimated local scale, we evaluate errors relative to the expected uncertainty in that region, allowing conformal prediction to adapt its interval width dynamically—widening where variability is high, and tightening where predictions are more stable.

Let us then understand this with another example scenario from the manufacturing side this time.

- In a factory process, **machine temperature** strongly affects **production yield**, with an optimal point (around 75 °C) where yields are stable and predictable.
- As temperature moves away from this optimum — either too low or too high — the process becomes unstable, and **yield variability increases**, creating a U-shaped noise pattern.
- A **standard absolute-residual conformal model** would assign the same interval width across all temperatures, ignoring that uncertainty grows at the extremes.
- The **normalized residual approach** divides each error by an estimate of local noise $\sigma(x)$, so errors are judged relative to the expected variability in that region.

- When intervals are formed, multiplying the conformal quantile back by **`sigma_hat`** makes them **narrow near the optimal temperature** (where predictions are reliable) and **wider at the extremes** (where the process is noisier).

```
import numpy as np
from sklearn.model_selection import train_test_split
from sklearn.ensemble import RandomForestRegressor,
GradientBoostingRegressor

def normalized_conformal_intervals(
    X_train, y_train, X_calib, y_calib, X_test, alpha=0.1
):
    # point prediction model
    point_model = RandomForestRegressor(random_state=0)
    point_model.fit(X_train, y_train)

    # calibration residuals
    calib_pred = point_model.predict(X_calib)
    abs_resid = np.abs(y_calib - calib_pred)

    # learn local scale (sigma_hat)
    scale_model = GradientBoostingRegressor(random_state=0)
    scale_model.fit(X_calib, abs_resid)

    sigma_cal = scale_model.predict(X_calib)
    sigma_test = scale_model.predict(X_test)

    # normalized nonconformity scores
    scores = abs_resid / (sigma_cal + 1e-9)
    q = np.quantile(scores, 1 - alpha)

    # adaptive intervals
    test_pred = point_model.predict(X_test)
    lower = test_pred - q * sigma_test
    upper = test_pred + q * sigma_test
    return lower, upper

# Synthetic manufacturing yield data (heteroskedastic)
np.random.seed(0)
X = np.linspace(50, 100, 600).reshape(-1, 1)
y = 95*np.exp(-0.5*((X.squeeze()-75)/8)**2) + np.random.
randn(600)*(2+0.08*(X.squeeze()-75)**2)

# Train / calibration / test split
X_tr_full, X_te, y_tr_full, y_te = train_test_split(X, y, test_
size=0.25)
X_tr, X_cal, y_tr, y_cal = train_test_split(X_tr_full, y_tr_full, test_
size=0.33)
```

```
alpha = 0.1
lower, upper = normalized_conformal_intervals(X_tr, y_tr, X_cal, y_cal,
X_te, alpha)
coverage = np.mean((y_te >= lower) & (y_te <= upper))

print("Empirical coverage:", coverage)
```

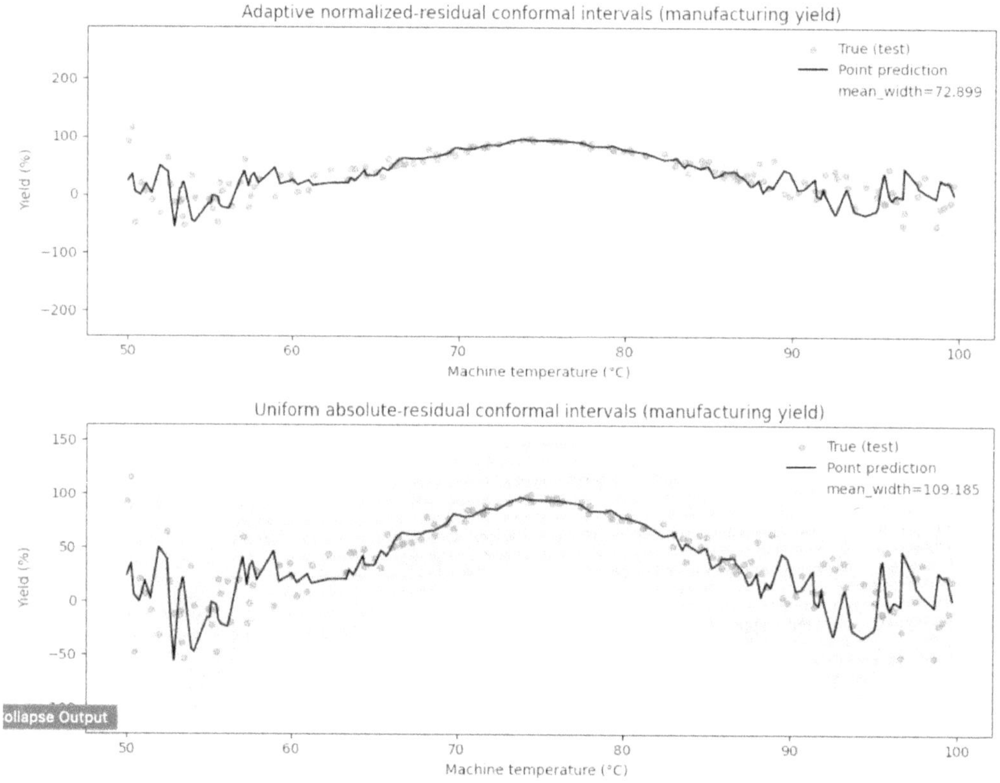

Figure 2.6: *CI Adaptiveness*

In the above example, we can clearly see how normalized residuals adapt to varying noise well as compared to fixed absolute errors, hence providing more dynamic intervals without hindering the accuracy significantly.

Probability Based Non-Conformity

While residual-based conformity scores mentioned above measure how *far* a model's prediction is from the truth, **probability-based scores** measure how *confident* the model is in its own prediction.

Instead of focusing on differences, these scores rely on the **predicted probability distribution** (or likelihood) produced by the model, asking a slightly different question:

"How surprised is the model by the true outcome, given what it believed beforehand?"

This is especially useful when models provide **probabilistic outputs**, such as predicted class probabilities for classification. In such cases, instead of looking at the magnitude of error, we measure **how much probability mass** the model assigned to what actually happened.

Let us now revisit our classroom scenario; this time projected as a classification problem of predicting whether students will pass or fail based on their study hours, attendance, and past grades. A probabilistic model (like logistic regression) doesn't just predict "pass" or "fail" — it outputs probabilities, say, 0.92 *for pass* and 0.08 *for fail*. If a student a ctually fails despite the model assigning only 8% probability to that event, the model was **very surprised**, it made a confident but wrong prediction. Another student with a 55%-45% probability split who fails does not shock the model as much; the model already expected that outcome to be somewhat likely.

For classification models, the probability-based nonconformity score is often defined as:

$$s_i = 1 - p(y_i \mid x_i)$$

Where $p(y_i \mid x_i)$ is the model's predicted probability for the *true class* of sample x_i

- If the model is confident and correct (probability near 1), s_i is small → high conformity.
- If the model is confident but wrong (probability near 0) s_i is large → low conformity.
- If the model is uncertain (probability ≈ 0.5), s_i is moderate → balanced conformity.

Let us now put some numbers behind our classroom performance example to better understand this scoring strategy. Suppose, we have a data from 600 students, where we assign pass or fail outcomes using a binomial distribution with probabilities that increase proportionally with study hours and attendance. We then split the dataset into training, calibration, and test sets as usual. During calibration, instead of computing residual errors, we evaluate how confident the model's predicted probabilities are for the true outcomes. The quantile in this case represents a **confidence threshold** — for example, a 90% level means that 90% of the predictions correspond to probabilities of 0.6 or higher for the correct class.

```
import numpy as np
from sklearn.linear_model import LogisticRegression
from sklearn.model_selection import train_test_split

# Simulated pass/fail data
np.random.seed(42)
X = np.column_stack([
```

```
    np.random.uniform(0, 10, 600),       # study hours
    np.random.uniform(0.5, 1.0, 600)     # attendance
])
true_prob = 1 / (1 + np.exp(-(0.8*X[:,0] + 3.5*(X[:,1]-0.7) - 3)))
y = np.random.binomial(1, true_prob)

# Train / calibration / test split
X_tr_full, X_te, y_tr_full, y_te = train_test_split(X, y, test_size=0.25)
X_tr, X_cal, y_tr, y_cal = train_test_split(X_tr_full, y_tr_full, test_
size=0.33)

# Probabilistic classifier
clf = LogisticRegression(max_iter=200)
clf.fit(X_tr, y_tr)

# Calibration nonconformity scores (1 - prob(true label))
calib_probs = clf.predict_proba(X_cal)
scores = 1 - calib_probs[np.arange(len(y_cal)), y_cal]

alpha = 0.1
q = np.quantile(scores, 1 - alpha)

# Prediction sets on test data
test_probs = clf.predict_proba(X_te)
pred_sets = [
    [cls for cls, p in enumerate(probs) if (1 - p) <= q]
    for probs in test_probs
]

coverage = np.mean([y_te[i] in pred_sets[i] for i in range(len(y_te))])
avg_size = np.mean([len(s) for s in pred_sets])

print("Empirical coverage:", coverage)
print("Average prediction set size:", avg_size)
```

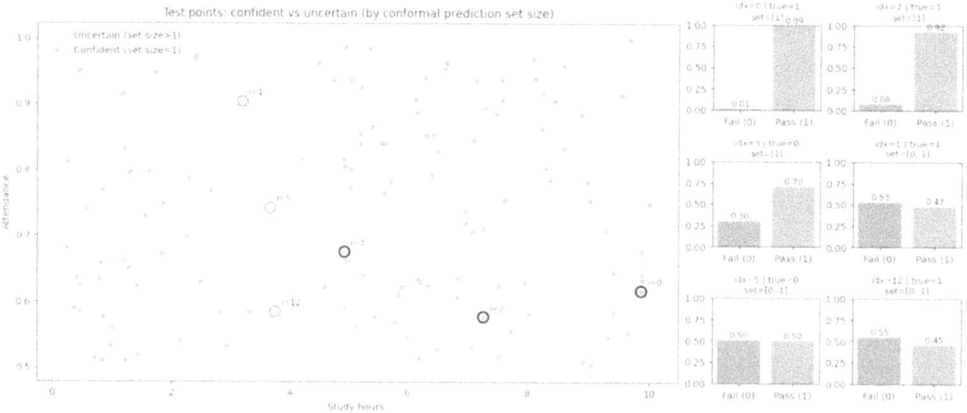

Figure 2.7: *Confidence Scores across Different Regions*

Here, we see prediction sets assigned to the test data based on the probability estimates across different ranges, we can clearly see in the middle area where students study less and attendance is also average there model fails to predict with confidence hence the uncertainty, and the best part is this uncertainty threshold is derived empirically from historical data without any assumptions. In fact, these interval sets make more sense when we have multiple classes, and the CP helps us identify most probable classes.

Validity and Coverage

All the principles we have explored so far – **exchangeability**, **model agnosticism**, and **nonconformity scoring** come together in one powerful outcome: **validity**.

Validity is the defining promise of conformal prediction, the assurance that when we say a prediction interval or set has 90% confidence, it truly covers the correct outcome 90% of the time. It's not an approximation, nor a hope based on assumptions, it's a statistical guarantee, derived purely from data. In classical machine learning, models can make accurate point predictions yet remain dangerously **overconfident** or **inconsistent** in their uncertainty estimates. For example, a neural network might assign 99% confidence to a misclassified image or an overfit regression model might produce narrow intervals that miss the true value too often. Conformal prediction corrects this imbalance. It doesn't claim perfect knowledge of the future; instead, it ensures **honesty** the frequency with which true outcomes fall inside predicted intervals matches the intended confidence level over time. At its core, validity is operationalized through **coverage**, the proportion of test instances where the true outcome lies within the conformal prediction region. Conformal prediction ensures that, under exchangeability, this coverage is statistically aligned with the chosen confidence level (for example, 90%, 95%) regardless of model type, data distribution, or complexity.

Validity is the reason you can trust conformal prediction.

This chapter explores what coverage means in both theoretical and practical terms, the difference between **marginal** and **conditional** validity, and why coverage can sometimes vary across subgroups or regions of the input space. We shall also discuss how conformal methods achieve this reliability without making distributional assumptions, and how practitioners can empirically check and improve coverage in real-world settings.

Imagine that we are building a regression model to predict house prices. For each prediction, conformal prediction does not just provide a single value, it produces an *interval*, say [320*k*, 360*k*], claiming to contain the true price with 90% confidence. **Coverage** tells us how often these claims are actually true. If, over many unseen houses, about 9 out of 10 actual prices indeed fall inside their respective intervals, the conformal predictor achieves **90% coverage**, and thus, **validity**.

In more formal terms, if $C(x_i)$ is the conformal prediction interval or set for an observation x_i and y_i is its true label, then the coverage is given by:

$$Coverage = P(y_i \in C(x_i))$$

A conformal predictor is said to be **valid at level** $(1 - \alpha)$ if:

$$P(y_i \in C(x_i)) \geq (1 - \alpha)$$

This means that the probability of the true outcome falling inside the predicted region is at least the intended confidence level (for example, 90% for α=0.1). Importantly, this guarantee does not rely on knowing the underlying data distribution or model correctness – it holds as long as the data points are **exchangeable**, meaning that past and future examples come from the same process.

Conclusion

In this chapter, we established the core principles that make conformal prediction both powerful and reliable: **exchangeability** as the foundational assumption, **model agnosticism** as the source of flexibility, **nonconformity scores** as the mechanism for converting model errors or probabilities into measurable uncertainty, and **validity and coverage** as the ultimate statistical guarantee. Together, these ideas form a complete framework for producing honest, distribution-free uncertainty estimates that remain trustworthy, regardless of the model or data complexity.

In the next chapter, we bring these foundations into practice by focusing specifically on **Conformal Prediction for Regression**. We will show how these principles translate into concrete interval-construction procedures, explore different scoring choices, examine interval sharpness and behavior under heteroskedastic noise, and demonstrate how conformal prediction provides robust, calibrated uncertainty estimates for continuous outcomes.

Points to Remember

- **Exchangeability is the foundation** of all conformal guarantees: coverage is valid as long as calibration and test data come from the same underlying process.
- **Conformal prediction is model agnostic**, meaning it can wrap around any predictive model such as: linear, tree-based, neural, or probabilistic, without altering its internal structure.
- **Nonconformity scores quantify uncertainty** by measuring how "strange" or "unusual" a new prediction is relative to the calibration data. Different score types adapt to different data characteristics.

- **Validity is expressed through coverage**, the fraction of true outcomes captured by the prediction region at a chosen confidence level (for example, 90%).

Chapter Resources

- Code Exercise

Multiple Choice Questions

1. Which assumption is essential for the validity guarantees in conformal prediction?
   a. Normality of residuals
   b. Exchangeability of data
   c. Independence between features
   d. Equal variance across the dataset
2. Conformal prediction is considered model-agnostic because:
   a. It requires linearity in the underlying model.
   b. It only works with probabilistic models.
   c. It can be applied to any model that produces predictions.
   d. It replaces the model's loss function.
3. What is the primary purpose of a nonconformity score?
   a. To measure the model's training error
   b. To quantify how unusual a new example is compared to calibration data
   c. To tune the hyperparameters of the underlying model
   d. To remove outliers from the dataset
4. Absolute residual non-conformity scores are most appropriate when:
   a. Noise varies significantly across the feature space.
   b. The dataset is homoskedastic.
   c. The model outputs calibrated probabilities.
   d. The data contains many missing values.
5. Normalized residual scores are used primarily to:
   a. Reduce training time of the base model
   b. Adjust for heteroskedastic noise

c. Improve the model's R^2

d. Replace the calibration split

6. In probability-based conformal prediction for classification, the non-conformity score is often computed as:

    a. The squared error between prediction and label.

    b. The number of classes predicted incorrectly.

    c. The negative log-likelihood of the true class.

    d. One minus the predicted probability of the true class.

7. Coverage in conformal prediction refers to:

    a. The percentage of features used in training.

    b. The proportion of outcomes captured by prediction sets or intervals.

    c. The accuracy of the underlying model.

    d. The number of calibration points required.

8. Which of the following best describes the role of non-conformity scores in conformal prediction?

    a. They convert model predictions into intervals or sets by measuring how unusual each example is.

    b. They replace the need for a calibration set entirely.

    c. They adjust the model weights during training.

    d. They ensure the dataset is exchangeable.

9. What happens to conformal prediction intervals if the calibration residuals become systematically larger?

    a. Intervals shrink because the model is more confident.

    b. Intervals become unstable and oscillate randomly.

    c. Intervals widen because the quantile of residuals increases.

    d. Intervals collapse to a single point.

10. A drop in empirical coverage most likely indicates:

    a. Too many calibration samples

    b. Better model accuracy

    c. Violation of exchangeability or distribution shift

    d. Excessive feature scaling

Answers

1. b
2. c
3. b
4. b
5. b
6. d
7. b
8. a
9. c
10. c

Key Terms

- **Exchangeability:** The fundamental assumption that past and future data points come from the same underlying process and can be permuted, without changing their joint behavior. This symmetry enables conformal prediction's coverage guarantees.
- **Model Agnosticism:** The ability of conformal prediction to work with any predictive model — from linear regression to deep neural networks, without requiring changes to the model itself or assumptions about its form.
- **Non-conformity Score:** A measure of how unusual or inconsistent a prediction is relative to the calibration data. It transforms model outputs into a standardized notion of uncertainty.
- **Coverage (Validity):** The proportion of true outcomes that fall within the conformal prediction region. Coverage reflects the accuracy of the stated confidence level (for example, 90%) and represents the core validity guarantee of conformal prediction.

References

1. A Review of Nonconformity Measures for Conformal Prediction in Regression Yuka Kato et al.

CHAPTER 3
Conformal Prediction for Classification

Introduction

In the previous chapters, we uncovered why uncertainty matters in machine learning, and how conformal prediction provides a principled, model-agnostic way to quantify it. We saw how point predictions, no matter how accurate, can be misleading when they fail to communicate uncertainty, and how conformal prediction transforms past model errors into statistically valid confidence guarantees. These ideas were introduced in a general setting, laying a common foundation that applies across different learning problems. In this chapter, we take the next step and focus on one of the most widely used and high-impact settings in machine learning: **classification**.

In real-world problems where machines are *asked to make choices rather than estimate numbers, uncertainty becomes even more important because those choices often lead to immediate and difficult-to-reverse actions*. When a model predicts a continuous value (regression), *small errors can sometimes be corrected or absorbed over time (though in some domains like healthcare, finance even small errors can be critical). But when a system must decide between categories such as approve or reject, safe or unsafe, or spam or legitimate, there is no gradual adjustment.* **A single decision can block a loan, delay medical care, flag a customer, or remove content.** Yet these decisions are still made under incomplete information and imperfect understanding of the world. Without a way to express how uncertain a decision truly is, the system appears more confident than it should be, increasing the risk of costly mistakes in exactly the borderline cases where caution matters most.

As discussed in the foundations chapter, conformal prediction provides a principled, model-agnostic way to quantify uncertainty using a model's past behavior, without relying on strong assumptions about data distributions or model structure. The same framework extends naturally to classification problems, where the consequences of uncertainty are often more severe. Instead of forcing a single label in every case, conformal prediction allows us to express uncertainty directly by returning a set of plausible classes whenever the model's confidence is not sufficiently supported by historical evidence. In this chapter, we build on the core ideas introduced earlier, and examine how conformal prediction works in classification settings, how prediction sets are constructed and interpreted, and how these sets provide meaningful, statistically valid guarantees that help classification systems behave more cautiously and reliably in real-world decision making.

Structure

This chapter is organized into the following sections:

- From Single Labels to Prediction Sets
- Building Conformal Predictors for Classification
- Conformal Prediction Algorithms
  - Inductive Conformal Prediction
  - Mondrian Conformal Prediction for Class Imbalance
  - Adaptive Conformal Prediction under Distribution Shift
- Evaluating Conformal Classifiers: Coverage and Set Size

From Single Labels to Prediction Sets

Traditional classification models are built to give a single answer/label for every input. *An email is labeled as spam or not spam, a transaction is flagged as fraud or legitimate, a customer is approved or rejected.* This design makes classification systems easy to use and easy to evaluate, but it also hides an important reality: many inputs do not clearly belong to just one category. In practice, data points often lie near decision boundaries, resemble multiple classes, or fall into regions the model has rarely seen before. When a classifier is forced to output exactly one label in such situations, *it presents a sense of certainty that the data itself does not justify, and hence, the need to output prediction sets specially in case of multi class/label settings provide the quantification of the uncertainty helping in making informed decisions.*

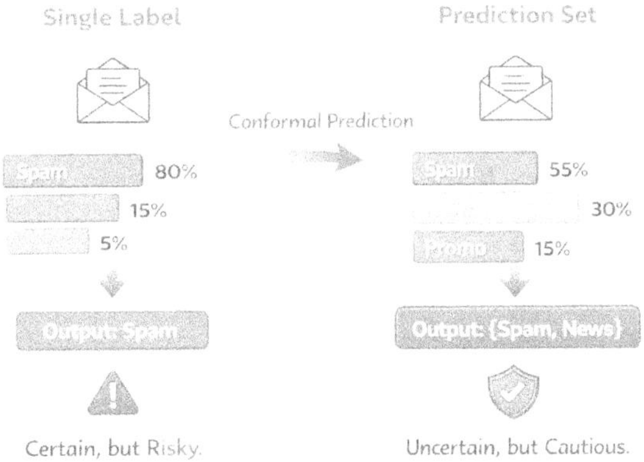

Figure 3.1: *Visual Illustration of CP in Classification*

Let us understand this with a setup using dummy data related to emails with multiple tags like spam, promotional, social, and important.

- Each email is first converted into numerical features using TF-IDF, allowing the classifier to work with raw text, while preserving the importance of informative words.
- A probabilistic multiclass classifier is trained so that, instead of only predicting a single label, it assigns a probability to every possible email category.
- A fixed probability threshold is then applied to these outputs, and all classes whose probability exceeds this threshold are included in the prediction set for that email.
- Emails with more than one class crossing the threshold are treated as uncertain cases, and their class probabilities are visualized using bar charts to show how belief is split across multiple, plausible labels.
- The horizontal threshold line makes it explicit which classes enter the prediction set, illustrating how ambiguity is revealed, rather than hidden by forcing a single prediction.

```
from sklearn.feature_extraction.text import TfidfVectorizer
from sklearn.linear_model import LogisticRegression

# Short email dataset
emails = [
    "Huge discounts available now",
    "Meeting rescheduled to tomorrow",
    "Exclusive deal from our partners",
    "Final reminder about your invoice"
]

label_names = ["spam", "promotional", "social", "important"]

# Vectorize text and train classifier
X = TfidfVectorizer(stop_words="english").fit_transform(emails)
clf = LogisticRegression(multi_class="multinomial", max_iter=300).fit(X,
[1, 3, 1, 3])

# Construct prediction sets using a probability threshold
probs = clf.predict_proba(X)
threshold = 0.3

prediction_sets = [
    [label_names[i] for i, p in enumerate(row) if p >= threshold]
    for row in probs
]
```

The full code link is provided at the end of this chapter.

The following are some of the sample emails where the model was not confident, and hence, provided a prediction set of possible outcomes instead of a single tag.

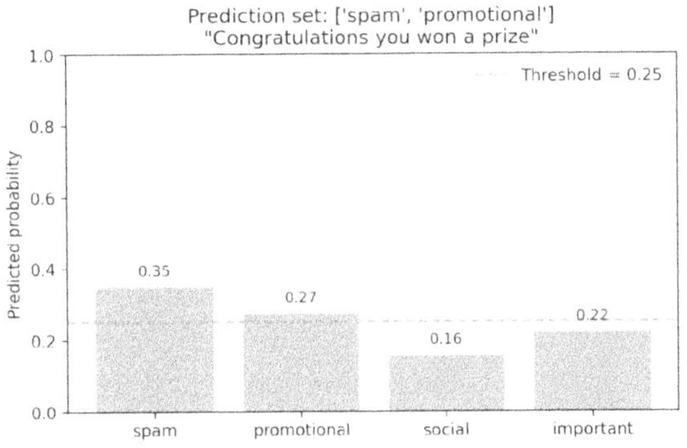

Figure 3.2: *Prediction Set for Sample 1*

The following is another example where the model confused between spam and promotional messages.

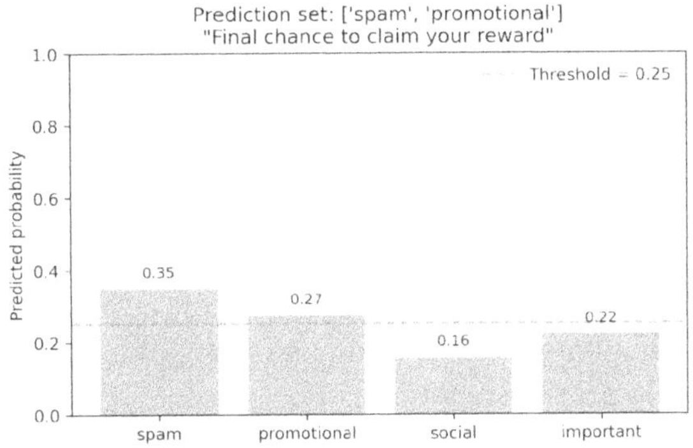

Figure 3.3: *Prediction Set for Sample 2*

Here is one more example solidifying the idea of the need of prediction sets in case of underconfident predictions.

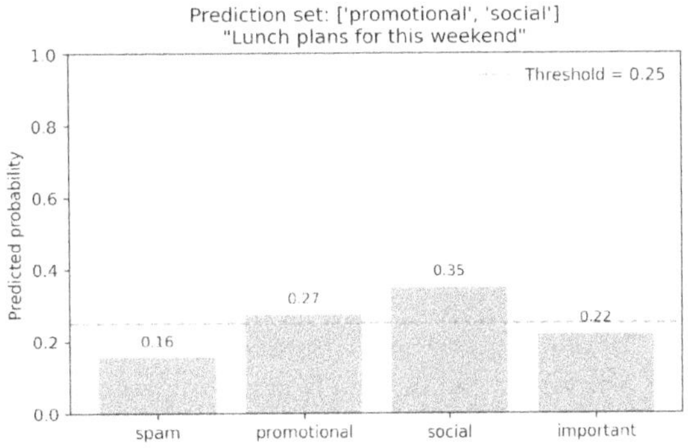

Figure 3.4: *Prediction Set for Sample 3*

These examples illustrate situations *where the model's uncertainty is not a weakness, but an accurate reflection of the data.* In each case, the classifier assigns meaningful probability to more than one class, **indicating that multiple interpretations are reasonable**. *Forcing a single label in such situations hides this uncertainty, and can lead to undesirable outcomes.* Prediction sets allow the model to communicate ambiguity explicitly, enabling more cautious and context-aware decisions. Let us do a breakdown of these example outputs to understand this concept intuitively.

- For "*Congratulations you won a prize*", the model is confused between **spam** and **promotional** because words like *congratulations*, *won*, and *prize* frequently appear in both spam emails and legitimate marketing campaigns. The TF-IDF representation captures these shared patterns, leading the classifier to assign comparable scores to both classes. A single-label prediction would likely mark it as spam, risking the loss of a genuine promotional message. The prediction set reflects that both interpretations are plausible, given the learned language patterns.

- In "*Final chance to claim your reward*", urgency-related phrases such as *final chance* and *claim* strongly influence the model. These phrases are highly predictive of spam, but they are also common in time-limited promotional emails. As a result, the classifier cannot clearly separate the two classes based on text alone. Returning the set {spam, promotional} communicates this uncertainty, and avoids an overconfident decision.

- For "*Lunch plans for this weekend*", the confusion lies between **social** and **important** because the message is short and context-dependent. Terms like *plans* and *weekend* are common in casual social conversations, but the timing and intent could still matter to the recipient. With no additional context, the model assigns similar probability to both classes. The prediction set {social, important} acknowledges this ambiguity, and allows downstream systems or user preferences to resolve it appropriately.

In real-world systems, classification outputs are rarely the final decision. They are often inputs to downstream actions that carry cost, risk, or user impact. An email classified as spam may be blocked entirely, a transaction flagged as fraud may be declined, a medical case labeled low risk may be deprioritized, and a content post marked harmful may be removed automatically. In such settings, the most damaging errors tend to occur not when the model is clearly wrong, but when it is **uncertain and forced to act confident**. Prediction sets help prevent this failure mode. By explicitly indicating when multiple outcomes remain plausible, *they allow systems to behave differently in borderline cases: triggering manual review, applying softer rules, delaying irreversible actions, or incorporating additional context.* This leads to more efficient decision making because resources such as human attention, alerts, and interventions are focused exactly where uncertainty is highest, rather than being wasted on cases where the model is already confident.

The examples in this section illustrate how prediction sets preserve critical information that single-label outputs discard. Instead of asking the model to choose one class at all costs, prediction sets allow it to say which classes still make sense given the data it has seen. This shift forms the core idea behind conformal prediction in classification. So far, we have used simple probability-based rules to motivate the concept. Conformal prediction builds on this intuition and replaces heuristic thresholds with a principled, data-driven procedure that guarantees how often the true label will appear in the prediction set. In the next sections, we will explore how these sets are computed formally, how confidence levels control their size, and how conformal prediction provides reliable uncertainty estimates for classification tasks in real-world systems.egories, and rarely to the others. The non-conformity scores encode this historical pattern in a numeric form, capturing which labels the model has struggled to distinguish in the past.

Building Conformal Predictors for Classification

In the previous section, *we saw how prediction sets provide a more faithful way to represent uncertainty in classification, especially in borderline cases where multiple labels remain plausible.* The natural next question is **how we decide *which* labels should enter this set, and which should be excluded**. In classification problems, this decision is closely tied to the *probabilities produced by the underlying model*. Rather than measuring uncertainty through errors or residuals, as we do in regression, *classification models express uncertainty through how they distribute probability mass across classes*. Probability-based non-conformity scores formalize this idea by turning class probabilities into a principled measure of how surprising or implausible a label is for a given input. In this section, we build on the intuition developed so far, and show how probabilistic outputs become the foundation for constructing prediction sets in conformal classification.

Probability-based non-conformity scores serve as *the bridge between a classifier's probabilistic output, and the prediction sets we saw earlier.* For a given input, the classifier assigns probabilities to all possible classes. These probabilities are then converted into nonconformity scores that reflect how poorly each candidate label fits the input. A simple *way to do this is to treat labels with low probability as more nonconforming and labels with high probability as more conforming.* In this sense, the non-conformity score can be thought of as a proxy for incompatibility that model makes during assigning classes.

Consider the email example where the model assigns similar probability to **spam** and **promotional** for a message like "*Final chance to claim your reward.*" Both labels receive relatively low non-conformity scores, while other classes such as **social** or **important** receive much higher scores. This reflects the model's past experience such as: messages with similar wording have often belonged to either spam or promotional.

Crucially, *Conformal Prediction evaluates them against non-conformity scores observed on past data*, effectively asking whether a **candidate label looks unusually incompatible compared to what the model has previously seen**. *Labels whose scores fall within the typical range of past errors are retained*, while those that appear too inconsistent are excluded. We can view probability-based non-conformity scores as a way of turning the model's past mistakes and uncertainties into a reusable signal. Now, we will dive into different techniques used to compute Probability based non-conformity scores. The following are some techniques used to compute this score, and we will understand all of them in detail using the usual way of understanding through dummy data.

Step 1: Training

We begin with a standard probabilistic classification model, and no notion of prediction sets. The model's only role is to learn how to assign probabilities to each possible class based on patterns in the training data. For every input, it produces a probability distribution over all , rather than a single label, capturing how plausible each label is relative to the others. These probability vectors form the common starting point for all probability-based non-conformity scores. In the steps that follow, we will keep this classifier fixed, and use its probabilistic outputs to demonstrate different ways of computing non-conformity scores within a single, continuous example.

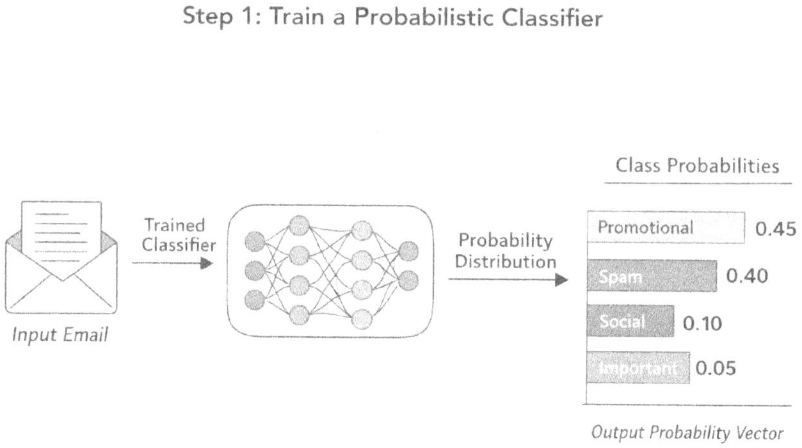

Figure 3.5: *Training the Classifier*

Step 2: Calibration

Once a probabilistic classifier has been trained, conformal prediction does not modify or retrain the model. Instead, it introduces a separate calibration step that uses a held-out dataset to understand *how the trained model behaves on unseen data*. The calibration set serves as a reference for the model's past uncertainty, capturing **how often and how severely the model assigns low probability to the correct label**. By *observing this behavior across many examples, conformal prediction builds an empirical picture of what constitutes typical and atypical model behaviors.* This reference will later be used to compute non-conformity scores, and eventually decide which labels should be included in a prediction set for new inputs, grounding uncertainty estimates in the model's own historical performance, rather than arbitrary thresholds.

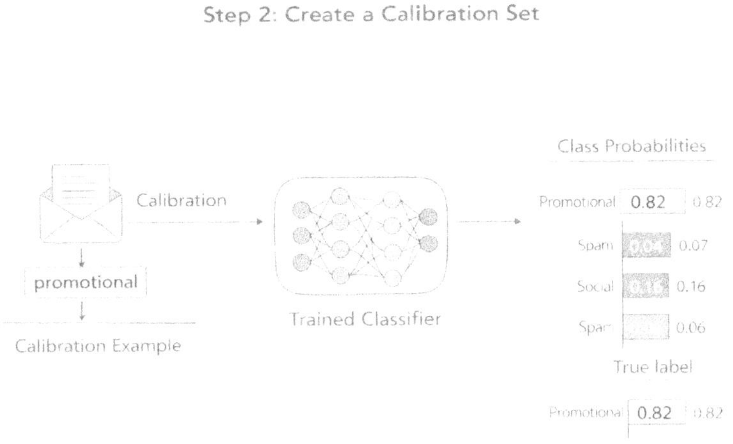

Figure 3.6: *Creating Calibration Set*

Step 3: Non-Conformity Scores

With the calibration examples passed through the trained classifier, the next step is to convert the model's probabilistic outputs into non-conformity scores. This step is where uncertainty is made explicit and quantifiable. For each calibration example, we focus on the probability assigned to its true label, and transform it into a non-conformity score using a chosen scoring rule. These scores summarize how well or how poorly the model has historically aligned with the correct labels on unseen data. Taken together across the calibration set, they form an empirical record of the model's past uncertainty, which will later serve as the reference for deciding which labels are acceptable for new inputs. [1]

Hinge Probability Based Score

The one-minus probability score defines the non-conformity of a candidate label as one minus the probability that the classifier assigns to that label.

$$s_i = 1 - p(y_i \mid x_i)$$

The intuition behind this definition is straightforward. Labels that receive high probability from the model are considered more compatible with the input, and therefore, have small non-conformity scores. Labels that receive low probability are treated as less compatible, and receive larger scores. This definition aligns naturally with the conformal prediction framework, where larger non-conformity values indicate greater disagreement between the model and the assumed label.

Hinge loss nonconformity score

Example	True label	Predicted probabilities for all classes	Prob-(true label)	Hinge loss nonconformity
1	promotional	(0.10, 0.70, 0.10,0.10)	0.70	0.30
2	spam	(0.45, 0.40, 0.10,0.05)	0.45	0.55
3	important	(0.15, 0.20, 0.10,0.55)	0.55	0.45
4	social	(0.20, 0.25, 0.35,0.20)	0.35	0.65
5	promotional	(0.30, 0.32, 0.28,0.10)	0.32	0.68

Figure 3.7: *One Minus Probability-Based Approach*

This is the most intuitive and widely used way to compute non-conformity scores in classification problems. The one-minus probability approach is a natural fit when the underlying model produces meaningful probability distributions over classes, as it directly reflects how strongly the model associates an input with a given label. By assigning low non-conformity to labels with high predicted probability and high nonconformity to unlikely labels, this score aligns closely with the idea of plausibility that underlies prediction sets.

This approach is especially suitable in multiclass settings where uncertainty arises from overlapping class patterns, rather than outright misclassification. It works well to expand the prediction sets in case the model was seen seriously under confident in predictions during calibration, and create concise prediction sets when probability generated by the model has been well calibrated representing the true likelihood of the actual outcome.

Margin-Based Probability Non-Conformity Score

The margin-based non-conformity score focuses on how strongly the model prefers the true label over its closest competitor. Instead of measuring how likely a label is in absolute terms, it measures how *separable* the true label is from the next most plausible alternative. This makes the margin score particularly sensitive to situations where the model is torn between two classes.

$$Margin_i = Max(p(y'_i/x_i)_{y'!=y}) - p(y/x_i)$$

Where y *= True Label*

Example	True label	Predicted probabilities for all classes	Prob (true label)	Margin nonconformity
1	promotional	(0.10, 0.70, 0.10,0.10)	0.70	0.10 - 0.70 = -0.60
2	spam	(0.45, 0.40, 0.10,0.05)	0.45	0.40 - 0.45 = -0.05
3	important	(0.15, 0.20, 0.10,0.55)	0.20	0.20 - 0.55 = -0.35
4	social	(0.20, 0.25, 0.35,0.20)	0.25	0.25 - 0.35 = -0.10
5	promotional	(0.30, 0.32, 0.28,0.10)	0.30	0.30 - 0.32 = -0.02

Figure 3.8: *Margin-Based Probability-Based Approach*

The margin-based non-conformity score captures a different kind of uncertainty than hinge loss. While hinge loss (1 – probability) measures how confident the model is in a label in absolute terms, the margin score measures how close that label is to being overtaken by its strongest competitor. In other words, hinge loss tells us *whether* the model is uncertain, whereas the margin score tells us *why* it is uncertain. When two labels receive nearly equal probabilities, the margin becomes small, signaling genuine ambiguity between specific alternatives, even if the overall confidence is low or moderate. This makes margin-based scoring especially useful in classification problems where errors arise from confusion between a small number of similar classes, leading to prediction sets that expand only when there is meaningful competition, rather than whenever the model's confidence happens to drop.

Cumulative Probability Non-Conformity Score

The cumulative probability score, often referred to as the **Adaptive Prediction Set (APS)** score, measures non-conformity by asking *how much total probability mass must be accumulated before reaching a given label.* Instead of focusing only on a single label's probability, or its closest competitor, this approach considers the *entire ordering* of class probabilities. Labels that appear early in this ordering are considered more conforming, while labels that require accumulating a large amount of probability mass before being reached are considered more non-conforming.

Concretely, for a given input, the classifier's predicted probabilities are sorted from highest to lowest. The nonconformity score for a candidate label is then defined as the sum of probabilities of all labels that have probability greater than or equal to that label. Labels near the top of the list have small cumulative scores, while labels lower in the ranking accumulate more probability mass, and therefore receive larger scores. This construction naturally adapts the size of prediction sets to the difficulty of the example: when probability mass is concentrated on a few labels, prediction sets remain small, and when probability mass is spread out, prediction sets expand.

The APS score is especially useful in multiclass problems with many labels, where uncertainty is not limited to a single competitor but distributed across several plausible alternatives. **Unlike hinge loss, which reacts to low absolute confidence, and margin-based scores, which focus on pairwise competition, APS captures *global uncertainty* by tracking how belief is distributed across the label space**. This makes it a strong choice when prediction sets should reflect the overall dispersion of model belief, rather than just the top contenders.

The following are a series of visual illustrations explaining the process, the first image shows threshold selection using a quantile based approach from the calibration set.

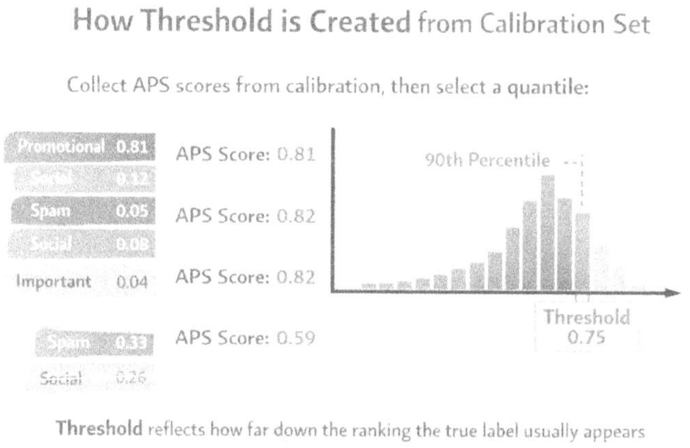

Figure 3.9: *Creating Threshold Using APS Scores*

This shows prediction set selection using the derived threshold for an underconfident example.

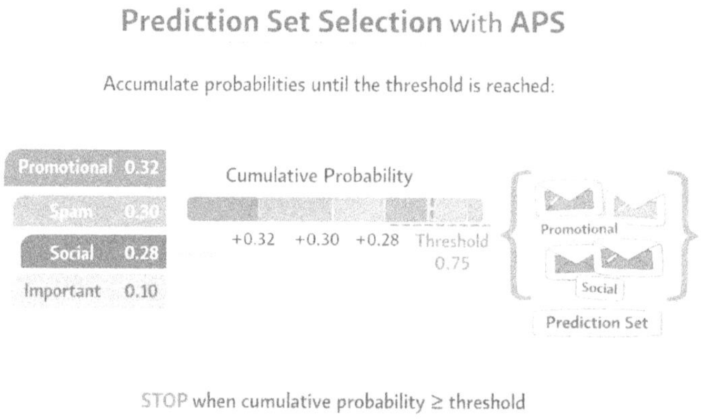

Figure 3.10: *Generating Prediction Set for a Vague Example*

Next, we see another example where the model was confident in its prediction, and hence, the prediction set adapted to contain a single class.

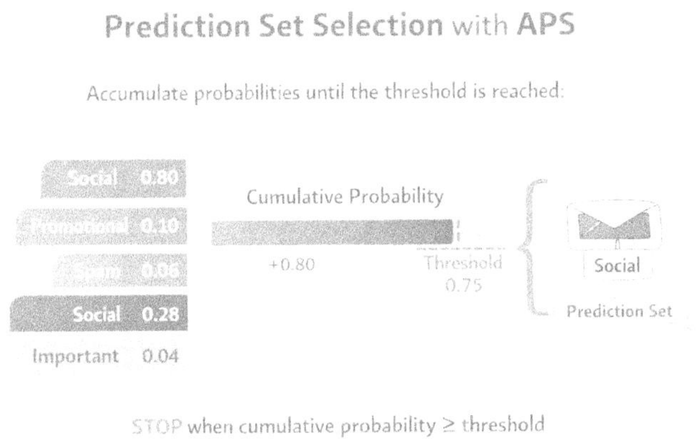

Figure 3.11: *Generating Prediction Set for a Confident Example*

- APS works by ordering labels by predicted probability, and accumulating probability mass until a calibration-derived threshold is reached. The labels included up to that point form the prediction set.
- In the first example, *probabilities are spread across multiple labels. The cumulative probability crosses the threshold only after adding several top labels, resulting in a multi-label prediction set that reflects genuine uncertainty.*
- In the *second example, one label dominates with high probability. The cumulative probability exceeds the threshold immediately, producing a singleton prediction set that signals strong conformity.*
- During calibration, APS scores are computed for each example by accumulating probabilities until the true label is reached. These scores summarize how far down the ranking the model typically needs to go.
- The threshold is chosen as a high percentile of calibration APS scores. It encodes the model's historical behavior, rather than any single prediction's confidence.
- At test time, prediction sets adapt automatically: confident examples stop early, while ambiguous ones expand, ensuring valid coverage, while remaining as informative as possible.

Step 4: Choosing the Threshold and Constructing Prediction Sets

We discussed in the APS section regarding threshold selection and prediction set creation. Here, we will summarize the process more formally. Currently, we have all the building blocks of conformal prediction for classification, and they are already in place. *We have a trained probabilistic classifier, a calibration set that reflects unseen data, and a collection of non-conformity scores that summarize how uncertain the model has historically been when it was actually correct.* What remains is to convert this historical information into a **decision rule** that can be applied consistently to new inputs. This is achieved by selecting a threshold from the calibration scores, and using it to construct prediction sets.

The central idea of this step is to replace arbitrary confidence cutoffs with a **data-driven notion of acceptability**. Instead of asking whether a class probability is "high enough," we ask a more meaningful question: *is this label as compatible with the input as the true labels typically were in the past?*

The following image illustrates how calibration thresholds are selected uniformly across different probability-based nonconformity scores using quantile selection. For each scoring method, non-conformity scores are first computed on the calibration set, producing an empirical distribution that reflects how uncertain the model has historically been when it was correct. A desired confidence level (1 – α) is then chosen, and the threshold is set as the $(1 - \alpha)^{th}$ quantile of this distribution, marked visually as a vertical cutoff. This cutoff separates typical, acceptable uncertainty from the most extreme calibration cases that we are willing to exclude. Importantly, the threshold is global and fixed, derived entirely from past data rather than the current test example. At prediction time, labels whose non-conformity scores fall below this threshold are included in the prediction set. In this way, the image shows how a single quantile-based rule converts historical uncertainty into a consistent, data-driven decision boundary for constructing prediction sets.

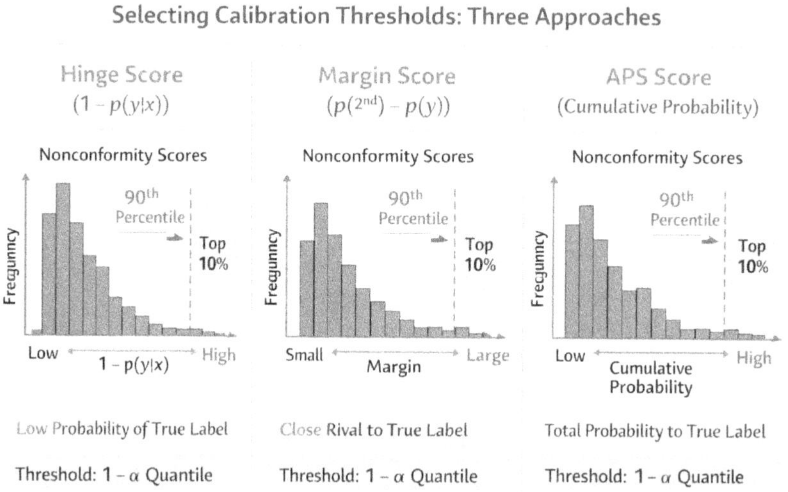

Figure 3.12: *Calibration Threshold Selection Summary*

Taken together, this step completes the conformal prediction pipeline for classification. By reducing threshold selection to a quantile operation on calibration non-conformity scores, conformal prediction replaces heuristic confidence rules with a principled, distribution-free decision mechanism. Regardless of whether hinge, margin, or APS-style scores are used, the logic remains the same: prediction sets are constructed by comparing test-time uncertainty against what was historically typical when the model was correct. The summary image highlights this unifying structure across all three approaches, emphasizing that differences lie only in how uncertainty is measured—not in how it is operationalized. This consistency is a key strength of conformal prediction such as: once nonconformity scores are defined, thresholding and prediction set construction follow a single, transparent rule that yields reliable uncertainty estimates across models, datasets, and application domains.

Conformal Prediction Algorithms

Up to this point in the chapter, we have built conformal predictions for classification step by step, developing the framework incrementally from first principles. We started with the motivation for prediction sets, introduced different types of probability-based non-conformity scores, and showed how calibration data is used to transform model uncertainty into statistically valid prediction sets. This progression focused on *what* each component does and *why* it is needed. The next step is to step back and organize these ideas into **concrete algorithms** that can be implemented, analyzed, and extended systematically.

Conformal prediction algorithms define **how the individual building blocks are assembled into a complete procedure**. They specify when the model is trained, how calibration data is used, how thresholds are computed, and how prediction sets are generated at inference time. Importantly, these algorithms do not introduce new sources of uncertainty or new modeling assumptions. Instead, they provide structured ways of applying the same conformal principles under different practical constraints and data conditions.

In classification, algorithmic choices matter because uncertainty is rarely uniform across the label space. Some problems are well balanced, where a single global notion of uncertainty is sufficient. Others are highly imbalanced or asymmetric, where rare classes require more careful treatment to avoid systematic under coverage. Different conformal algorithms address these realities by controlling **how calibration information is pooled and reused**, while preserving the same underlying coverage guarantees.

In this section, we introduce the foundational conformal prediction algorithms for classification. Inductive Conformal Prediction (ICP) formalizes the basic workflow using a single global calibration threshold, offering simplicity, efficiency, and ease of deployment. Mondrian Conformal Prediction builds directly on ICP by conditioning calibration on class labels, allowing coverage guarantees to hold more evenly in imbalanced settings. We then extend this framework to Adaptive Conformal Prediction, which relaxes the assumption of a static data distribution by allowing calibration and thresholds to evolve over time. Together, these approaches form the core toolkit for conformal classification, providing a progression from basic uncertainty quantification to methods that remain reliable under class imbalance and distribution shift, and serving as the foundation for more advanced extensions explored later in the chapter.

Inductive Conformal Prediction

Having already established how prediction sets are constructed from probabilistic outputs, calibration data, and non-conformity scores, we now package this workflow into its first complete algorithmic form: **Inductive Conformal Prediction (ICP)**. The purpose of this section is not to introduce new ideas, but to show how the previously discussed components interact when deployed together in a real system.

We now present Inductive Conformal Prediction for classification through a **single executable example**, where each stage of the algorithm is paired with a visualization that explains *what is happening at that step*. The emphasis here is not on re-deriving theory, but on showing how the ICP structure emerges naturally from the workflow we have already developed. [2]

Imports and Data Generation

We begin by setting up a simple binary classification problem: predicting whether a student will **pass or fail** based on study hours and attendance.

```
import numpy as np
import matplotlib.pyplot as plt
from sklearn.linear_model import LogisticRegression
from sklearn.model_selection import train_test_split

np.random.seed(42)

# Generate synthetic data
n = 600
study_hours = np.random.uniform(0, 10, n)
attendance = np.random.uniform(0.5, 1.0, n)
X = np.column_stack([study_hours, attendance])

# True probability of passing (unknown to the model)
true_prob = 1 / (1 + np.exp(-(0.8*study_hours + 3.5*(attendance - 0.7) - 3)))
y = np.random.binomial(1, true_prob)

plt.figure(figsize=(6,5))
plt.scatter(study_hours, attendance, c=y, cmap="coolwarm", s=20,
alpha=0.7)
plt.xlabel("Study hours")
plt.ylabel("Attendance")
plt.title("Synthetic pass/fail data")
plt.colorbar(label="Label (0=fail, 1=pass)")
```

```
plt.tight_layout()
plt.show()
```

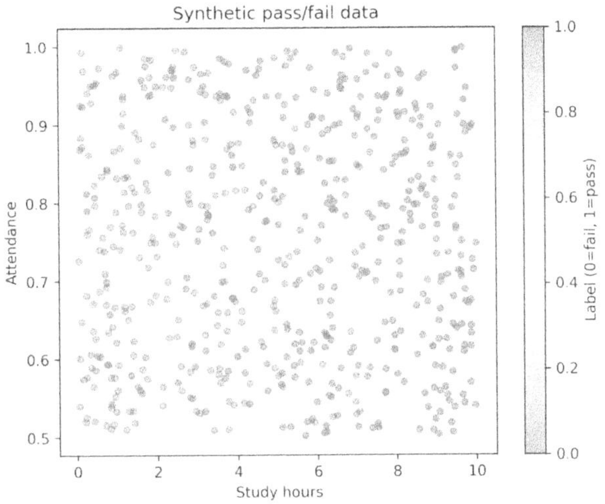

***Figure 3.13**: Synthetic Data with Overlapping Classes*

We are trying to model data with the following characteristics to capture uncertainty clearly:

- Overlapping classes with no sharp boundary
- Regions where uncertainty is unavoidable
- A realistic setting where prediction sets are meaningful

Train and Freeze Classifier

ICP explicitly separates **learning**, **uncertainty estimation**, and **evaluation**, and then train a probabilistic classifier as well as immediately **freeze it**. From this point onward, the model will not change.

```
X_train_full, X_test, y_train_full, y_test = train_test_split(
    X, y, test_size=0.25, random_state=1
)

X_train, X_calib, y_train, y_calib = train_test_split(
    X_train_full, y_train_full, test_size=0.33, random_state=2
)
clf = LogisticRegression(max_iter=200)
clf.fit(X_train, y_train)

xx, yy = np.meshgrid(
    np.linspace(0, 10, 200),
    np.linspace(0.5, 1.0, 200)
)
```

```
grid = np.c_[xx.ravel(), yy.ravel()]
probs_grid = clf.predict_proba(grid)[:,1].reshape(xx.shape)
plt.figure(figsize=(6,5))
plt.contourf(xx, yy, probs_grid, levels=20, cmap="viridis")
plt.colorbar(label="P(pass)")
plt.xlabel("Study hours")
plt.ylabel("Attendance")
plt.title("Frozen classifier: predicted probability surface")
plt.savefig('prob_dist.png'.format(index), dpi=300, bbox_inches="tight")
plt.tight_layout()
plt.show()
```

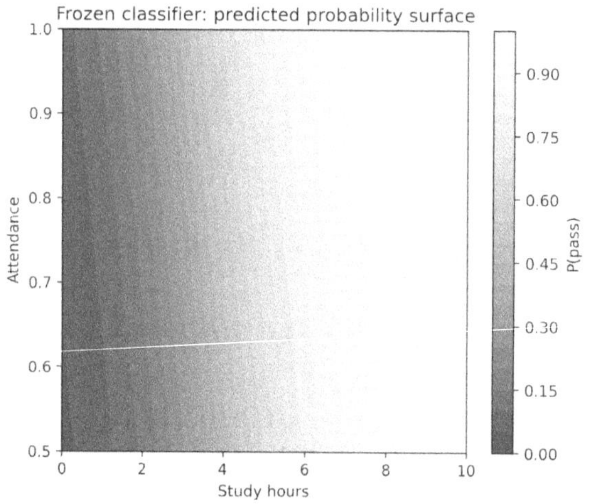

Figure 3.14: *Prediction Probability Surface*

This visualization shows the raw probability surface produced by the trained classifier before any conformal calibration is applied. Each point corresponds to a combination of study hours and attendance, and the color indicates the model's predicted probability of passing, transitioning smoothly from low to high values, rather than changing abruptly. The gradual color bands reveal regions where the model is naturally uncertain, especially around the mid-range probabilities where no clear separation between pass and fail exists. These areas correspond to inputs near the model's implicit decision boundary, where forcing a single label would conceal meaningful ambiguity. At this stage, the probabilities express only the model's internal belief based on training data, and carry no formal reliability guarantees. This surface, therefore provides the baseline over which conformal prediction will later operate, without altering the model itself, but by calibrating how much uncertainty is acceptable, given its past behavior.

Calibration: Measuring Historical Uncertainty

We now evaluate how uncertain the frozen model was on unseen calibration data using **hinge non-conformity scores**.

```
calib_probs = clf.predict_proba(X_calib)
scores_calib = 1 - calib_probs[np.arange(len(y_calib)), y_calib]
plt.figure(figsize=(6,4))
plt.hist(scores_calib, bins=25, edgecolor="k", alpha=0.7)
plt.xlabel("Nonconformity score (1 - p(true label))")
plt.ylabel("Count")
plt.title("Calibration nonconformity distribution")
plt.tight_layout()
plt.show()
```

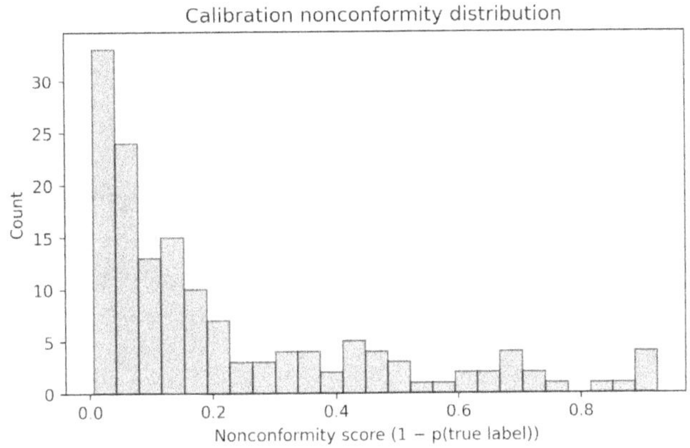

Figure 3.15: *Non-Conformity Scores on Calibration Set*

This plot shows us:

- This distribution encoded by the past behavior.
- Typical uncertainty occupies the left region (~20% uncertainty region).
- Rare, high-surprise cases form the right tail.

Threshold Selection

ICP converts the calibration distribution into a **single global threshold** using quantiles.

```
alpha = 0.1
q = np.quantile(scores_calib, 1 - alpha)
plt.figure(figsize=(6,4))
plt.hist(scores_calib, bins=25, edgecolor="k", alpha=0.6)
plt.axvline(q, color="red", linestyle="--", linewidth=2,
            label=f"q (1-α) = {q:.2f}")
plt.xlabel("Nonconformity score")
plt.ylabel("Count")
plt.title("Calibration threshold selection")
plt.legend()
```

```
plt.tight_layout()
plt.show()
```

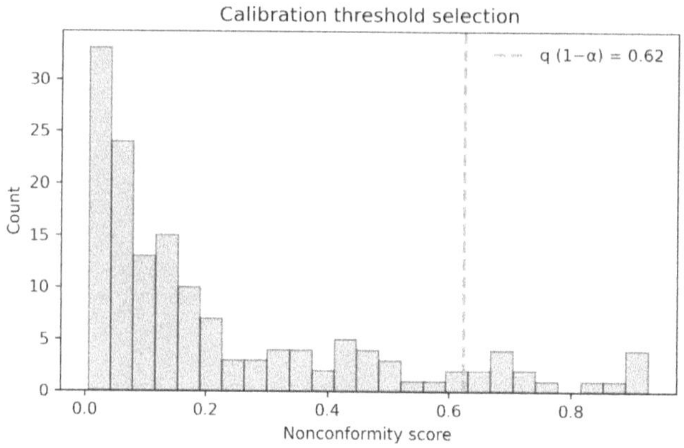

Figure 3.16: *Threshold Selection Using Quantile*

This plot shows us clearly that historically 90% of the prediction errors are under 60%, that is any prediction whose probability/confidence is less than 40% can be excluded from the prediction set.

Prediction Sets

At inference time, the ICP simply checks whether candidate labels fall within the acceptable uncertainty region.

```
test_probs = clf.predict_proba(X_test)

prediction_sets = [
    [cls for cls, p in enumerate(probs) if (1 - p) <= q]
    for probs in test_probs
]

set_sizes = np.array([len(s) for s in prediction_sets])

plt.figure(figsize=(6,5))
plt.scatter(X_test[set_sizes==1,0], X_test[set_sizes==1,1],
            c="teal", s=25, label="Confident (|set|=1)", alpha=0.7)
plt.scatter(X_test[set_sizes>1,0], X_test[set_sizes>1,1],
            c="orange", s=25, label="Uncertain (|set|>1)", alpha=0.7)

plt.xlabel("Study hours")
plt.ylabel("Attendance")
plt.title("Prediction set size across input space")
plt.legend()
plt.tight_layout()
plt.show()
```

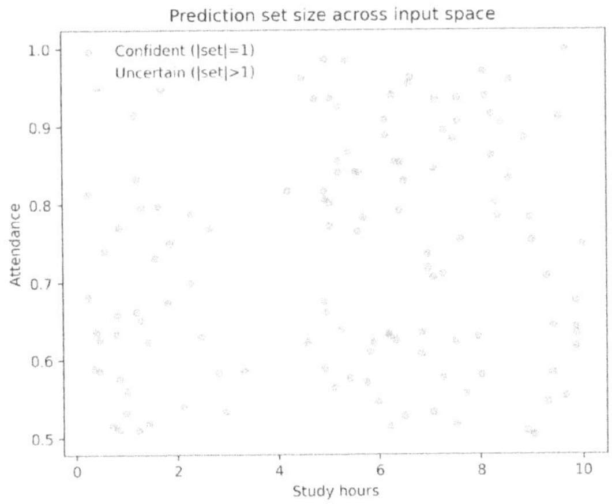

Figure 3.17: *Creating Prediction Sets*

This plot shows how prediction set sizes vary across the input space, once the Inductive Conformal Prediction (ICP) is applied. Each point represents a test example, with well separated/high probability points indicating **confident cases** where the prediction set contains a single label and orange points indicating **uncertain cases** where multiple labels are included. The uncertain points cluster in a narrow band of the feature space, corresponding to regions where the classifier's probabilities are split and the model historically struggled to be decisive (students spending ~4 hours do not clearly define their performance). In contrast, areas far from this boundary remain confidently classified, even though the same global, conformal threshold is used everywhere. This demonstrates a key property of ICP such as: although uncertainty control is governed by a single calibration-derived rule, the resulting prediction sets adapt **locally** to the difficulty of individual inputs, expanding only where the data genuinely supports ambiguity, rather than uniformly across the space.

The visual examples in this section show that, despite relying on a global threshold, ICP adapts locally to the input space, that is, **prediction sets remain small and decisive where the model is consistently confident, and expand only in genuinely ambiguous regions.** This behavior allows the model to communicate uncertainty explicitly, instead of hiding it behind forced single-label decisions. At the same time, the use of a single global calibration pool highlights a limitation in imbalanced settings, motivating class-conditional extensions such as Mondrian Conformal Prediction, which we will explore next.

Mondrian Conformal Prediction for Class Imbalance

Class imbalance is one of the most common and persistent challenges in real-world machine learning. *In many practical applications, the classes of greatest interest are also the rarest: fraudulent transactions among millions of legitimate ones, critical medical conditions among routine cases, unsafe content among vast volumes of benign posts, or system failures among long periods of normal operation.* As a result, learning algorithms are often trained on data where some classes dominate in frequency, while others appear only sporadically. This imbalance affects not only model accuracy, but also how uncertainty is expressed and interpreted.

Just as traditional Machine Learning models are sensitive to class imbalance, conformal prediction is not immune to its effects. Although conformal prediction provides distribution-free coverage guarantees, these guarantees are typically **marginal**, *meaning they hold on average over the entire data distribution.* **When classes are imbalanced, the calibration data is dominated by majority classes, and the conformal threshold learned from this data primarily reflects the uncertainty behavior of those classes.** Minority classes, which may exhibit very different uncertainty patterns, contribute relatively little to the calibration process.

This imbalance creates a subtle but important issue in conformal classification. A single global threshold may achieve the desired overall coverage, while still systematically under-covering rare classes or over-inflating prediction sets for the common ones. In high-stakes settings, this is particularly problematic because minority classes often correspond to rare but critical events where reliable uncertainty estimates matter most. Understanding how and why class imbalance affects conformal prediction is therefore essential before deploying conformal methods in realistic classification systems.

- In a dataset with **100,000 transactions** (**98,000 legitimate**, **2,000 fraudulent**), suppose Inductive Conformal Prediction is applied with $\boldsymbol{\alpha} = \mathbf{0.1}$, and the **global calibration threshold** is learned as **q = 0.20** (meaning probabilities as low as 0.80 for the true label were historically acceptable, mostly for legitimate cases).
- Because **98% of calibration examples are legitimate**, this threshold mainly reflects their behavior; for fraud cases, the model is typically less confident, and often assigns the fraud label probabilities around **0.60–0.70**, corresponding to non-conformity scores of **0.30–0.40**, which exceed the global threshold.
- At prediction time, this causes the **fraud label to be excluded** from many fraud prediction sets, even though the model's uncertainty is expected and reasonable for such rare cases.
- The result is **≈90% overall coverage**, but only **≈70–75% coverage for fraud**, showing how a single global threshold can look correct on average, while failing systematically for the minority class—motivating, class-conditional conformal approaches.

To address this limitation, **Mondrian Conformal Prediction** refines the inductive framework by changing only one aspect: **how calibration information is pooled.**

Instead of using a single global calibration distribution to set the threshold, Mondrian Conformal Prediction partitions the calibration data by class, and computes **separate thresholds for each class**. In the fraud example, this means learning one threshold from legitimate transactions, and a different threshold from fraudulent ones. As a result, uncertainty for rare classes is judged against the model's historical behavior *on that class itself*, rather than being overshadowed by majority-class patterns. This preserves the same inductive structure and coverage guarantees of ICP, but shifts them from global, marginal coverage to **class-conditional reliability**, making conformal prediction better aligned with the realities of imbalanced and high-risk classification problems.

Now, let us understand the workflow of Conformal Prediction using dummy data.

Imports and Imbalanced Data Generation

KPI-Driven Fraud Example (Two Continuous Drivers)

We model fraud as a rare event driven by **two continuous business KPIs**, both common in real payment systems:

- **KPI-1: Transaction Risk Score**

  (aggregated from amount deviation, device mismatch, velocity, and so on)

- **KPI-2: Behavioral Anomaly Score**

  (distance from user's historical spending pattern)

Fraud becomes more likely as **either KPI increases**, but remains noisy and overlapping with legitimate behavior.

```
import numpy as np
from sklearn.linear_model import LinearRegression
from sklearn.ensemble import RandomForestRegressor
from sklearn.model_selection import train_test_split
import numpy as np
import matplotlib.pyplot as plt
from sklearn.linear_model import LogisticRegression
from sklearn.model_selection import train_test_split

np.random.seed(0)
n = 10000
fraud_rate = 0.02
# ----------------------------
# KPI 1: Transaction risk score
# ----------------------------
risk_legit = np.random.gamma(shape=2.0, scale=1.0, size=int((1-fraud_
rate)*n))
```

```
risk_fraud = np.random.gamma(shape=5.0, scale=1.2, size=int(fraud_
rate*n))
# --------------------------------
# KPI 2: Behavioral anomaly score
# --------------------------------
anomaly_legit = np.random.normal(loc=0.0, scale=1.0, size=len(risk_
legit))
anomaly_fraud = np.random.normal(loc=2.0, scale=1.5, size=len(risk_
fraud))

X = np.column_stack([
    np.concatenate([risk_legit, risk_fraud]),
    np.concatenate([anomaly_legit, anomaly_fraud])
])

y = np.array([0]*len(risk_legit) + [1]*len(risk_fraud))  # 1 = fraud

plt.figure(figsize=(6,5))
plt.scatter(X_legit[:,0], X_legit[:,1], s=10, alpha=0.3,
label="Legitimate")
plt.scatter(X_fraud[:,0], X_fraud[:,1], s=30, alpha=0.8, label="Fraud")
plt.xlabel("Transaction amount deviation (KPI-1)")
plt.ylabel("Behavior / velocity deviation (KPI-2)")
plt.title("Imbalanced fraud dataset driven by two KPIs (98% vs 2%)")
plt.legend()
plt.tight_layout()
plt.show()
```

The following is how the class distribution of this synthetic data looks like:

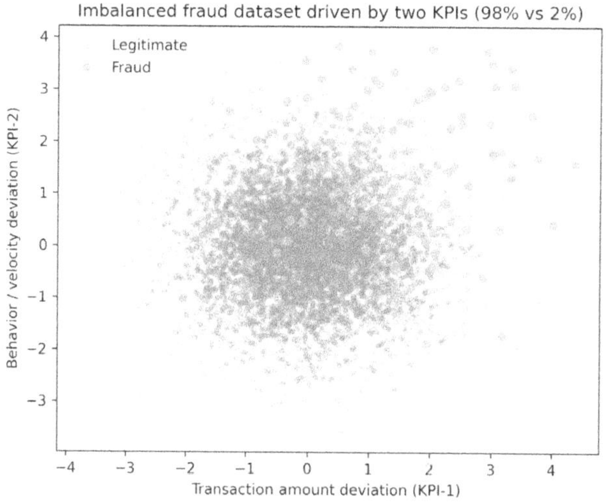

Figure 3.18: *Synthetic Data with Imbalance*

This data-generation setup is designed to reflect how fraud is influenced by **two continuous risk-driving signals** in real systems, while remaining noisy, overlapping, and highly imbalanced. For **KPI 1 (transaction risk score)**, legitimate transactions are sampled from a Gamma distribution with a low average value, representing normal spending behavior with occasional mild deviations. Intuitively, a Gamma distribution is useful here because it produces **only positive values**, with most observations being small and a **long right tail** that allows for rare but large values, much like transaction amounts or risk scores in practice. Fraudulent transactions are drawn from a Gamma distribution with a higher average and wider spread, capturing the fact that fraud tends to involve larger or more abnormal amounts, while still overlapping with legitimate behavior.

For **KPI 2 (behavioral anomaly score)**, legitimate activity is modeled using a normal distribution centered near zero, corresponding to stable and expected user behavior, whereas fraud is modeled with a shifted and noisier normal distribution to represent irregular timing, velocity, or behavioral changes. Importantly, neither KPI cleanly separates fraud from legitimate activity on its own; fraud simply becomes more likely as these values increase. This intentional overlap creates a realistic setting with inherent uncertainty and strong class imbalance, making it well suited for studying how conformal prediction behaves in practical fraud-detection scenarios.

Train and Freeze the Model

This part is similar to the Inductive setup, so we will just visualize the probability surface across the two KPIs to confirm if the Classifier learnt the underlying patterns from the different classes, the full code can be found at the github repo whose link is provided at the end of this Chapter under the Resources section.

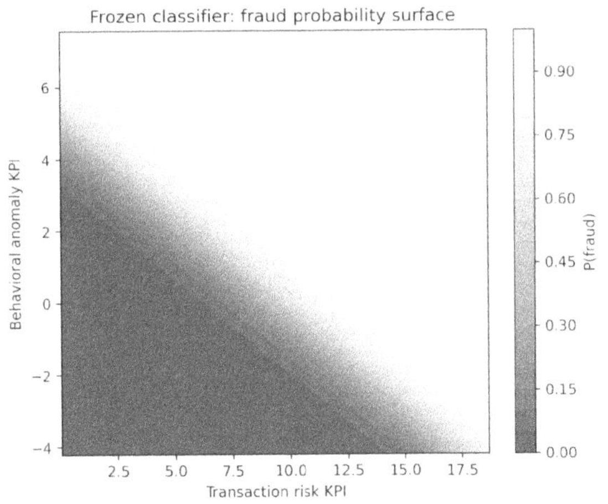

Figure 3.19: *Probability Surface for Trained Classifier*

Here, we can clearly see that the classifier learns the underlying patterns assigning high probabilities to high-risk score customers and vice versa.

Global Calibration Threshold

We compute hinge non-conformity scores on calibration data, over a full calibration set ignoring the class imbalance, first.

```
# Nonconformity scores on test data
scores = 1 - test_probs[np.arange(len(y_test)), y_test]
scores_legit = scores[y_test == 0]
scores_fraud = scores[y_test == 1]

# Global conformal threshold
q = q_global

# Empirical CDF plot
plt.figure(figsize=(6,4))
for s, lbl, col in [(scores_legit, "Legitimate", "teal"),
                    (scores_fraud, "Fraud", "orange")]:
    x = np.sort(s)
    y = np.arange(1, len(x)+1) / len(x)
    plt.plot(x, y, label=lbl, color=col)

plt.axvline(q, color="red", linestyle="--", label="Global threshold")

# Class-conditional coverage
cov_legit = np.mean(scores_legit <= q)
cov_fraud = np.mean(scores_fraud <= q)

plt.xlabel("Nonconformity score (1 - p(true label))")
plt.ylabel("Empirical CDF")
plt.title("Class-conditional coverage under global conformal
calibration")
plt.legend()
plt.tight_layout()
plt.show()
```

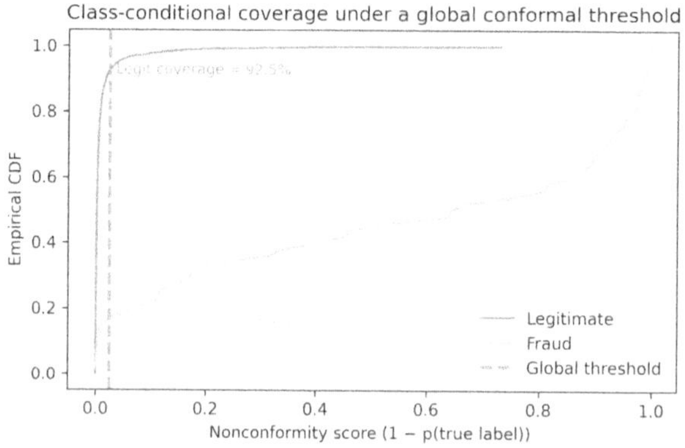

Figure 3.20: *CDFs Showing Coverage from Global Threshold*

This figure brings together both **how coverage is computed** and **why a single global conformal threshold is insufficient in this imbalanced fraud example**. For each test transaction, a non-conformity score is calculated which measures how uncertain the model is about the true label. A transaction is considered *covered* if its non-conformity score is less than or equal to the global threshold; coverage for a class is simply the fraction of its examples satisfying this condition. In the CDF plot, this corresponds exactly to the height of each class's curve at the vertical threshold line. While the legitimate class achieves coverage close to the target level, **the fraud class curve lies much lower at the same threshold, indicating substantially reduced coverage.**

This discrepancy occurs because the global threshold is calibrated primarily on majority-class behavior, and therefore, reflects what is typical uncertainty for legitimate transactions. As *a result, many fraud cases where higher uncertainty is expected fall above the threshold and have the fraud label excluded from their prediction sets.* The example shows that although global conformal prediction satisfies marginal coverage on average, it can be systematically unreliable for minority classes, motivating class-conditional approaches such as Mondrian Conformal Prediction.

Class-wise/Mondrian Thresholds

A simple fix around this problem is to create a class-wise calibration threshold accounting for variable uncertainty across classes, and hence, handling the imbalance.

```
q_legit = np.quantile(scores[y_calib==0], 1-alpha)
q_fraud = np.quantile(scores[y_calib==1], 1-alpha)
```

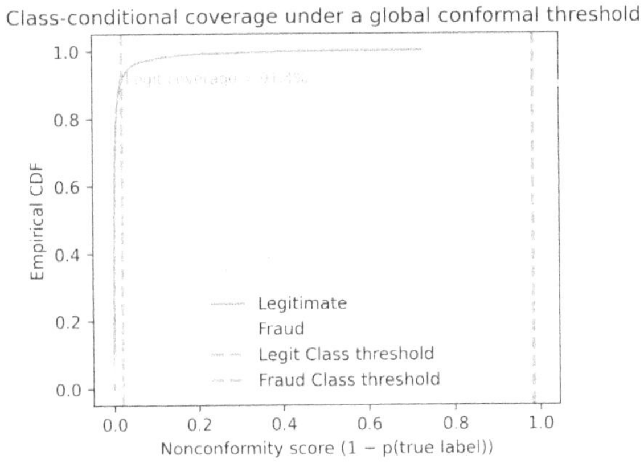

Figure 3.21: *CDFs Showing Coverage from Class-Level Thresholds*

This visualization shows the effect of applying class-conditional (Mondrian) Conformal Thresholds instead of a single global threshold. Separate non-conformity score distributions are constructed for legitimate and fraudulent transactions, and each class uses its own quantile as the acceptance threshold. As a result, coverage is now computed independently for each class by checking whether the class-specific non-conformity score falls below its corresponding threshold. The CDF plot makes this explicit, that is, at the legitimate-class threshold q_{legit} the legitimate curve reaches the target coverage level, and similarly, at the fraud-class threshold q_{fraud} the fraud curve also reaches the same target level. This confirms that Mondrian calibration restores class-conditional coverage, eliminating the systematic under-coverage of the minority class observed under global calibration.

Note:

- *The fraud-class threshold is higher because fraud cases are* ***inherently more uncertain and variable****, and conformal prediction is correctly accounting for this by allowing greater uncertainty to meet the coverage guarantee.*
- *A higher threshold can lead to* ***larger or more ambiguous prediction sets*** *for fraud, which, while statistically valid, may be less useful for systems that require decisive actions.*
- *This behavior is* ***not a failure of conformal prediction*** *but an honest reflection of the difficulty of the underlying problem; when the signal is weak, valid uncertainty guarantees necessarily come at the cost of wider prediction sets.*
- *In practice, this trade-off can be managed by improving the base model to better separate minority classes, using* ***class-specific or asymmetric coverage targets****, or combining conformal prediction with* ***cost-sensitive learning*** *to align uncertainty with business risk.*
- *The key takeaway is that conformal prediction provides reliable uncertainty estimates, but their practical usefulness depends on modeling choices; with appropriate adjustments, meaningful guarantees for minority classes can be achieved without making the system overly conservative.*

This section demonstrated how class imbalance interacts with conformal prediction, and why a single global calibration threshold can be insufficient in realistic, high-imbalance settings. When calibration data is dominated by a majority class, the resulting global threshold primarily reflects majority-class uncertainty. Although marginal coverage may still hold, minority classes often the most important in practice can suffer systematic under-coverage, as illustrated through the fraud-detection example.

Mondrian conformal prediction resolves this issue by conditioning calibration on class labels, and learning **separate uncertainty thresholds for each class**. This simple structural change *preserves the inductive conformal framework and its finite-sample guarantees*, while shifting the notion of reliability from global averages to class-conditional behavior. The visualizations showed that, under Mondrian calibration, each class achieves its intended coverage level, eliminating the failure mode observed with global calibration.

At the same time, the example highlights an important practical insight: restoring coverage for highly variable minority classes that often requires accepting higher uncertainty, which can lead to wider or more ambiguous prediction sets. Rather than being a flaw, this reflects an honest assessment of model limitations. In practice, this trade-off can be managed through better base models, class-specific coverage targets, adaptive or normalized non-conformity scores, and cost-sensitive learning. Together, these tools allow Mondrian Conformal Prediction to serve as a principled and flexible foundation for uncertainty quantification in imbalanced classification problems, making it a natural extension of Inductive Conformal Prediction for real-world applications.

Adaptive Conformal Prediction under Distribution Shift

In many real-world applications, the assumption that future data will follow the same distribution as past data is often violated. *Customer behavior evolves, fraud patterns change, user preferences drift, sensors degrade, and policies or external conditions shift over time. This phenomenon, broadly referred to as* ***distribution shift****, poses a fundamental challenge not only for predictive accuracy but also for the reliability of uncertainty estimates.*

Conformal prediction, in its standard inductive and Mondrian forms, relies on an **exchangeability assumption** between calibration data and future test data. **When this assumption holds, the coverage guarantees are exact. However, under distribution shift, calibration data may no longer be representative of the uncertainty encountered at prediction time**. As a result, fixed thresholds learned from historical calibration sets can become stale, leading to either systematic under-coverage (overconfidence) or overly conservative prediction sets.

Adaptive conformal prediction addresses this issue by allowing the conformal procedure itself to **evolve in response to the changing data**, rather than remaining static after calibration. Instead of treating uncertainty calibration as a one-time operation, adaptive methods update thresholds, scores, or calibration windows over time, using recent data to better reflect the current uncertainty conditions. The goal is not to eliminate distribution shift, which is often unavoidable but to maintain meaningful coverage guarantees *as the data-generating process changes*.

In this section, we explore how conformal prediction can be extended to handle distribution shift in a principled way. We focus on adaptive techniques that retain the spirit of conformal prediction such as: minimal assumptions and transparent uncertainty, while relaxing the strict requirement of full exchangeability. This sets the stage for practical conformal systems that remain reliable in dynamic, real-world environments. Thus, let us dive into the core ideas of adaptive conformal prediction, next.

The defining feature of adaptive conformal prediction is a shift in perspective: **calibration is no longer treated as a one-time, offline step**, but as an ongoing process that evolves with the data. Instead of fixing a single threshold based on a static calibration set, adaptive methods allow the conformal mechanism to update itself as new observations arrive. At a high level, this adaptivity is achieved by **tying the conformal threshold to recent model behavior, rather than historical behavior**. The non-conformity scores computed on new data are used directly or indirectly to adjust the future thresholds, **so that the notion of "typical uncertainty" tracks the current data distribution.** This allows the conformal predictor to remain sensitive to gradual changes, sudden shifts, or recurring seasonal patterns. Crucially, adaptive conformal prediction does not aim to fully restore the original exchangeability assumption. Instead, it relaxes it in a controlled way by introducing **local or temporal notions of validity**. Coverage guarantees are no longer interpreted globally over an indefinite future, but over **moving windows, recent time horizons, or stochastic processes** that better reflect how data evolves in practice.

This change reframes the role of conformal prediction in dynamic systems. Rather than asking, "*Is this prediction valid under the original data distribution?*", adaptive methods ask, "*Is this prediction calibrated with respect to what the model is encountering right now?*" The rest of this section builds on this idea by showing concrete mechanisms—such as rolling calibration windows and online threshold updates—that operationalize adaptivity, while retaining the interpretability and transparency of conformal prediction.

Let us demonstrate **adaptive conformal prediction for classification** using a simple synthetic example with **distribution shift over time**. We will start with a standard inductive conformal setup, and then show how **updating the conformal threshold using recent data** restores reliable coverage when uncertainty patterns change.

- Simulate a **non-stationary classification problem**
- Show how a **fixed conformal threshold fails over time**
- Introduce a **rolling / adaptive conformal threshold**
- Visualize how adaptivity restores coverage

The key idea:

Uncertainty changes over time, so calibration must change too.

Data Generation: A Realistic Setting with Distribution Shift

We generate the dummy data with the following characteristics:

- A **time index** to represent transaction order.
- Each transaction has a **risk score**.
- **Fraud probability** depends on this risk score.
- Crucially, the **strength of this relationship decays over time**.

So, the data becomes harder, not because labels flip randomly, but because the signal weakens.

```
import numpy as np
import matplotlib.pyplot as plt

np.random.seed(0)

T = 3000                          # number of transactions over time
time = np.arange(T)

# Risk indicator (e.g., amount / behavior deviation)
risk_score = np.random.normal(0, 1, T)

# Signal strength decays over time (distribution shift)
signal_strength = np.linspace(10, 3, T)

# Fraud probability depends on both risk and time
true_prob = 1 / (1 + np.exp(-(signal_strength * risk_score)))

# Binary fraud labels
y = np.random.binomial(1, true_prob)
```

This data-generation process simulates a time-evolving fraud detection scenario with gradual distribution shift. Each transaction arrives in sequence (time) and is associated with a continuous risk score, representing signals such as amount deviation or behavioral anomaly, drawn from a stable distribution. *The key source of non-stationarity is the signal strength, which decreases over time, modeling how fraud patterns become harder to detect as adversaries adapt. The fraud probability is then computed by passing the product of the risk score and the time-varying signal strength through a logistic function, ensuring probabilities remain between 0 and 1.* Finally, *binary fraud labels are sampled from these probabilities, introducing realistic uncertainty and overlap between fraud and legitimate transactions. This setup creates a controlled but realistic environment where the model remains fixed,* yet uncertainty increases over time, precisely the setting where adaptive conformal prediction becomes necessary. The following is a visualization of how the signal strength weakens with time, showing our setup is done as expected.

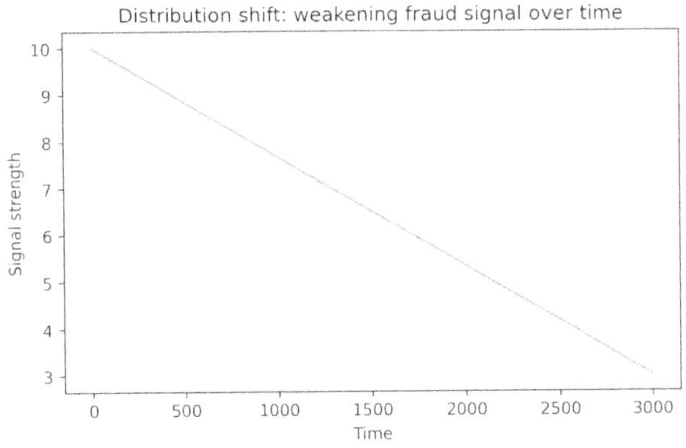

Figure 3.22: *Decaying Signal Strength with Time*

The y-axis represents **how predictive the risk score is such as**:

- Early in time: Small changes in risk score strongly affect fraud probability.
- Later in time: The same risk score carries much less information.
- This mimics real systems where:
    - attackers adapt
    - behavior distributions drift
    - uncertainty grows gradually

Importantly, nothing is wrong with the data:

- Labels are generated consistently.
- There is no noise injection trick.
- The difficulty increases naturally.

Train a Static Model on Early Data

In real systems, models are usually trained on historical data, and then deployed for long periods without retraining. To mirror this, we:

- train a classifier using early transactions only
- freeze the model
- apply it unchanged to the future data

This lets us isolate one phenomenon clearly: the data distribution changes, but the model does not.

```
from sklearn.linear_model import LogisticRegression

# Train on early transactions only
train_end = 800

clf = LogisticRegression()
clf.fit(risk_score[:train_end].reshape(-1, 1),
        y[:train_end])

pred_probs = clf.predict_proba(
    risk_score.reshape(-1, 1)
)[:, 1]

plt.figure(figsize=(6,4))
plt.scatter(time, pred_probs, c=y, s=5, alpha=0.5)
plt.xlabel("Time")
plt.ylabel("Predicted fraud probability")
plt.title("Frozen model confidence degrades over time")
plt.tight_layout()
```

```
plt.savefig('class_dist.png'.format(index), dpi=300, bbox_inches="tight")
plt.show()
```

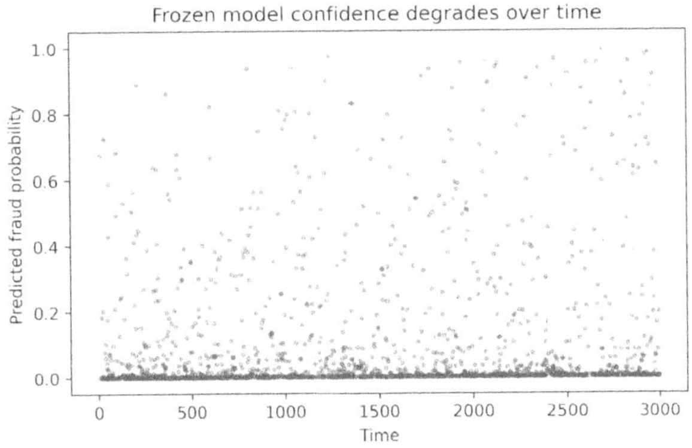

Figure 3.23: *Class Separation Reducing with Time*

This plot illustrates how a classifier trained on early data behaves as the data distribution evolves over time. Each point represents a transaction, with the predicted probability of fraud shown on the vertical axis and time on the horizontal axis, and colors indicating the true class. Early in time, the model produces more confident predictions, with probabilities clustered closer to 0 or 1 and clearer separation between fraudulent and legitimate transactions. As time progresses, the predicted probabilities increasingly concentrate around intermediate values, and the two classes overlap more heavily. This indicates that the model is becoming less confident, not because it is malfunctioning, but because the underlying signal that links the risk score to fraud has weakened. The plot highlights a key challenge for uncertainty estimation: even when a model remains fixed and reasonably accurate, the structure of uncertainty can drift over time, causing any static uncertainty calibration—such as a fixed conformal threshold—to become outdated.

A fixed conformal threshold assumes that the distribution of nonconformity scores remains stable over time. In this plot, predictions gradually become less extreme and increasingly concentrated away from 0 and 1, reflecting growing uncertainty as the data distribution evolves. For example, a threshold calibrated when most predictions were highly confident may become too strict later, causing many otherwise valid observations with intermediate probabilities (for example, 0.4–0.6) to exceed the fixed threshold. As a result, the prediction sets no longer achieve the desired coverage, demonstrating why conformal thresholds must adapt as uncertainty changes over time.

Uncertainty Thresholds at Different Calibration Windows

In this section, we consider two calibration strategies. The first mirrors the standard approach by selecting calibration points uniformly at random from the available data, while the second uses only the most recent observations. The latter is designed to reflect the current, weaker signal regime, and therefore, captures the increased uncertainty induced by signal decay.

```
alpha = 0.1
calib_size = 400

# --------------------------
# Option 1: Random calibration
# --------------------------
np.random.seed(1)
random_idx = np.random.choice(
    np.arange(train_end, T), size=calib_size, replace=False
)

calib_probs_rand = clf.predict_proba(
    risk_score[random_idx].reshape(-1,1)
)
calib_y_rand = y[random_idx]

scores_rand = 1 - calib_probs_rand[
    np.arange(len(calib_y_rand)), calib_y_rand
]

q_random = np.quantile(scores_rand, 1 - alpha)

# --------------------------
# Option 2: Recent calibration
# --------------------------
recent_idx = np.arange(T - calib_size, T)

calib_probs_recent = clf.predict_proba(
    risk_score[recent_idx].reshape(-1,1)
)
calib_y_recent = y[recent_idx]

scores_recent = 1 - calib_probs_recent[
    np.arange(len(calib_y_recent)), calib_y_recent
]

q_recent = np.quantile(scores_recent, 1 - alpha)
```

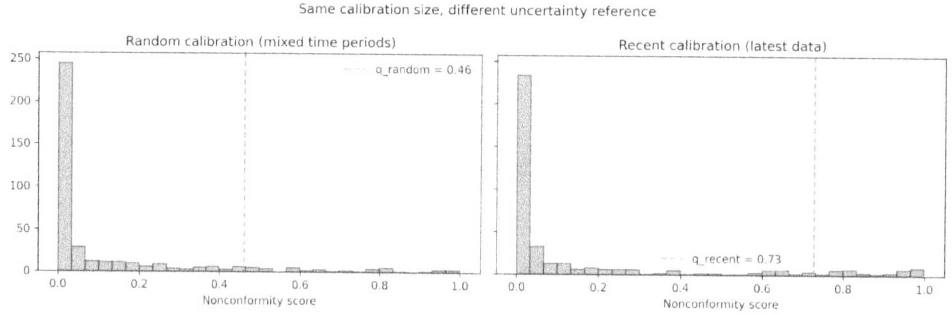

Figure 3.24: *Threshold at Random versus Recent Calibration Window*

This comparison clearly illustrates the adaptive nature of conformal prediction under distribution shift. When calibration is aligned with the recent data, **the conformal algorithm automatically adjusts by widening its uncertainty band to reflect the weakened signal and increased ambiguity in the current regime**. Rather than relying on a fixed notion of uncertainty, the method responds directly to changes in the underlying data distribution, expanding prediction sets when confidence decreases. This behavior highlights how conformal prediction can adapt to drift in a principled, data-driven manner, without requiring retraining of the underlying model.

While recent-window calibration provides a simple and effective way to adapt conformal prediction under distribution shift, it represents only one of the several possible adaptive strategies. More sophisticated approaches include **weighted or exponentially decayed calibration schemes**, which assign greater importance to the recent observations; **online conformal prediction methods**, which update calibration thresholds sequentially as new data arrives; and **risk-controlling conformal prediction formulations**, which dynamically adjust calibration to maintain a desired error rate even under distribution drift. [3]

Evaluating Conformal Classifiers: Coverage and Set Size

In the previous sections, we examined coverage across different CP algorithms, how conformal classifiers guarantee that the true label is contained in the prediction set with a user-specified probability, and how this guarantee behaves under class imbalance and distribution shift. With this foundation in place, we now turn to a more complete evaluation of conformal classifiers by pairing coverage with a second, equally important dimension: **prediction set size**.

While coverage tells us whether a conformal classifier is statistically reliable, it does not tell us whether it is practically useful. In real applications, the value of a conformal predictor depends not only on *how often it is correct*, but also on *how specific its predictions are*. A conformal classifier that achieves the desired coverage by frequently outputting large or ambiguous prediction sets may satisfy theoretical guarantees, while offering limited operational value. Set size, therefore, acts as a measure of efficiency, complementing coverage by quantifying how much uncertainty the system is forced to express.

This section builds incrementally on the earlier discussion by focusing on the **joint behavior of coverage and set size**. We examine how these metrics interact, how they respond to modeling choices and data conditions, and how they should be interpreted differently in technical validation versus business decision-making contexts. The goal is to provide a unified lens for evaluating conformal classifiers—not just as statistically valid constructs, but as decision-support tools whose uncertainty outputs must be both trustworthy and actionable.

Coverage Revisited

Although coverage has already been introduced as the core theoretical guarantee of conformal prediction, its role in evaluation goes beyond simply checking whether a target level (for example, 90% or 95%) is met. In practice, coverage should be treated as a **diagnostic signal**, rather than a single pass–fail criterion. Empirical coverage can be monitored across different slices of the data such as classes, time periods, or regions of the feature space to reveal where uncertainty estimates remain reliable and where they may degrade. This perspective is especially important given the earlier discussions on class imbalance and distribution shift, where marginal coverage may hold globally, while failing locally.

From a technical standpoint, deviations from the target coverage can indicate violations of underlying assumptions, stale calibration, or model drift. From a business standpoint, uneven coverage often maps directly to risk: under-coverage in rare or high-impact cases can be far more costly than mild over-coverage in common, low-risk scenarios. As such, coverage should be evaluated not only in aggregate, but also conditionally, aligned with the structure of the application.

Prediction Set Size as a Measure of Efficiency

Prediction set size captures the **cost of uncertainty** expressed by a conformal classifier. Smaller sets indicate more decisive predictions, while larger sets reflect ambiguity that the model is unwilling to resolve. Unlike coverage, which is constrained by design, set size is a free outcome that depends on the quality of the underlying model, the chosen non-conformity score, the calibration strategy, and the data distribution itself.

Technically, average set size provides a first-order summary of efficiency, but it is often more informative to examine the **distribution of set sizes**. For example, a system that produces singleton sets most of the time but occasionally outputs large sets behaves very differently from one that consistently outputs sets of size two. These differences can have significant downstream implications, even if average set size appears similar.

The Coverage–Set Size Trade-off

Coverage and set size are inherently linked through a trade-off. Increasing the target coverage level generally requires allowing larger prediction sets, while pushing for smaller sets risks excluding the true label more often. Conformal prediction makes this trade-off explicit and tunable through the choice of the miscoverage level. Rather than hiding uncertainty behind point predictions, it forces practitioners to decide how much uncertainty they are willing to tolerate and where.

Importantly, this trade-off is not uniform across all settings. In well-separated regions of the feature space, high coverage can often be achieved with small sets. In ambiguous or noisy regions, maintaining coverage necessarily leads to larger sets. Evaluating a conformal classifier, therefore, means understanding *where* large sets occur and *why*, not just how many there are on average.

Interpreting Set Size in Business Contexts

From a business perspective, prediction set size often translates directly into operational actions. Singleton sets may enable full automation, while larger sets may trigger manual review, secondary checks, or conservative fallback decisions. In this sense, set size can be interpreted as a confidence signal that is more actionable than a raw probability score, because it comes with a formal reliability guarantee.

This makes it useful to evaluate conformal classifiers using metrics such as the fraction of singleton prediction sets, the rate at which full-label sets occur, or the expected decision cost induced by uncertainty. These metrics bridge the gap between statistical evaluation and real-world deployment, helping stakeholders assess whether a conformal system is not only valid, but also economically and operationally viable.

Bringing the Metrics Together

Ultimately, evaluating a conformal classifier requires looking at coverage and set size together, not in isolation. Coverage answers the question, "Can I trust this system's uncertainty guarantees?" Set size answers, "How useful are those guarantees in practice?" By jointly analyzing these metrics—across classes, time, and operating conditions we obtain a more complete picture of performance, one that reflects both the theoretical promises of conformal prediction and the practical realities of decision-making under uncertainty.

In the remainder of this section, we will use concrete examples to illustrate how coverage and set size behave under different modeling and calibration choices, and how these evaluation criteria can be aligned with real-world objectives.

Practical Evaluation Workflow

To make coverage and set size actionable, it is helpful to adopt a structured evaluation workflow rather than relying on a single summary statistic. A typical evaluation begins by verifying **global coverage** on a held-out test set, ensuring that the conformal classifier meets the nominal guarantee. This step establishes baseline validity. Next, coverage should be examined **conditionally**, for example by class, time period, or risk segment, to detect uneven reliability that may be hidden by aggregate metrics. As discussed earlier, this step is crucial in imbalanced or non-stationary settings, where marginal coverage can mask important failure modes.

Once reliability has been assessed, attention can shift to **set size behavior**. This includes computing the average set size, but also inspecting its distribution and identifying where large sets concentrate. Are large sets associated with specific classes, regions of the feature space, or time windows? Answering these questions helps distinguish unavoidable uncertainty from correctable modeling issues, such as weak features or outdated calibration.

Monitoring in Deployment

In deployed systems, evaluation does not end at validation time. Coverage and set size can also serve as **monitoring signals**. Sudden drops in empirical coverage or systematic increases in set size often indicate distribution shift, model drift, or changes in data quality. Because conformal prediction externalizes uncertainty, these changes are often visible earlier than drops in accuracy, making conformal metrics a useful early-warning system.

From a business standpoint, monitoring the rate of large or ambiguous prediction sets can also reveal operational stress. An increase in such sets may translate to higher manual review costs or delayed decisions, signaling the need for recalibration, retraining, or threshold adjustment.

Evaluating conformal classifiers requires moving beyond traditional accuracy-centric metrics and adopting a dual focus on coverage and set size. Coverage ensures statistical reliability, while set size captures practical efficiency and decision readiness. Together, they provide a transparent and principled way to assess uncertainty-aware models.

The key takeaway is that a conformal classifier should not be judged solely by whether it meets its coverage guarantee, but by how economically it achieves that guarantee. By systematically analyzing coverage and set size globally, conditionally, and over time—practitioners can align conformal prediction with both technical rigor and real-world decision-making needs, completing the evaluation loop for conformal classification systems.

Conclusion

In this chapter, we developed conformal prediction for classification from first principles to practical deployment considerations. Beginning with the construction of prediction sets and the role of nonconformity scores, we showed how conformal methods transform probabilistic classifiers into systems that produce **explicit, reliable uncertainty estimates**. Through inductive conformal prediction, we established the basic mechanism for achieving marginal coverage, and through Mondrian Conformal Prediction, we addressed the critical limitations that arise in imbalanced classification settings by restoring class-conditional reliability.

We then extended this framework to more realistic, non-stationary environments, where distribution shift invalidates static calibration assumptions. Adaptive conformal prediction illustrates how uncertainty estimation can evolve with the data, allowing prediction sets to widen or contract in response to changing signal quality, without retraining the underlying model.

Finally, we focused on evaluation, emphasizing that conformal classifiers must be assessed not only by their coverage guarantees but also by the efficiency of their prediction sets. By jointly analyzing coverage and set size, and by interpreting these metrics through both technical and business lenses, we framed conformal prediction as a decision-support tool, rather than a purely statistical construct. Large or ambiguous prediction sets are not failures; they are signals often indicating genuine uncertainty, model limitations, or evolving data regimes.

Taken together, this chapter showed that conformal prediction for classification is not a single algorithm, but a flexible framework. Its behavior depends on choices about calibration, conditioning, adaptivity, and evaluation, all of which can be aligned with real-world objectives and constraints. With this foundation in place, in the next chapter, we will talk about how Conformal Prediction fits into the next Supervised Class of Algorithms, that is, Regression, and provides uncertainty estimates along with prediction outputs.

Points to Remember

- **Conformal Prediction** for classification outputs **prediction sets**, not point predictions, providing explicit and reliable uncertainty quantification.
- The central guarantee of conformal prediction is **coverage**, which ensures that the true label is contained in the prediction set with a user-specified probability under appropriate assumptions.
- **Inductive Conformal Prediction (ICP)** provides marginal coverage but can fail silently in imbalanced settings, where minority classes may be systematically under-covered.
- **Mondrian Conformal Prediction** addresses class imbalance by calibrating uncertainty separately for each class, restoring class-conditional coverage.
- Under **distribution shift**, static calibration becomes outdated; uncertainty can change even when model accuracy appears stable.
- **Adaptive Conformal Prediction** updates calibration using the recent data, allowing prediction sets to expand or contract in response to the evolving uncertainty.
- Coverage alone is not sufficient for evaluation; **prediction set size** is equally important as a measure of efficiency and practical usefulness.
- Large prediction sets are not errors but signals of genuine ambiguity, model limitations, or changing data regimes.

- Evaluating conformal classifiers requires analyzing **coverage and set size jointly**, both globally and conditionally (by class, time, or risk segment).
- **Conformal Prediction is a flexible framework**, rather than a single algorithm, and its effectiveness depends on thoughtful choices around non-conformity scores, calibration strategy, and evaluation aligned with real-world decision-making needs.

Chapter Resources

- Code Exercise

Multiple Choice Questions

1. Which assumption is essential for the validity guarantees in conformal prediction?
    a. Normality of residuals
    b. Exchangeability of data
    c. Independence between features
    d. Equal variance across the dataset
2. Conformal prediction is considered model-agnostic because:
    a. It requires linearity in the underlying model.
    b. It only works with probabilistic models.
    c. It can be applied to any model that produces predictions.
    d. It replaces the model's loss function.
3. What is the primary purpose of a non-conformity score in conformal prediction?
    a. To measure the model's training error
    b. To quantify how unusual an example is relative to the calibration data
    c. To tune the hyperparameters of the model
    d. To remove noisy observations
4. In inductive conformal prediction for classification, calibration data is used to:
    a. Retrain the underlying model
    b. Estimate class probabilities
    c. Determine the non-conformity threshold
    d. Balance the class distribution

5. Marginal coverage in conformal prediction guarantees:
   a. Equal coverage for all classes.
   b. Coverage conditional on features.
   c. Average coverage over the entire data distribution.
   d. Coverage only on the training set.
6. Why can marginal coverage be problematic in imbalanced classification settings?
   a. It increases prediction set size uniformly.
   b. It overfits the majority class.
   c. It can hide under-coverage of minority classes.
   d. It violates the exchangeability assumption.
7. Mondrian conformal prediction modifies standard ICP by:
   a. Using multiple calibration sets
   b. Conditioning calibration on class labels
   c. Retraining the model for each class
   d. Optimizing prediction set size
8. In class-imbalanced problems, Mondrian conformal prediction primarily helps by:
   a. Improving model accuracy
   b. Reducing calibration sample size
   c. Restoring class-conditional coverage
   d. Eliminating uncertainty altogether
9. What typically happens to conformal prediction sets when the underlying data distribution shifts?
   a. They automatically shrink.
   b. They remain unchanged.
   c. Their coverage may degrade if calibration is static.
   d. They become deterministic.
10. Adaptive conformal prediction addresses distribution shifts by:
    a. Updating calibration or thresholds using the recent data
    b. Modifying the loss function
    c. Retraining the model continuously
    d. Enforcing stricter assumptions

11. Why might recent calibration outperform random calibration under distribution shift?
    a. It uses more data.
    b. It reduces variance in predictions.
    c. It reflects current uncertainty in a better way.
    d. It improves feature representations.
12. In adaptive conformal prediction, widening prediction sets usually indicates:
    a. Improved model accuracy
    b. Decreasing uncertainty
    c. Increased ambiguity in recent data
    d. Failure of the calibration procedure
13. Which metric is most directly associated with the efficiency of a conformal classifier?
    a. Coverage
    b. Accuracy
    c. Prediction set size
    d. Precision
14. From a business perspective, large prediction sets most commonly imply:
    a. Increased manual review or conservative decisions
    b. Higher revenue
    c. Faster automation
    d. Better user experience
15. Which statement best summarizes the goal of conformal prediction for classification?
    a. To maximize predictive accuracy
    b. To eliminate uncertainty from predictions
    c. To provide reliable, distribution-free uncertainty guarantees
    d. To replace probabilistic classifiers entirely

Answers

1. b
2. c

3. b
4. c
5. c
6. c
7. b
8. c
9. c
10. a
11. c
12. c
13. c
14. a
15. c

Key Terms

- **Prediction Set:** The set of labels output by a conformal classifier for a given input, constructed so that the true label is included with high probability.
- **Coverage:** The proportion of times the true label lies within the prediction set. In conformal prediction, coverage is controlled by design through the miscoverage level.
- **Miscoverage Level (〈):** A user-specified tolerance for error, where $1-\alpha$ is the target coverage level.
- **Calibration Set:** A held-out dataset used to compute non-conformity scores, and determine conformal thresholds, separate from the model training data.
- **Marginal Coverage:** Coverage guaranteed on average over the entire data distribution, without conditioning on classes or subgroups.
- **Class-Conditional Coverage:** Coverage guarantees that hold separately within each class, rather than only on average across all data.
- **Distribution Shift:** A change in the data-generating process over time or across environments, which can invalidate static calibration assumptions.
- **Rolling / Recent Calibration:** A calibration strategy that uses the most recent data points to better reflect the current uncertainty conditions.
- **Prediction Set Size:** The number of labels in a prediction set, used as a measure of efficiency and practical usefulness.

- **Coverage-Set Size Trade-off:** The inherent balance between reliability (coverage) and informativeness (smaller prediction sets) in conformal classification.

References

1. The Penalized Inverse Probability Measure for Conformal Classification Paul Melki et. al.
2. Inductive Conformal Prediction: A Straightforward Introduction with Examples in Python Martim Soursa
3. Adaptive Conformal Inference Under Distribution Shift by Issac Gibbs et.al.

CHAPTER 4
Conformal Prediction for Regression

Introduction

In the previous chapter, we explored how conformal prediction *reshapes classification by moving beyond single, overconfident labels to statistically valid prediction sets.* We saw how uncertainty in classification is best expressed not as a number, but as a set of plausible outcomes, especially in borderline or ambiguous cases. This shift fundamentally changed how we interpret model outputs. Instead of asking, "What is the correct class?", we learned to ask "Which classes remain plausible given what the model has seen before?"

In this chapter, we turn our attention to regression, the setting where models predict continuous values such as prices, demand, duration, or quantities. At first glance, regression may appear simpler than classification. After all, instead of choosing between categories, the model only needs to estimate a number. *But in practice, regression is often where uncertainty matters most. A single numeric prediction, whether it is a sales forecast, a credit loss estimate, or a medical dosage, can be dangerously misleading when presented without context about how wrong it could be.*

Traditional regression models are optimized to predict a central tendency, usually the mean or median of the target variable. Loss functions such as mean squared error or mean absolute error reward accuracy on average, but they say nothing about how reliable an individual prediction is. *Two inputs with identical predicted values may carry vastly different levels of risk, volatility, or unpredictability. Yet classical regression models typically report both predictions with equal confidence, masking this distinction entirely.*

This is precisely where conformal prediction becomes indispensable. Conformal prediction for regression transforms a point-predicting model into an uncertainty-aware predictor by attaching a prediction interval to each estimate. Instead of stating that a future demand will be 500 units, the model can say that the demand is expected to lie between 430 and 580 units with 90% confidence. *Crucially, this confidence statement is not based on distributional assumptions or model-specific variance estimates. It is derived empirically from how the model has actually behaved on the past data.*

While the core principles of conformal prediction remain the same, exchangeability, calibration, non-conformity scores, and validity, the regression setting introduces its own subtleties. Unlike classification, where uncertainty is expressed through sets of labels, regression requires us to reason about interval width, error symmetry, and how uncertainty varies across the input space. Questions that naturally arise include why some prediction intervals are wide, while others are narrow, and how uncertainty should adapt when noise changes with input features. Also, what it means for a regression interval to be both valid and informative.

In this chapter, we address these questions step by step. We begin with the simplest and most widely used conformal regression method based on absolute residuals, building intuition around how historical errors translate into future uncertainty. From there, we explore more advanced constructions that adapt interval widths to heteroskedastic data, allowing uncertainty to expand in noisy regions, and contract where predictions are stable. Along the way, we examine how interval sharpness, coverage, and calibration interact, and why achieving validity alone is not enough for practical usefulness.

By the end of this chapter, you will have a clear understanding of how conformal prediction operates in regression settings, how different design choices affect the resulting intervals, and how to interpret these intervals responsibly in real-world decision-making. Most importantly, you will see how conformal prediction turns regression models from tools that merely predict numbers into systems that communicate uncertainty honestly and reliably, a requirement for any model that aims to be trusted beyond the laboratory.

Structure

This chapter is organized into the following sections:

- From Point Predictions to Conformal Prediction Intervals
- Quantifying Uncertainty from Past Errors
- Training Strategies
- From Valid Intervals to Reliable Decisions

From Point Predictions to Conformal Prediction Intervals

Most regression models are designed to answer a single question: what is the best numerical estimate for the target variable given the input features? Whether we are predicting sales, prices, energy consumption, or risk scores, the output of a regression model is typically a single number. This point prediction is often treated as the final answer and, in many systems, it is the only information passed downstream for decision making.

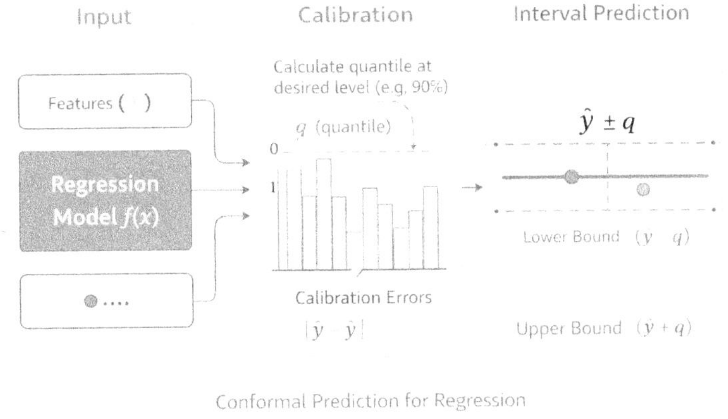

Figure 4.1: *Visual Illustration of CP in Regression*

However, as we discussed in the earlier chapters, a point prediction by itself hides an important fact, that is, the same predicted value can be associated with very different levels of uncertainty. Two inputs may both receive a prediction of 500, yet one may correspond to a highly stable and predictable situation, while the other lies in a noisy or poorly understood region of the data. Traditional regression models do not distinguish between these cases. They are optimized to minimize average errors, not to communicate how wrong a specific prediction might be. To make this idea more concrete, let us look at the following scenario: imagine a retail demand forecasting model predicting weekly sales for two different products.

- For **Product A**, sales have been consistently around 500 units every week for the past year, with only small fluctuations caused by minor day-to-day variations. The model has seen many similar situations before, and its past prediction errors in this region are small and stable.

- For **Product B**, sales are also predicted to be 500 units, but historical demand has been highly volatile. Some weeks the sales were as low as 200 units, while in others, they spiked above 900 due to promotions, stockouts, or external events. The model has fewer comparable examples, and has historically made larger errors in this region.

- Despite these very different histories, a traditional regression model reports the same output, 500 (central tendency), for both products. The prediction looks equally precise, even though the underlying uncertainty is vastly different.

- Because the model is trained to minimize average error across all products and time periods, *it has no mechanism to express that Product B's prediction is riskier or less reliable than Product A's.*

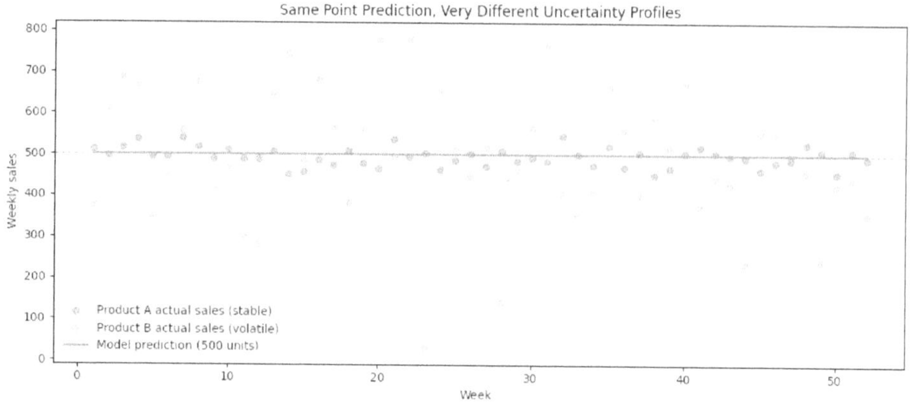

Figure 4.2: *Impact of Uncertainty in Regression*

As a result, downstream decisions such as inventory planning or supply allocation treat both predictions as equally trustworthy, potentially leading to overstock for one product and stockouts for the other. This example highlights a core limitation of point prediction models. They compress all uncertainty into a single number, and optimize for overall accuracy, but they do not communicate how uncertain a specific prediction is. Conformal prediction addresses this gap by attaching uncertainty directly to each prediction, allowing two identical point estimates to carry very different levels of confidence when warranted by historical behavior.

A natural way to address this gap is to replace point predictions with prediction intervals. Instead of producing a single value □, the model produces a range within which the true outcome is expected to lie with a specified level of confidence. For example, the following plot shows a range of demands for the two products with the band naturally being higher for Product B capturing the fluctuation in demand due to external factors. So, instead of saying the demand would be 500 units, now, we say the demand could be anywhere between 300 - 700 units; hence, allowing the company to plan the inventory accordingly for both products.

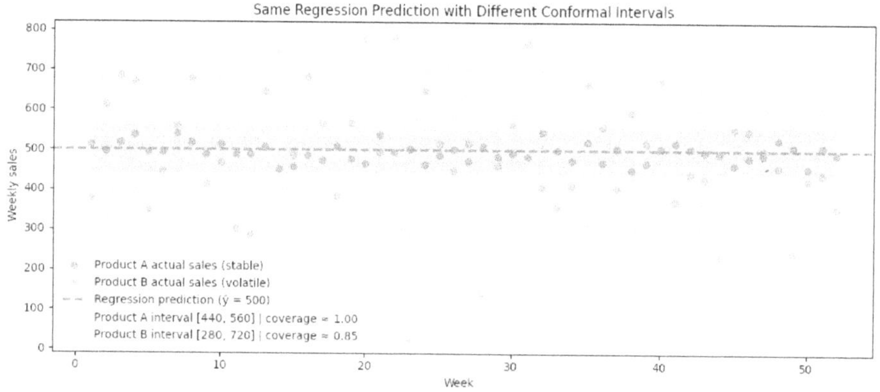

Figure 4.3: *Uncertainty Band around Prediction*

Conformal prediction, instead of relying on theoretical assumptions, about the data or the model, it uses the model's own historical errors to quantify uncertainty. The central idea is simple: if a model has tended to make errors of a certain magnitude on past data, then future predictions should be allowed to deviate by a similar amount. By calibrating uncertainty empirically, conformal prediction turns any regression model into an interval-producing model with statistically valid coverage guarantees.

This shift from point predictions to conformal prediction intervals mirrors the transition we saw in classification from single labels to prediction sets. In both cases, the goal is not to replace the underlying model, but to wrap it with a layer that communicates uncertainty honestly. *For regression, this means expressing uncertainty as an interval whose width reflects how the model has behaved in similar situations before, rather than how confident it appears internally.*

In the sections that follow, we will see how these intervals are constructed in practice, starting with simple residual-based methods and gradually extending them to handle more complex situations such as varying noise levels across the input space. Throughout, the emphasis will remain on intuition, empirical behavior, and practical interpretation, ensuring that prediction intervals are not only valid, but also meaningful for real-world decision making.

Quantifying Uncertainty from Past Errors

Every regression model makes mistakes. In most machine learning workflows, these mistakes which are often called as cost in the Machine Learning lingo are treated as something to minimize, once the training is complete. Metrics such as mean squared error or mean absolute error compress all prediction errors into a single number, *offering a high-level sense of model quality but discarding information about how those errors are distributed and where they occur.*

From the perspective of uncertainty, this discarded information is precisely what we need. The magnitude and variability of past errors tell us how reliable the model has been in different situations. A model that has consistently made small errors in a particular region of the input space deserves more trust there than in regions where its errors have been large or erratic. Rather than viewing residuals as failures, conformal prediction treats them as empirical evidence about the model's uncertainty.

In regression settings, this perspective is especially natural. Unlike classification, where uncertainty is expressed through competing labels, regression uncertainty manifests as deviation in magnitude. The question is not whether the model chose the wrong category, but how far its numerical prediction deviated from reality. Residuals capture this deviation directly, making them a natural starting point for building prediction intervals.

To make this idea concrete, we now examine how uncertainty is quantified from the model's past performance. Rather than relying on a single definition, we will look at several complementary ways of interpreting and summarizing past errors, each shedding light on a different aspect of model reliability. These perspectives build progressively, starting from simple notions of error magnitude, and moving toward more structured views that connect residual behavior to prediction intervals. Together, they form the foundation for residual-based conformal prediction in regression.

Absolute Residuals

The most fundamental way to quantify uncertainty in regression is to examine the **residual**, defined as the difference between the actual observed value and the model's prediction. For a given input, the residual measures how much reality deviated from the model's expectation. It is the raw, unprocessed expression of prediction error.

Unlike aggregated error metrics, residuals preserve information at the level of individual observations, making them a powerful diagnostic tool for understanding how a model behaves across different cases.

From the perspective of uncertainty, residuals provide a historical record of model performance. Each residual represents a concrete instance where the model was either accurate or inaccurate. Taken together, they reveal patterns such as bias, asymmetry, and variability that are invisible when errors are summarized into a single number.

Consider a real estate company using a regression model to estimate the **market price of individual residential properties**. Each property is characterized by features such as location, floor area, age of the building, amenities, and proximity to transport hubs. The model outputs a predicted sale price for each property.

After a property is sold, the **actual transaction price** becomes known. Each property sale represents an independent regression instance. There is no temporal dependency or forecasting involved.

For each property, the residual is computed as the difference between the actual sale price and the predicted price.

- A positive residual indicates that the property sold for more than expected. **The model undervalued the property**.
- A negative residual indicates that the property sold for less than expected. **The model overvalued it**.

Each residual is directly interpretable, and captures how much the model's valuation deviated from the true market outcome for that specific property giving key insights of pricing of the property as per the market demand. Let us solidify this with a code example using dummy data.

```
# ------------------------------
#Generate dummy property data
```

```
# ------------------------------
n = 300

# Feature: floor area in square feet
floor_area = np.random.uniform(500, 3500, size=n)

# True (unknown) market price function (in lakhs)
true_price_mean = 0.045 * floor_area

# Market-driven noise
# Larger properties have higher variability in prices
noise_std = 8 + 0.02 * floor_area
actual_price = true_price_mean + np.random.normal(0, noise_std)
```

The dummy dataset is constructed by modeling housing prices as a linear function of floor area, with additional noise that grows with property size, capturing the real-world tendency for larger houses to exhibit greater price variability.

```
# ------------------------------
# Residuals
# ------------------------------

# Residual = Actual - Predicted
residuals = actual_price - predicted_price
abs_residuals = np.abs(residuals)

# 90% empirical error quantile
q90 = np.quantile(abs_residuals, 0.90)

lower_band = predicted_price - q90
upper_band = predicted_price + q90
```

Figure 4.4: *Housing Prices Dummy Data*

Using the fitted model, we then compute absolute residuals to quantify the uncertainty introduced during the synthetic data generation process, and subsequently, construct confidence intervals around point predictions to make them practically usable.

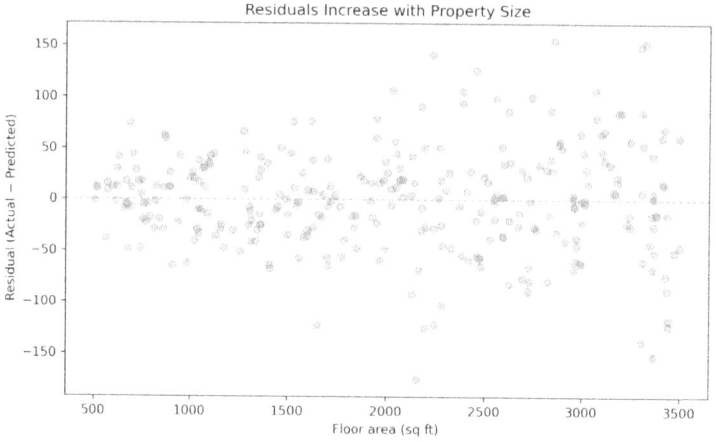

Figure 4.5: *Residuals against the Floor Area*

As shown above, residuals reflect the changing noise structure in the data, with larger variability at higher prices. This indicates that the model captures the dominant linear trend, and the residuals isolate the remaining random variation. The residuals are then used at the end to create a simple quantile-based confidence interval around housing prices prediction, making it more reliable.

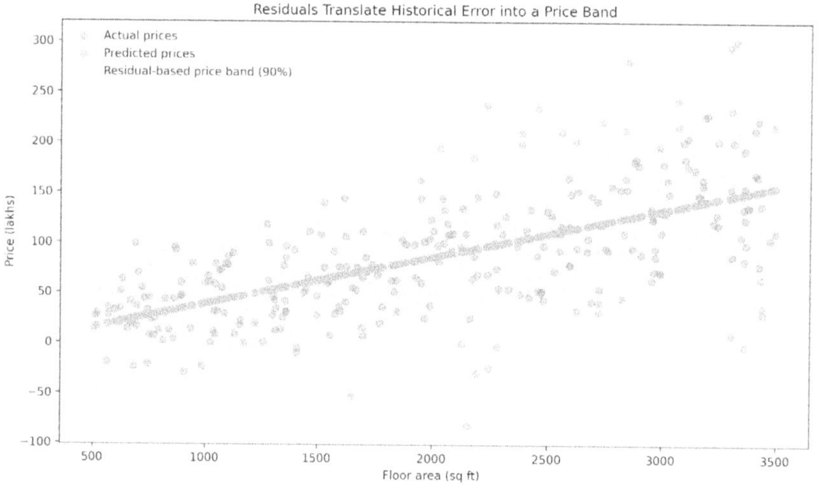

Figure 4.6: *Error Variability*

This illustrates why residuals occupy a central role in uncertainty quantification for regression. Far from being mere errors to minimize, residuals provide an empirical record of how the model has historically deviated from reality. By examining their magnitude and structure, we are able to recover meaningful information about uncertainty that is invisible in point predictions alone.

The residual-based price band demonstrates how this information can be translated into a practical decision-making tool. Instead of committing to a single estimated price, the business gains a range that reflects plausible market outcomes based on past behavior. Such bands can guide pricing strategies, negotiation buffers, risk assessment, allowing decisions to explicitly account for uncertainty, rather than treating all predictions as equally precise.

Locally Scaled Residuals

The residual-based intervals constructed so far rely on a single global notion of uncertainty. By aggregating residuals across the entire calibration set, we implicitly assume that prediction uncertainty is uniform across the input space. *While this assumption simplifies interval construction and preserves coverage guarantees, it is often unrealistic in practical regression problems.*

In many real-world settings like our previous housing pricing example, uncertainty varies systematically with the input. Some regions of the feature space are well represented in the data and yield stable, predictable outcomes. Other regions are sparse, noisy, or influenced by unobserved factors, leading to larger and more erratic prediction errors. A single global residual quantile cannot distinguish between these regimes. As a result, global conformal intervals tend to be overly conservative in stable regions, and insufficiently wide in noisy ones.

Locally scaled residuals address this limitation by conditioning the notion of uncertainty on the input itself. Instead of measuring deviation using raw absolute residuals alone, residuals are normalized by a local estimate of uncertainty. This scaling allows prediction intervals to adapt to the difficulty of individual predictions, while retaining the distribution-free guarantees that make conformal prediction attractive.

From a conformal perspective, the key idea is simple. Rather than asking how large a typical error is across all observations, we ask how large an error is relative to what is expected in that specific region of the input space. Residuals that are large in absolute terms may be unsurprising in high-variance regions, while much smaller deviations may be significant in regions where predictions are usually accurate. Local scaling makes this distinction explicit.

This section introduces locally scaled residuals as a natural extension of absolute-residual conformal prediction. We will examine how local uncertainty estimates can be obtained, how they are incorporated into conformal nonconformity scores, and why this approach leads to more informative and better aligned prediction intervals in heterogeneous data settings.

For the same housing prices example where price varied more for bigger houses, this perfectly fits in to explain the varied noise.

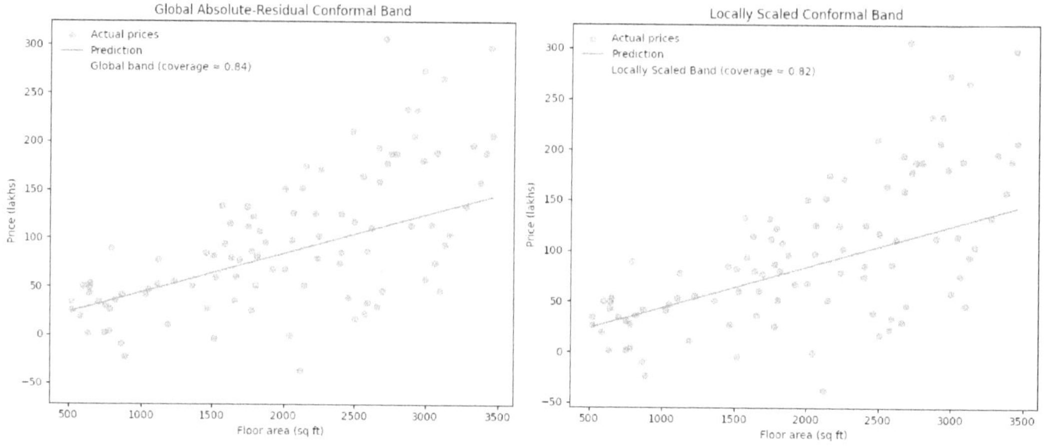

Figure 4.7: *Thresholds Techniques Compared*

To account for input-dependent uncertainty, we estimate a local scale function $\sigma(x)$ that reflects how large prediction errors are typically expected to be for a given input. This function is learned empirically from the training data by examining how absolute residuals vary with the input feature. *In the housing example, we observe that residual magnitudes increase with floor area, indicating higher uncertainty for larger properties. A simple regression is therefore fit between floor area and absolute residuals to capture this trend, yielding a smooth estimate of local error scale across the input space.* Each residual is then normalized by this local scale, producing locally scaled residuals that measure deviation relative to what is expected in that region. Conformal calibration is performed on these normalized scores, and the resulting quantile is rescaled by $\sigma(x)$ at prediction time, producing intervals that are narrow where the model is reliable and wider, and where uncertainty is inherently higher.

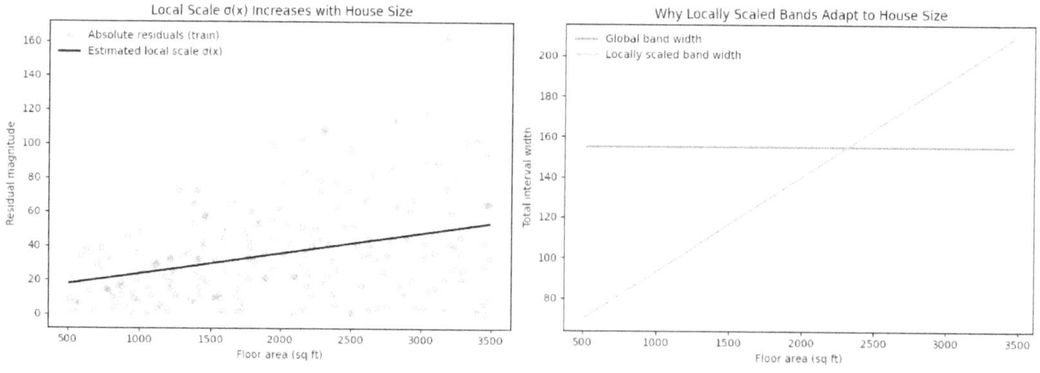

Figure 4.8: *Local Scale*

In the following figure, we see how a locally scaled residual adjusts looking at two different types of houses.

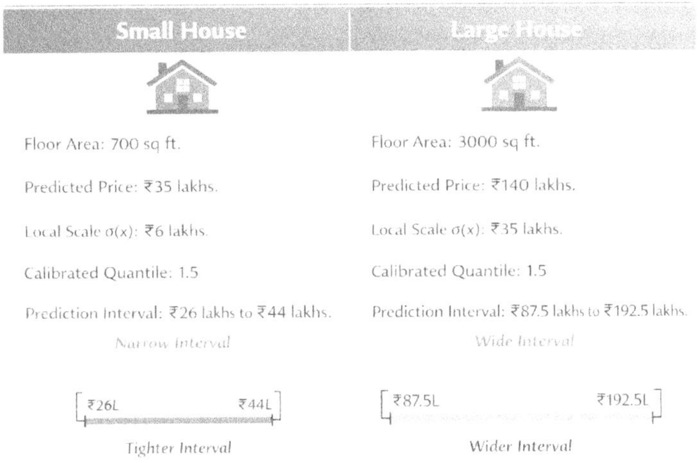

Figure 4.9: *Comparison of Data Points*

Locally scaled residuals extend conformal prediction beyond a one-size-fits-all notion of uncertainty by explicitly acknowledging that some predictions are inherently harder than others. By normalizing residuals using an empirically learned local scale, this approach allows prediction intervals to adapt to input-dependent variability, while preserving the distribution-free coverage guarantees of conformal prediction. The result is a more faithful representation of uncertainty: tight intervals where the model is consistently reliable, and wider intervals where the data itself is volatile. Importantly, this adaptivity is achieved without changing the underlying model or relying on parametric assumptions. Locally scaled residuals therefore strike a practical balance between validity and informativeness, making them especially well-suited for real-world regression problems with heterogeneous noise.

Training Strategies

So far, we have examined different **non-conformity scores** for regression, and how they capture uncertainty through past prediction errors. These scores define *what* aspect of error is measured and compared, but they do not, by themselves, constitute a complete conformal prediction method.

A conformal prediction algorithm is defined by the **entire pipeline** such as: how the model is trained, how data is partitioned, how non-conformity scores are computed, and how calibration is performed. The choice of score is one component of this pipeline, and in this section, we shift focus from individual scores to full-fledged **conformal prediction algorithms for regression**. These algorithms differ primarily in how they use the available data to train models, and compute conformity scores. Some rely on a simple train–calibration split, while others reuse data through leave-one-out or cross-validation schemes. Importantly, just like in classification, these algorithms are agnostic to the underlying regression model.

Understanding these training strategies clarifies how conformal prediction operates as a complete system. It also reveals the trade-offs between simplicity, computational cost, and statistical efficiency. In the sections that follow, we introduce the most commonly used conformal regression algorithms, and show how previously discussed scores can be incorporated into each of them.

Split Conformal Prediction

Split conformal prediction is the simplest, and most widely used conformal algorithm for regression. It serves as the baseline against which more advanced conformal methods are compared. The defining characteristic of split conformal prediction is its strict separation of the data into two disjoint parts: one used to train the predictive model, and the other used exclusively to calibrate uncertainty. [1]

- A regression model is trained and tuned on the training set.
- The remaining data is then passed through this trained model to compute non-conformity scores, typically based on residuals or their variants.
- These scores are aggregated using a quantile to determine the width of the prediction interval. The same trained model and calibrated quantile are subsequently used to produce prediction intervals for new inputs.

This separation of roles is what makes split conformal prediction attractive. It is easy to implement and, computationally efficient. Because calibration is performed on data that was not used for training, the resulting prediction intervals enjoy finite-sample, distribution-free coverage guarantees under minimal assumptions.

Let us continue with the housing prices example, and plug in all the major steps to perform a full CP pipeline for regression.

Step 1: Splitting the Data

Here, we first break down our dataset into three subsets.

- **Training data:** Used to train and fine tune the hyperparameters of the model using strategies like K- Fold Cross Validation.
- **Calibration data:** Captures the uncertainty of the trained model on a hold out set using different non-conformity scoring strategies as discussed in the previous section.
- **Test set:** Finally, give the predictions along with the intervals learnt using the calibration data on the unseen dataset.

The split is typically performed **randomly**, ensuring that the training and calibration sets are exchangeable samples from the same underlying distribution. This exchangeability is the key assumption that enables conformal prediction to provide valid coverage guarantees. In practice, common choices allocate a larger fraction of the data to training, and a smaller but sufficient portion to calibration, balancing predictive accuracy with reliable uncertainty estimation.

```
# ----------------------------------------------------
#Percentage-based random split
# ----------------------------------------------------

idx = np.random.permutation(n)

train_frac = 0.6
calib_frac = 0.2   # remaining 0.2 is test

n_train = int(train_frac * n)
n_calib = int(calib_frac * n)

train_idx = idx[:n_train]
calib_idx = idx[n_train:n_train + n_calib]
test_idx  = idx[n_train + n_calib:]

X_train, y_train = floor_area[train_idx], price[train_idx]
X_calib, y_calib = floor_area[calib_idx], price[calib_idx]
X_test,  y_test  = floor_area[test_idx],  price[test_idx]
```

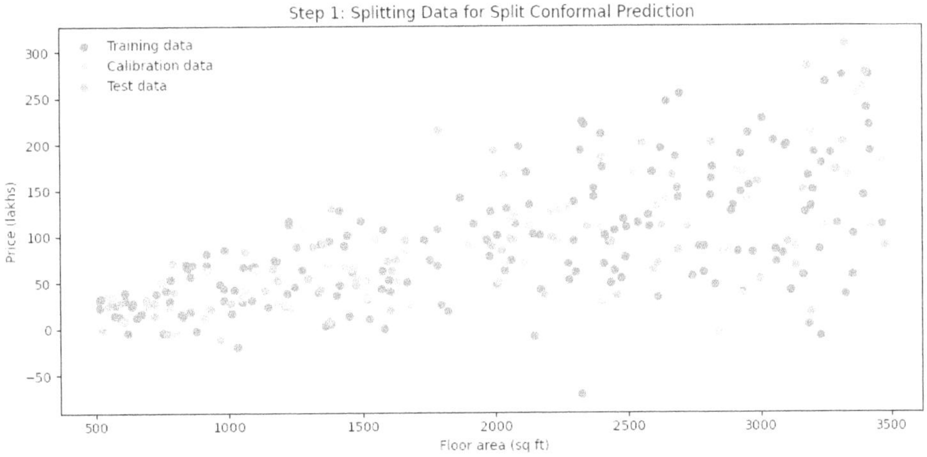

Figure 4.10: *Splitting the Data*

Step 2: Calibration

Once the predictive model has been trained, *it is applied to the calibration set to evaluate how it performs on the previously unseen data. For each calibration point, a non-conformity score is computed, typically based on the discrepancy between the observed outcome and the model's prediction. These scores form an empirical record of the model's past errors under conditions that mirror future use.*

Calibration proceeds by *aggregating these scores, and selecting a threshold that corresponds to the desired coverage level. This threshold is obtained as a high quantile of the calibration score distribution, and represents the largest error the model is willing to tolerate while remaining statistically honest.* Importantly, this choice is entirely data-driven: no assumptions are made about the distribution of errors or the correctness of the underlying model. The selected threshold encapsulates how much uncertainty must be added to predictions, so that based on historical evidence, only a small fraction of future outcomes are expected to fall outside the resulting interval.

```
# ------------------------------------------------
# Compute calibration residuals
# ------------------------------------------------

calib_predictions = model(X_calib)
scores = np.abs(y_calib - calib_predictions)

alpha = 0.1
q = np.quantile(scores, 1 - alpha)
```

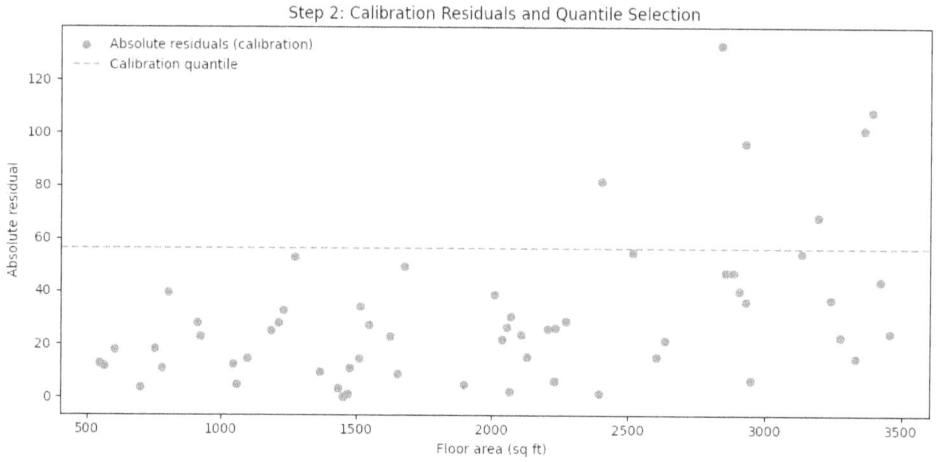

Figure 4.11: *Calibration and Threshold Selection*

Step 3: Prediction Intervals

With the calibration threshold determined, prediction intervals can now be constructed for new inputs. For any input value, **the trained regression model first produces a point prediction, representing its best estimate of the outcome. This point prediction is then expanded by the calibrated threshold on both sides to form an interval**. The resulting range reflects the amount of uncertainty that must be added to the model's prediction in order to remain consistent with the model's historical error behavior observed during calibration.

This construction is deliberately simple. The same calibrated threshold is applied uniformly across all new predictions, translating past out-of-sample errors into a future uncertainty guarantee. Under the assumption that future data is exchangeable with the calibration data, this interval is guaranteed to contain the true outcome with the specified probability. Importantly, no retraining or re-calibration is required at prediction time, making split conformal prediction easy to deploy in practice.

```
# --------------------------------------------------
# Prediction intervals on test data
# --------------------------------------------------

test_predictions = model(X_test)
lower_bound = test_predictions - q
upper_bound = test_predictions + q
```

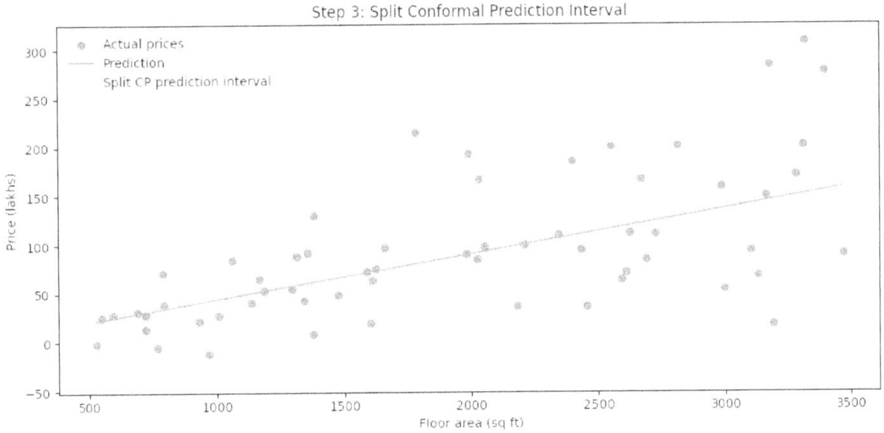

Figure 4.12: *Prediction Intervals*

Split conformal prediction provides a simple and effective way to transform point predictions into uncertainty-aware prediction intervals with finite-sample coverage guarantees. By clearly separating training and calibration, it ensures that uncertainty is calibrated using genuine out-of-sample errors, making the procedure transparent, model-agnostic, and easy to deploy. Its strength lies in this simplicity: any regression model and any non-conformity score can be incorporated without altering the underlying learning process.

While split conformal prediction is simple and reliable, its rigid use of data leaves room for improvement. The model is trained only once, and a fixed subset of data is reserved for calibration, which means the resulting intervals do not reflect how predictions might change if the training data were slightly different. This can lead to intervals that are more conservative than necessary. To address this, conformal methods have been developed that reuse data more effectively by retraining models in a structured way, while still maintaining coverage guarantees. The next section introduces these approaches, and shows how they lead to more efficient and informative prediction intervals.

Jackknife+

Split conformal prediction establishes a simple and reliable baseline, but its reliance on a single train–calibration split limits how fully it can exploit the available data. In particular, it treats the trained model as fixed, and does not account for how predictions might change if the training data were slightly perturbed. Jackknife+ addresses this limitation by changing not the non-conformity score, but the **training strategy** itself.

The central idea behind Jackknife+ is to reuse the data more aggressively by repeatedly retraining the model on slightly different versions of the dataset. Instead of fitting one model, Jackknife+ fits multiple models, each leaving out a single data point. These leave-one-out models are then used to assess how both predictions and errors vary across small changes in the training data.

From a conformal perspective, this procedure produces a richer set of information. Each data point contributes not only an error term, but also a version of the model that reflects what the predictor would look like if that point were absent. By aggregating predictions and residuals across these leave-one-out models, Jackknife+ constructs prediction intervals that reflect both empirical error behavior and sensitivity to the training data.

Importantly, Jackknife+ preserves the same distribution-free coverage guarantees as split conformal prediction, while often producing intervals that are more robust to model instability. This makes it particularly appealing in settings where datasets are small, models are flexible, or individual observations exert a strong influence on the fitted predictor.

In the sections that follow, we unpack Jackknife+ step by step, beginning with its intuition and algorithmic structure, before examining how it differs from split conformal prediction in practice.

We use the same data generation process as last time, and create a small housing prices dataset with noise:

```
n = 120  # small dataset to highlight instability

floor_area = np.random.uniform(600, 3200, size=n)

true_price = 0.05 * floor_area
noise_std = 5 + 0.03 * floor_area   # heteroskedastic noise
price = true_price + np.random.normal(0, noise_std)
n_train = len(x_train)
```

After generating the dataset, we first split it into training and test sets, and then train leave-one-out models exclusively on the training data.

```
n_train = len(X_train)

loo_preds_test = []
loo_residuals = []

for i in range(n_train):

    mask = np.ones(n_train, dtype=bool)
    mask[i] = False

    X_loo = X_train[mask]
    y_loo = y_train[mask]

    coef_loo = np.polyfit(X_loo, y_loo, deg=1)

    def model_loo(x):
        return np.polyval(coef_loo, x)

    # LOO residual
    pred_i = model_loo(X_train[i])
    loo_residuals.append(abs(y_train[i] - pred_i))

    # Predictions for test set
    loo_preds_test.append(model_loo(X_test))

loo_preds_test = np.array(loo_preds_test)
loo_residuals = np.array(loo_residuals)

# Quantile of residuals
q_jack_mm = np.quantile(loo_residuals, 1 - alpha)

# Minmax interval
jack_mm_lower = np.min(loo_preds_test - q_jack_mm, axis=0)
jack_mm_upper = np.max(loo_preds_test + q_jack_mm, axis=0)
```

The preceding code implements the Jackknife-Minmax conformal prediction method by explicitly constructing Leave-One-Out (LOO) models, and aggregating their predictions in a conservative min-max fashion. The procedure begins by iterating over each training observation, and temporarily removing it from the dataset. For each index i, the model is refitted using all data points except (X_i, Y_i). This produces a leave-one-out estimator, which represents the model trained without the influence of the ith observation.

Once the leave-one-out model is fitted, two quantities are computed.

- First, the LOO residual for the excluded point is calculated. This residual measures how well the model predicts a point it has not seen during training, making it an approximately exchangeable error estimate. These residuals form the empirical distribution from which uncertainty is quantified.

- Second, each leave-one-out model generates predictions for all test points. These predictions are stored so that, for every new input X_{n+1}, we have a collection of predictions $\mu_{-1}(X_{n+1}), \mu_{-2}(X_{n+1})$ and so on. This captures how sensitive the model's prediction is to the removal of individual training points.

After computing all LOO residuals, the method extracts the empirical quantile:

$$q_{1-\alpha} = \text{Quantile}_{1-\alpha}\left(R_1^{\text{LOO}}, \ldots, R_n^{\text{LOO}}\right)$$

Figure 4.13: *Identifying Empirical Quantiles*

This single quantile represents a worst-case error level that controls the desired coverage rate. Finally, the prediction interval for each test point is constructed using a min–max envelope:

$$[min_{i=1,..,n}\hat{\mu}_{-i}(X_{n+1}) - q_{1-\alpha}, max_{i=1,..,n}\hat{\mu}_{-i}(X_{n+1}) + q_{1-\alpha}]$$

Figure 4.14: *Prediction Intervals*

Operationally, this corresponds to shifting every leave-one-out prediction downward by the same quantile, and taking the minimum as the lower bound, as well as shifting every prediction upward by the same quantile, and taking the maximum as the upper bound. The result is an interval that encloses all LOO-based uncertainty simultaneously.

Conceptually, this construction does two things at once. *The residual quantile accounts for predictive error, while the min–max aggregation accounts for model instability across different training subsets.* The cost of this robustness is conservativeness: the interval is typically wider since it inflates every leave-one-out prediction by the same worst-case residual, and then takes the outer envelope across all models.

The following is a side-by-side comparison of jackknife+ against split on the same housing dataset, where we can clearly see the jackknife+ interval that ensures a better coverage with a small increase in the width.

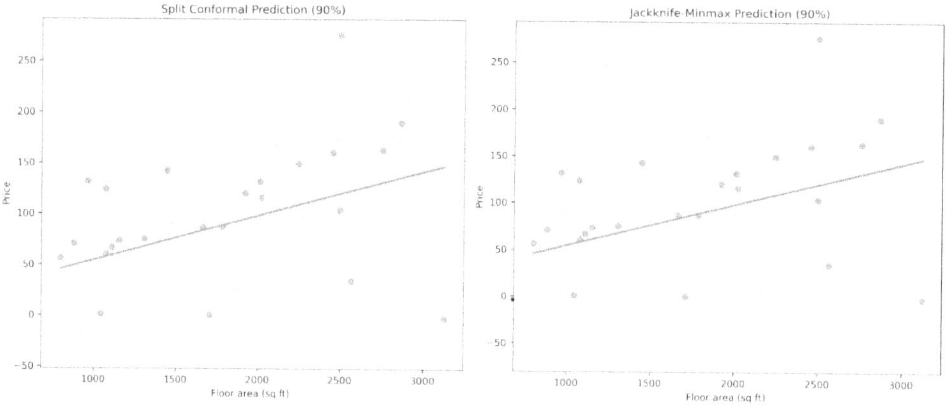

Figure 4.15: *Split and Jackknife+ Prediction Intervals*

Split Conformal Prediction is attractive because of its simplicity and strong finite-sample guarantee. The method divides the dataset into two parts: one portion is used to *train the predictive model, and the remaining portion is used to estimate uncertainty through calibration residuals. The final prediction interval takes the form of the model prediction plus or minus a constant quantile of calibration residuals. This construction guarantees marginal coverage of at least 1 – α under exchangeability, regardless of the underlying regression algorithm. However, this simplicity comes at a cost. Because a portion of the data is withheld for calibration, the predictive model is trained on less data than is actually available. In small or unstable datasets, this reduction in training data can noticeably degrade predictive accuracy.* [2]

Jackknife+ addresses this inefficiency by eliminating the explicit data split. Instead of reserving a calibration set, it trains leave-one-out models such as: for each observation in the training set, a model is fit without that observation. The residual for each point is computed using the model that excluded it. For a new test point, each leave-one-out model produces a prediction, and these predictions are combined with their corresponding residuals to form an interval via a min–max aggregation. Conceptually, Jackknife+ uses *all* the available data for both model fitting and uncertainty quantification, without discarding any points for calibration.

The key advantage of Jackknife+ over Split Conformal is statistical efficiency. Because Split Conformal trains on only a subset of the data, its point predictions can be noisier, which directly translates into wider intervals. Jackknife+, by contrast, effectively leverages nearly the full dataset in every leave-one-out fit, resulting in more stable predictions.

Another important distinction lies in how model instability is handled. Split Conformal assumes the trained model is fixed after fitting; all uncertainty is captured through calibration residuals. Jackknife+ explicitly accounts for model variability by incorporating the spread across leave-one-out predictions. If the model is unstable—meaning small changes in the training data significantly alter predictions—Jackknife+ intervals automatically widen to reflect that instability. This makes Jackknife+ more adaptive to the behavior of the underlying algorithm.

In summary, Split Conformal is computationally simple and theoretically clean, but it sacrifices data efficiency. Jackknife+ is computationally more demanding, since it requires fitting the model multiple times, yet it often produces narrower and more adaptive intervals because it uses all the available data for learning. When computational cost is manageable and data are limited or models are unstable, Jackknife+ typically provides a more statistically efficient alternative to Split Conformal, while preserving rigorous distribution-free guarantees.

From Valid Intervals to Reliable Decisions

Up to this point, we have focused on how to construct conformal prediction intervals for regression. We began by understanding the methods to quantify the uncertainty by using simple residual-based methods, extended them to locally scaled variants, and later examined training strategies such as split conformal and Jackknife+. At each stage, the emphasis was on validity – ensuring that prediction intervals achieve the desired coverage under exchangeability.

But once we have valid intervals, a deeper question emerges: What makes a conformal interval not just valid, but useful?

Up to now, we have seen these intervals in action through simplified examples. In this section, we formally define how they should be used in practice. Because in the end, uncertainty estimates matter only when they inform better business decisions.

This final section shifts perspective. Rather than asking *how to construct intervals*, we now ask:

1. What does coverage really guarantee?
2. When are intervals informative?
3. How should conformal predictors be evaluated in practice?
4. What happens when assumptions fail?
5. How do we move from statistical validity to decision reliability?

Understanding these questions is what transforms conformal prediction from a clever algorithm into a trustworthy decision framework.

Marginal Coverage versus Conditional Reality

Conformal prediction guarantees **marginal coverage**. Formally, if we choose a miscoverage level α, then under exchangeability:

$$P(Yn + 1 \in C(Xn + 1)) \geq 1 - \alpha$$

Figure 4.16: *Marginal Coverage*

This statement is powerful. It does not depend on:

- The correctness of the regression model.
- Any parametric assumptions.
- The distribution of the data.

However, the guarantee is **marginal**, it holds on average across the entire data distribution.

Marginal Coverage Meaning

Suppose, we construct 90% conformal intervals for housing prices. *If we apply this model to many unseen properties drawn from the same distribution, approximately 90% of true prices will fall inside their respective intervals.*

But this does not mean:

- Every type of house gets 90% coverage.
- Every neighborhood achieves equal reliability.
- Every price range is equally well calibrated.

Coverage is guaranteed in aggregate, not necessarily within every subgroup. Imagine a demand forecasting system for retail products.

- For stable, high-volume products, the model performs consistently, and intervals are tight.
- For volatile, low-volume products, the model struggles and intervals are wider.

Now, suppose:

- Stable products achieve 95% empirical coverage.
- Volatile products achieve only 82% coverage.

If stable products dominate the dataset, *the overall empirical coverage can still appear close to 90%*. In other words, when we average performance across all products, the conformal guarantee seems to be working exactly as promised. From a purely statistical standpoint, the requirement is satisfied. But here is where intuition becomes important.

Imagine that 80% of your products are stable, predictable, and low-variance. The model performs very well on them, and intervals contain the true value almost all the time, say around 95% of the time. The remaining 20% are volatile, heavily promoted, or highly seasonal products where predictions are much harder. For these, coverage drops to 80%. When we average across all products, the strong performance on stable products compensates for the weaker performance on the volatile ones. The overall coverage might still come out close to 90%. On paper, everything looks correct.

But in practice, the products where the system struggles are exactly the ones where uncertainty matters most. *Stable products rarely cause operational surprises. Volatile products do.* They are the ones that create stockouts, overproduction, lost revenue, and emergency decisions. If intervals are systematically too narrow for those difficult cases, the business risk is concentrated precisely where it hurts the most. This is the difference between marginal validity and conditional reliability.

Marginal validity means that across the entire population, the coverage rate is correct on average. Conditional reliability asks a more practical question: "Is the system reliable for this specific type of case?"

A conformal model can be globally valid but locally unreliable. It can meet its mathematical promise, while still under-covering important subgroups. This is not a flaw in conformal prediction, it is a consequence of its design. The guarantee is distribution-wide, not subgroup-specific. *But from a decision-making perspective, we must look beyond averages. We need to examine how coverage behaves across different segments, risk levels, or product types.* Validity tells us that the system is honest overall. Conditional analysis tells us whether it is trustworthy where it matters most.

In real-world systems, marginal coverage should be treated as a baseline guarantee, not a final validation step. It tells us that, on average, across the entire data distribution, the system behaves as promised. That is important because it protects us from systematic overconfidence, and provides statistical reassurance. *However, averages can conceal important structure in the data. A system can satisfy its overall coverage target, while consistently failing in specific regions of the feature space. In practice, those regions are often the ones that carry the highest business risk.*

Subgroup reliability is equally important. Different populations can behave very differently under the same predictive system. New customers may have less historical data, volatile products may display unpredictable patterns, and rare feature combinations may not be well represented in the calibration set. If certain subgroups consistently receive narrower-than-appropriate intervals, the system may technically meet its marginal guarantee, while being unreliable where uncertainty is the highest.

Coverage must also be monitored over time. Real-world data distributions are not static. Seasonality, market shifts, operational changes, or broader economic factors can gradually alter the behavior of the system. A conformal predictor that achieved its target coverage at deployment may begin to under-cover months later if the underlying data distribution drifts. Ongoing monitoring ensures that validity remains aligned with current conditions, rather than past assumptions.

Finally, systematic under-coverage in specific regions should be investigated rather than dismissed as random noise. If intervals repeatedly fail for volatile products, high-demand periods, or rare feature combinations, this signals structural miscalibration. Addressing it may require redesigning the non-conformity score, updating the calibration strategy, or incorporating additional modeling adjustments. Marginal validity provides statistical reassurance, but reliability demands deeper scrutiny. Validity is the floor because it ensures that the system is not recklessly overconfident. It is not the ceiling because a trustworthy system must also be stable across segments, responsive to change, and informative precisely where uncertainty matters most. Only then does conformal prediction move from a theoretical guarantee to a decision framework that organizations can confidently rely upon.

A Diagnostic Toolkit for Conformal Regression

Once prediction intervals are constructed, the real work begins. Conformal regression provides a statistical guarantee, but responsible deployment requires systematic evaluation. A single coverage number is not enough to assess reliability. *Just as we would not evaluate a regression model using only overall mean squared error, we should not evaluate a conformal predictor using only marginal coverage*. A diagnostic toolkit is essential. It helps answer a deeper question: not just whether the system is valid, but whether it is behaving sensibly, consistently, and usefully across different situations.

Empirical Coverage

The first and most fundamental diagnostic is empirical coverage on a held-out test set. *We measure the proportion of test points whose true value falls inside the predicted interval*. This number should be close to the desired confidence level. However, this should not be treated as a binary pass or fail metric. Slight deviations may occur due to finite sample variability. What matters is whether the coverage is consistently near the target across multiple splits or resampling runs. Large or unstable deviations suggest that calibration may be insufficient or that exchangeability assumptions may be strained. Empirical coverage answers the question: "Is the system broadly behaving as promised?"

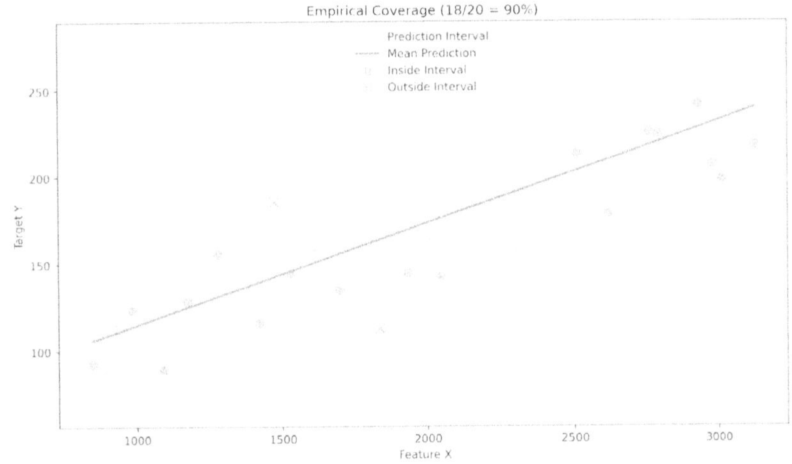

Figure 4.17: *Empirical Coverage*

Conditional Coverage

Empirical coverage tells us how often our prediction intervals contain the true values on average. If we target 90% coverage, and observe something close to 90% on the test set, the conformal predictor has satisfied its statistical guarantee. From a global perspective, the system appears reliable. *However, business decisions are rarely made "on average." They are made for specific customers, specific products, specific regions, and specific risk categories. This is where conditional coverage becomes important.*

Conditional coverage asks a more refined question: *is the model equally reliable across different parts of the feature space?* Instead of computing a single overall coverage number, we divide the data into meaningful segments, and compute coverage separately within each group. These segments can be defined by predicted value ranges, feature quantiles, product types, customer risk categories, geographic regions, or time periods. This approach reveals whether the system is uniformly reliable, or whether a strong average is masking weaknesses in specific regions.

Lending portfolios provide an intuitive example. Suppose, we construct conformal intervals for predicting expected loan loss amounts and evaluate coverage across borrower segments such as salaried professionals, gig economy workers, and first-time borrowers. It is common to observe strong coverage for salaried borrowers, where income streams are stable and historical data is abundant, but weaker coverage for gig workers or first-time borrowers due to income volatility and limited credit history. The model may appear globally valid, yet be overconfident in segments that carry higher behavioral uncertainty. For financial institutions exposed to these higher-risk borrowers, such imbalance can lead to underestimated provisioning and increased portfolio vulnerability.

In practice, conditional coverage analysis is straightforward. The test data can be partitioned into bins based on predicted values, feature quantiles, operational risk tiers, or time windows based on the business requirement. Coverage is then computed separately within each bin and compared to the target level. Some variation is expected due to finite sample noise, but systematic under-coverage in specific regions signals structural miscalibration. It may indicate that the non-conformity score does not adapt sufficiently to heteroskedasticity, that calibration data is sparse in certain areas, or that distribution shift has affected particular segments differently.

An intuitive way to think about conditional coverage is to compare it to insurance. Marginal coverage says that across all claims, 90% are reimbursed. Conditional coverage asks whether high-risk claims are reimbursed at the same rate, or whether the system mostly protects low-risk cases while failing in complex scenarios. A system that performs well in easy situations but struggles in difficult ones may satisfy its statistical guarantee, yet still be operationally unreliable.

When conditional coverage deviates meaningfully from the target in important segments, several remedies may be considered. These include using locally scaled non-conformity scores to better capture heteroskedasticity, increasing the calibration set size, applying stratified or Mondrian conformal approaches, or designing segment-specific calibration procedures. Thus, the goal is not to eliminate all variations, which is impossible in finite samples, but to ensure that reliability does not collapse in high-impact regions.

Marginal validity provides statistical reassurance. Conditional coverage analysis provides operational insight. Marginal coverage answers whether the system is valid, overall. Conditional coverage answers whether the system is reliable where decisions truly matter. In production environments, both perspectives are essential for transforming conformal prediction from a theoretical guarantee into a trustworthy decision framework. The following is an explanation.

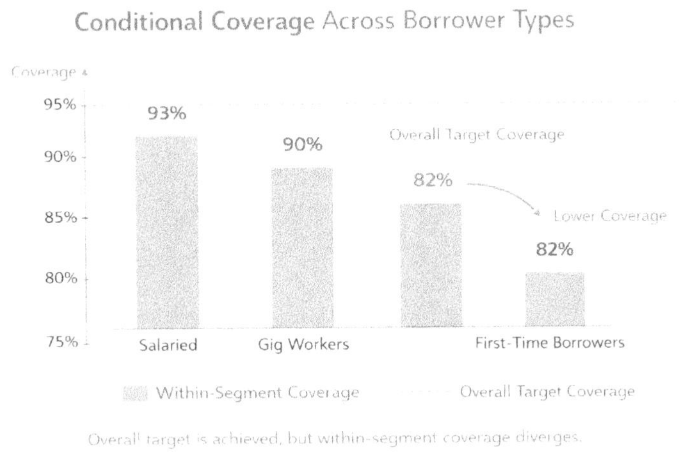

Figure 4.18: *Conditional Coverage*

This figure illustrates conditional coverage for the example, we discussed above, across different borrower segments for a regression model predicting expected loan loss amount. While the overall target coverage for the intervals is 90%, the achieved coverage varies across borrower types. Some segments exceed the target, while others fall below it, indicating uneven reliability. This highlights how marginal validity can mask subgroup-level under-coverage, especially in higher-risk borrower categories.

Once we identify that coverage is uneven (say borrower segments in this case), the goal is not to question conformal prediction itself, but to refine how we apply it. The first step is to recognize if different segments behave differently. For example, gig workers, first-time borrowers, and high-risk applicants may exhibit more variability than salaried individuals with stable income histories when it comes to risk. If we use a single global error quantile for all borrowers, we implicitly assume that uncertainty behaves the same everywhere, which is rarely true in practice. The following are some remedies to rectify this.

- *One simple approach is to calibrate separately across meaningful borrower segments.* Rather than computing one universal threshold, we can compute calibration quantiles within groups such as salaried, gig, or first-time borrowers. This prevents stable segments from "diluting" the uncertainty required for more volatile ones.
- Data representation also plays a critical role. If certain borrower types are underrepresented in the calibration set, the intervals for those segments may not accurately reflect their variability. Thus, *improving coverage sometimes requires something very basic: better, more balanced data.*

Finally, in high-stakes environments like lending, monitoring should be continuous. Coverage should be tracked across segments over time. If under-coverage begins to appear consistently in a particular borrower group, recalibration or model refinement should be triggered before portfolio risk accumulates.

The key idea is simple. When marginal coverage looks fine but segment-level coverage does not, the solution is not to abandon the framework. The solution is to make uncertainty modeling more aligned with how risk actually behaves across different parts of the business.

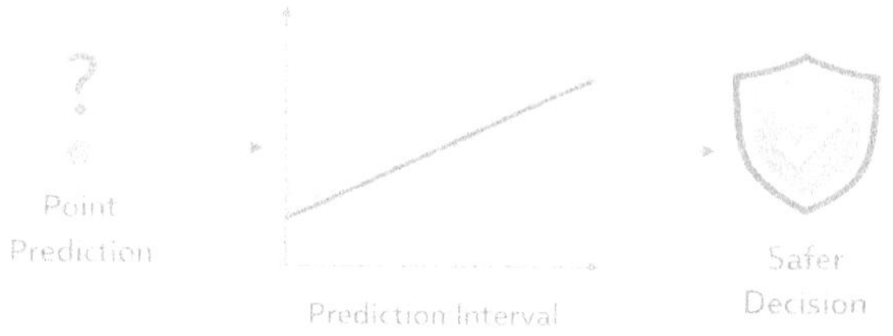

Figure 4.19: *Conformal Regression Workflow*

The figure above provides a simplified visual overview of the conformal prediction workflow for regression.

Conclusion

In this chapter, we moved beyond point predictions, and explored what it truly means to make reliable regression estimates. We saw how a single number, no matter how accurate on average, can hide substantial uncertainty beneath it. By leveraging conformal prediction, we transformed historical model errors into statistically valid prediction intervals, allowing regression systems to communicate not just what they expect, but how uncertain that expectation is.

We began by constructing simple residual-based intervals, and gradually refined them through calibration strategies, locally adaptive approaches, and practical diagnostics. Along the way, we learned that achieving marginal coverage is only the starting point. True reliability requires examining how intervals behave across segments, how wide they are, and whether they adapt intelligently to varying levels of uncertainty. We also saw that validity alone is not enough. An interval that achieves its nominal coverage but fails in high-risk segments can create a false sense of security. That is why diagnostics such as conditional coverage, and monitoring over time are essential in real-world systems. Conformal prediction provides the mathematical guarantee, but responsible deployment requires thoughtful evaluation and continuous oversight.

At its core, conformal regression represents a shift in mindset. Traditional machine learning focuses on optimizing error metrics. Conformal prediction asks a different question: given how wrong the model has been in the past, how cautious should we be about the next prediction? This simple yet powerful idea transforms regression models from confident estimators into accountable decision tools. *Thus, the journey from point estimates to calibrated intervals reflects the broader theme introduced at the beginning of this book: the illusion of certainty. Models will always produce numbers. But numbers without quantified uncertainty can mislead, especially in high-stakes domains such as finance, healthcare, and forecasting. Conformal prediction does not eliminate uncertainty. Instead, it makes uncertainty explicit, measurable, and usable.*

As we close this chapter, one principle should remain clear. A prediction becomes trustworthy not when it is precise, but when its uncertainty is honestly expressed.

In the next chapter, we will extend these ideas further: exploring how conformal prediction adapts to sequential data, and wrap conformal intervals around forecasting related problems.

Points to Remember

- Point predictions alone are incomplete. A single number without quantified uncertainty can create false confidence in high-stakes decisions.
- Conformal prediction transforms historical model errors into statistically valid prediction intervals without modifying the underlying model.
- Marginal coverage guarantees **reliability on average**, but does not ensure fairness or reliability across all subgroups.
- Conditional coverage analysis is essential to uncover hidden under-coverage in specific feature regions or business segments.
- **Interval width is as important as coverage**. Extremely wide intervals may be valid, but not necessarily useful for decision-making.
- Heteroskedasticity matters. If uncertainty varies across the feature space, interval construction must adapt accordingly.
- Calibration quality directly affects reliability. Poorly constructed calibration sets can distort interval guarantees.
- Monitoring coverage over time is critical in dynamic environments where data distributions shift.
- The ultimate goal of conformal regression is not just valid intervals, but trustworthy decisions grounded in transparent uncertainty.

Chapter Resources

- Code Exercise

Multiple Choice Questions

1. What is the primary limitation of point predictions in regression models?
    a. They require too much computation.
    b. They cannot handle large datasets.

   c. They do not communicate uncertainty.
   d. They always overfit.

2. Conformal prediction intervals are constructed using:
   a. Future unseen errors
   b. Parametric distribution assumptions
   c. Past model residuals
   d. Bayesian priors

3. Marginal coverage guarantees that:
   a. Every subgroup achieves the exact coverage.
   b. Coverage holds on average across the data distribution.
   c. All predictions are correct.
   d. The model is unbiased.

4. If a conformal model achieves 90% coverage, overall but only 75% for a specific segment, this indicates:
   a. Perfect calibration
   b. Conditional under-coverage
   c. Overfitting
   d. Data leakage

5. Why is interval width important in conformal regression?
   a. Narrower intervals always guarantee better models.
   b. Width determines the training speed.
   c. Valid intervals can still be uninformative if too wide.
   d. Width is unrelated to usefulness.

6. Increasing calibration set size generally:
   a. Reduces interval width drastically
   b. Stabilizes quantile estimation
   c. Removes the need for diagnostics
   d. Eliminates distribution shift

7. Conditional coverage analysis involves:
   a. Re-training the base model
   b. Checking coverage across feature-based segments

   c. Removing outliers
   d. Adjusting the learning rate

8. Heteroskedastic data refers to:
   a. Data with missing values.
   b. Data with constant variance.
   c. Data where noise variance changes across inputs.
   d. Data with categorical features.

9. Locally adaptive conformal methods primarily aim to:
   a. Reduce the computational cost.
   b. Capture varying uncertainty across the feature space.
   c. Remove calibration step.
   d. Replace regression models.

10. Under distribution shift, conformal guarantees may weaken because:
    a. Exchangeability assumptions may be violated.
    b. The regression model becomes linear.
    c. Calibration becomes unnecessary.
    d. Residuals disappear.

11. Empirical coverage is calculated as:
    a. Total predictions divided by the calibration size.
    b. Points inside interval divided by the total test points.
    c. Mean squared error.
    d. Interval width divided by alpha.

12. A model with 99% coverage when targeting 90% likely has:
    a. Underfitting
    b. Perfect conditional coverage
    c. Overly wide intervals
    d. Data leakage

13. Why is monitoring coverage over time important?
    a. Models never change.
    b. Business conditions and data distributions evolve.

   c. It improves the training speed.
   d. It increases model accuracy.

14. The key advantage of conformal prediction is that it is:
   a. Model-specific
   b. Distribution-dependent
   c. Model-agnostic and assumption-light
   d. Only applicable to linear regression

15. The ultimate objective of conformal regression is to:
   a. Minimize residual variance
   b. Replace all statistical models
   c. Provide honest and reliable uncertainty for decision-making
   d. Eliminate prediction errors

Answers

1. c
2. c
3. b
4. b
5. c
6. b
7. b
8. c
9. b
10. a
11. b
12. c
13. b
14. c
15. c

Key Terms

- **Prediction Interval:** A range around a regression prediction that is expected to contain the true value with a specified confidence level.

- **Marginal Coverage:** The guarantee that, on average across the entire data distribution, the true outcome falls inside the prediction interval at the desired rate (for example, 90%).
- **Conditional Coverage:** Coverage evaluated within specific subgroups or feature regions, rather than across the full dataset.
- **Non-Conformity Score (Regression):** A measure of how unusual a prediction error is, often defined using absolute residuals.
- **Calibration Set:** A held-out dataset used to compute residual quantiles that determine the interval width.
- **Empirical Coverage:** The observed proportion of test points whose true values lie inside the constructed prediction intervals.
- **Sharpness:** The tightness or width of prediction intervals; narrower intervals are sharper and generally more informative.
- **Heteroskedasticity:** A condition where the variance of prediction errors changes across different regions of the input space.
- **Locally Adaptive Conformal Prediction:** A conformal approach that adjusts interval width based on local variability or predicted uncertainty.
- **Distribution Shift:** A change in data distribution between training/calibration data and deployment data, potentially weakening guarantees.
- **Exchangeability:** The assumption that calibration and future data points are drawn from the same underlying distribution.
- **Rolling Calibration:** Periodically updating calibration quantiles using the recent data to maintain validity in dynamic environments.
- **Coverage–Width Trade-off:** The balance between maintaining target coverage, and keeping intervals sufficiently narrow to remain useful.
- **Under-Coverage:** When empirical coverage falls below the target level, indicating overconfidence.
- **Over-Coverage:** When empirical coverage exceeds the target level, often resulting in unnecessarily wide intervals.

References

1. Split Conformal Prediction and Non-Exchangeable Data by Roberto I. Oliveira et al.
2. Predictive inference with the jackknife+ by Rina Foygel Barber et al.

CHAPTER 5
Conformal Prediction for Forecasting

Introduction

In the previous chapters, we explored how conformal prediction extends machine learning models with reliable uncertainty guarantees in both regression and classification settings. In regression, we transformed point estimates into valid prediction intervals. In classification, we replaced single labels with statistically guaranteed prediction sets. In both cases, the central idea remained consistent: use past model behavior to quantify uncertainty for future predictions without relying on strong distributional assumptions. In this chapter, we move to a setting where uncertainty becomes even more critical and more complex such as: **forecasting**. Forecasting is fundamentally different from standard regression or classification. Instead of predicting independent observations, we predict **future values that are sequentially connected to the past**. Time introduces structure. Observations are no longer exchangeable in the classical sense — they are ordered, dependent, and often evolving.

When forecasting, Retail teams plan **inventory** for upcoming weeks, Financial analysts estimate **market movements**, Energy providers forecast **demand fluctuations**, and Supply chain systems **anticipate future shortages.**

In all these scenarios, a single point forecast is rarely sufficient. Saying that next week's demand will be 10,000 units means very little without knowing whether the plausible range is 9,800–10,200 or 7,000–13,000. Decisions depend not only on the prediction, but on how wide the range of plausible futures is. And here lies the core challenge.

Unlike regression tasks **where data points are assumed exchangeable**, forecasting deals with temporal dependence, trends, seasonality, growing uncertainty with horizon. Because of this structure, **uncertainty in forecasting is dynamic**. It evolves over time. It accumulates across horizons. It may shrink during stable periods, and explode during volatile ones. In simple terms, conformal forecasting asks:

"How wrong has this model been recently, and what does that tell us about future uncertainty?"

However, applying conformal prediction to forecasting is not straightforward. The exchangeability assumption that underpins standard conformal prediction is fragile in time series settings. **Data cannot be freely shuffled. Residuals may be autocorrelated.** Errors may grow with horizon. Therefore, conformal forecasting requires adaptations like: Rolling calibration windows, Horizon-wise residual handling, Local exchangeability assumptions, and so on.

In this chapter, we will systematically build the theory and practice of conformal prediction for forecasting.

Structure

This chapter is organized into the following sections:

- From Point Forecasts to Conformal Forecast Intervals
- Why Forecasting is Different from Regression
- Building Conformal Intervals for Forecasting

From Point Forecasts to Conformal Forecast Intervals

In supervised learning, regression models are **typically built under the assumption that observations are independent**. Each input output pair is treated as a separate instance, and the model learns a relationship between features as well as targets without considering order. *Forecasting, however, operates in a fundamentally different setting. In time series problems, data points are sequentially connected.* The value at time, **t** depends directly or indirectly, on values at earlier time steps. *Patterns such as trend, seasonality, cycles, and regime changes introduce temporal structure that cannot be ignored.*

Despite this structural difference, forecasting systems often behave similarly to regression models in one important way: they produce a **single number** for the future. *A time series model analyzes historical observations, captures recurring patterns, and outputs a point forecast for the next step or for multiple steps ahead. This forecast becomes the central input to operational decisions such as: inventory planning, revenue projections, staffing allocation, financial risk management, or energy distribution. The output appears precise and actionable.*

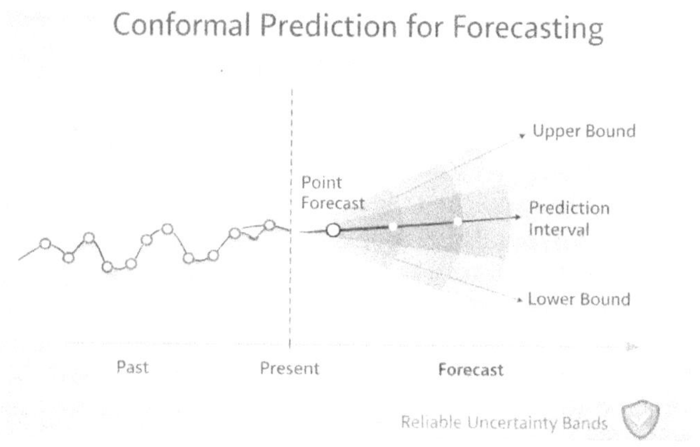

Figure 5.1: *Visual Illustration of Conformal Forecasting*

Yet that single number represents only one possible realization of the future. Consider a retail demand forecasting system predicting that next week's sales for a product will be 1,200 units. This value may indeed be the model's best estimate, given the historical data. But it does not answer deeper questions that decision-makers implicitly care about.

- Have similar forecasts in the past missed by 20 units or by 300? Does uncertainty systematically widen during festive periods?
- Does demand become more volatile after promotional price changes? Is next week historically stable or highly unpredictable?

The point forecast conceals all of this information. The limitation becomes even more pronounced in forecasting than in regression because uncertainty evolves over time. In regression, prediction errors are often treated as identically distributed across observations. *In forecasting, error behavior can change depending on the time horizon, recent volatility, or structural shifts. Multi-step forecasts typically accumulate uncertainty as the horizon increases.* External shocks can suddenly alter historical patterns. A model that appears accurate during stable periods may behave unpredictably during regime changes. The temporal dimension amplifies the consequences of ignoring uncertainty.

The key idea as touched upon in the previous section is simple: examine how large the model's recent forecast errors have been, and use that historical behavior to determine how wide future forecast intervals should be. By grounding uncertainty estimates in observed forecasting performance, conformal methods provide finite-sample coverage guarantees under appropriate assumptions, even when the underlying forecasting model is complex or unspecified.

The shift from point forecasts to conformal forecast intervals represent a change in how forecasting systems communicate risk. Rather than presenting a single trajectory into the future, the system provides a range of plausible outcomes whose width reflects historical error behavior. When recent forecasts have been stable and accurate, intervals naturally shrink. When volatility increases or the model struggles, intervals widen automatically. Uncertainty becomes data-driven, adaptive, and transparent. The following is an example showing how simply relying on point forecasts fails to capture the demand variability and the need of conformal intervals around them.

In this synthetic retail example, we construct sales mimicking real world patterns, including trend and seasonality. We first create a time index, t representing 150 sequential weeks, which allows us to model temporal behavior. *The term trend = 2. * It introduces steady linear growth, reflecting how retail sales often increase over time due to expansion, inflation, or brand maturity. The seasonality = 20 * sin(2πt / 12) component captures recurring cyclical patterns such as monthly demand fluctuations, festive peaks, or periodic buying behavior. To simulate unpredictable promotional effects, we randomly select eight weeks between week 20 and 130, and inject large positive spikes (80–150 units) into those weeks, mimicking discounts or marketing campaigns that temporarily boost sales.* Finally, we add noise drawn from a normal distribution whose variance increases over time (15 + 0.3 * t), modeling heteroscedasticity – a common real-world phenomenon where volatility grows as the business scales. The final sales series is therefore a realistic blend of trend, seasonality, promotion shocks, and time-varying uncertainty, making it ideal for demonstrating why a single point forecast cannot fully capture retail demand variability.

```
# -------------------------
# 1. Generate retail sales data
# -------------------------
n = 150
t = np.arange(n)

trend = 2 * t
seasonality = 20 * np.sin(2 * np.pi * t / 12)

promo = np.zeros(n)
promo[np.random.choice(np.arange(20, 130), 8, replace=False)] =
np.random.uniform(80, 150, 8)

noise = np.random.normal(0, 15 + 0.3 * t, n)

sales = 200 + trend + seasonality + promo + noise


# -------------------------
# 2. Fit Holt-Winters model
# -------------------------
model = ExponentialSmoothing(
    train,
    trend="add",
    seasonal="add",
    seasonal_periods=12
```

```
).fit()

y_pred_test = model.forecast(len(test))

# ------------------------
# 3. Build simple conformal-style interval
# ------------------------
residuals = np.abs(train - model.fittedvalues)
q = np.quantile(residuals, 0.90)

lower = y_pred_test - q
upper = y_pred_test + q
```

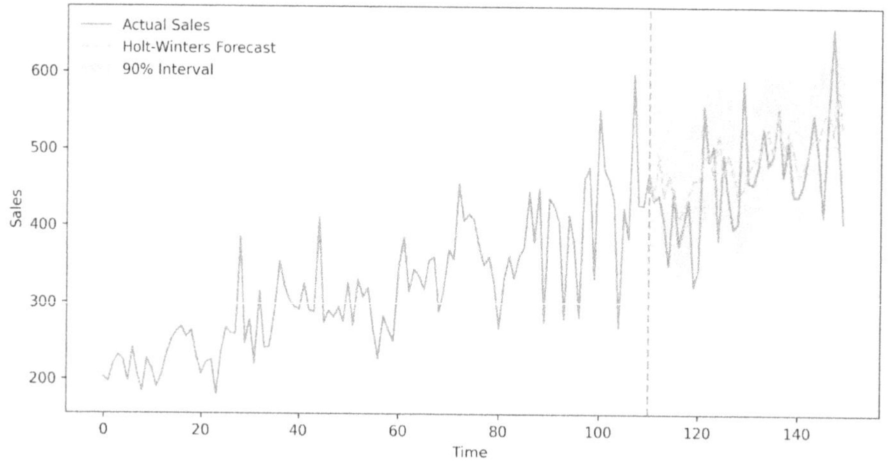

Figure 5.2: *Demand Forecast Uncertainty*

Through the above plot, we can clearly see the importance of a conformal band on top of the point forecast to handle the sales variability efficiently.

In the sections that follow, we will examine how this transformation is achieved in time series settings. We will explore why the exchangeability assumption requires careful treatment in sequential data, how conformal methods can be adapted using rolling calibration strategies, and how uncertainty evolves across forecasting horizons. The goal is not simply to attach intervals to forecasts, but to construct intervals that are statistically valid, practically interpretable, and robust to the temporal realities of forecasting problems.

Why Forecasting is Different from Regression

In the previous chapters, we applied conformal prediction to regression and classification settings where observations were treated as independent data points.

In those problems, the order of the data did not fundamentally change the learning task. Whether a housing record appeared first or last in the dataset did not affect the statistical assumptions underlying conformal prediction. The exchangeability assumption that data points are interchangeable without changing their joint distribution was both natural and reasonable in such settings.

Forecasting operates under a very different structure. In time series problems, observations are sequentially dependent. The value at time t is often influenced by values at earlier time steps. *Sales this week depend on last week's demand. Electricity consumption today is influenced by yesterday's temperature. Stock prices react to past movements. The data is no longer a collection of independent pairs; it is a temporally linked process.*

This temporal dependence immediately challenges one of the core ideas behind classical conformal prediction: exchangeability. When we shuffle regression data, the joint distribution remains unchanged. *But if we shuffle a time series, we destroy its structure. Trend disappears. Seasonality vanishes. Autocorrelation is lost. In forecasting, the past and the future are not symmetric, and this asymmetry changes how we must think about uncertainty.*

Another crucial difference lies in how errors behave. In regression, each prediction error is tied to an independent input. In forecasting, especially multi-step forecasting, errors compound over time. A mistake in predicting tomorrow's value can propagate into the prediction for the day after tomorrow. As the forecast horizon increases, uncertainty typically grows. This phenomenon does not appear in standard regression, where each prediction is made independently of previous predictions. Moreover, time series often exhibit non-stationarity. Retail demand may shift due to new competitors. Economic regimes may change. Consumer behavior may evolve. The data-generating process itself may drift over time. In regression, we often assume that the training and test data are drawn from the same distribution. In forecasting, this assumption is frequently violated. The future may not look like the past.

These differences create a fundamental tension. Classical split conformal prediction relies on a fixed calibration set drawn from the same distribution as future test points. But in forecasting, future observations are inherently "later" in time, and may follow slightly different dynamics. *If volatility increases or structural breaks occur, calibration errors from the distant past may underestimate future uncertainty.*

This does not mean conformal prediction fails in forecasting. It means we must adapt to it. Instead of treating calibration as a static, one-time step, forecasting often requires rolling or sequential calibration strategies. *Instead of assuming global exchangeability, we may rely on local or approximate exchangeability within moving windows. Instead of producing a single interval width, we may allow horizon-dependent uncertainty that widens over time.*

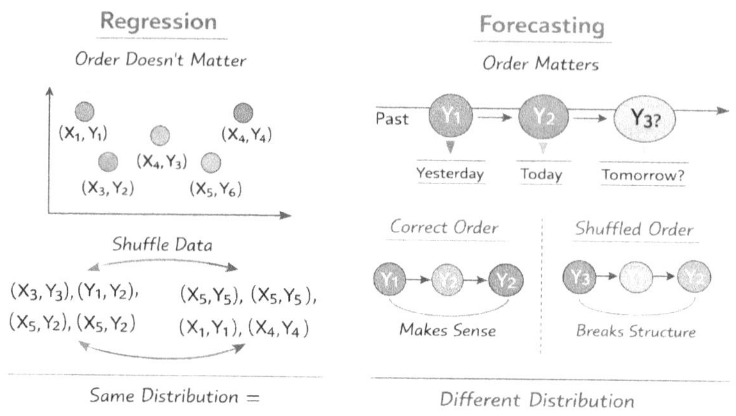

Figure 5.3: *Forecasting versus Regression*

The core idea remains unchanged: use past forecast errors to quantify future uncertainty. But the mechanics must respect the temporal structure. In the sections that follow, we will examine how conformal prediction can be carefully adapted to forecasting settings. We will begin with one step ahead forecasting under rolling calibration, and gradually extend the framework to multi-step horizons and non-stationary environments.

The Breakdown of Exchangeability in Time Series

In regression settings, exchangeability is often a reasonable assumption because data points are treated as independent realizations from the same underlying distribution. Whether a housing transaction appears at the beginning or end of the dataset does not change the joint probability structure. As we discussed earlier, the joint probability of the dataset can be written as a product of individual probabilities, and reordering those terms does not alter the result. This symmetry is what allows conformal prediction to guarantee coverage under minimal assumptions. In forecasting, this symmetry no longer exists.

Time introduces direction. The past influences the future, but the future does not influence the past. Sales today may depend on yesterday's demand, but yesterday's demand does not depend on tomorrow's outcome. This one-way dependency breaks the interchangeability of observations. Once temporal dependence enters the system, shuffling observations alters the conditional relationships that define the data-generating process.

Consider weekly retail demand. Suppose, the sales gradually increase due to a trend. The probability of observing 120 units in week three depends on the fact that week one and week two showed 100 and 110 units respectively. That upward movement provides context. If we randomly reorder the weeks, the logical structure collapses. The probability model must now evaluate values without the temporal conditions that originally produced them. The statistical environment changes. This breakdown becomes even more pronounced when seasonality is present. A December sales spike is meaningful because it follows November, and precedes January. Its probability is tied to its position within a yearly cycle. If we treat that December observation as if it occurred in July, the joint distribution no longer represents the true generating mechanism.

From the perspective of conformal prediction, this creates a challenge. Classical split conformal methods assume that calibration data and future test points are exchangeable. In time series, however, future observations are systematically "later", and potentially drawn from a slightly shifted or evolving distribution. The act of time passing introduces structural drift. This does not mean forecasting data is unpredictable. It means the assumption that all observations are interchangeable must be weakened or localized. Instead of global exchangeability across the entire dataset, we may only have approximate exchangeability within short time windows. Thus, recent weeks may resemble the near future more closely than distant historical periods.

Recognizing this breakdown is crucial. It clarifies why static calibration: using a single fixed calibration set from the past may underestimate uncertainty in evolving systems. It also motivates rolling and sequential conformal approaches, where calibration adapts over time, rather than remaining fixed. Here, we simulate a dummy time series data with inherent trend and seasonality, and shuffle the data to show the importance of ordering in time series data. [1]

```
# ------------------------
# Forecasting Setup (Sequential Data)
# ------------------------

t = np.arange(100)

# Time-dependent structure
series = (
    50
    + 0.5 * t
    + 10 * np.sin(2 * np.pi * t / 12)
    + np.random.normal(0, 2, 100)
)

# Shuffle time order
series_shuffled = series[np.random.permutation(len(series))]
```

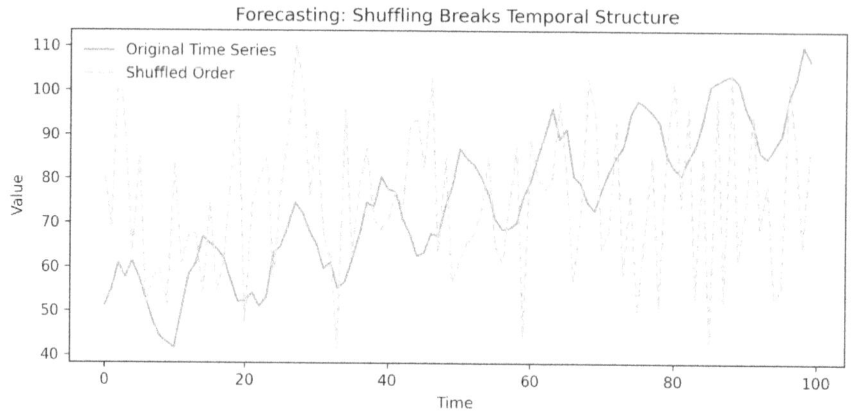

Figure 5.4: *Exchangeability Failure in Time Series*

To understand the above behavior further, we need to understand *where* structure lives in regression versus forecasting to solidify the understanding. Although both settings may visually display trends or patterns, the source of that structure is fundamentally different. In regression, structure is cross-sectional. Each observation represents an independent entity: a house, a customer, a product, or a transaction. *The relationship we model exists between variables within the same row. For example, house price depends on size, number of rooms, and location. If we shuffle the dataset, we are merely reordering independent observations. The relationship between size and price remains intact* **because it is embedded within each pair.**

The dataset is a collection of independent samples drawn from the same joint distribution. Order is incidental; it carries no meaning. In forecasting, structure is temporal. Each observation is not just a value but a position in time. The value at time t derives meaning from its placement relative to earlier points. A *sales value in December is not just another number; it follows November and precedes January. A gradual upward movement is not just a pattern between variables but a pattern across time. Seasonality, trend, momentum, and volatility clustering all depend on ordered continuity. The dataset is no longer a set of interchangeable rows; it is a sequence governed by progression.*

This distinction explains why shuffling affects forecasting so dramatically. In regression, shuffling preserves the underlying cross-sectional relationship. In forecasting, shuffling dismantles the mechanism that generated the data. Adjacent points no longer reflect temporal neighbors. Trends disappear because "later" no longer follows "earlier." Seasonal cycles collapse because periodic structure depends on consistent ordering. The graph changes not because the values changed, but because their relationships changed. Putting differently, regression models learn a mapping between inputs and outputs. Forecasting models learn dynamics over time. While forecasting can certainly be multivariate, incorporating multiple external features such as price, promotions, weather, or economic indicators, its core structure is still sequential. The model is not merely learning a relationship between variables within a single row; it is learning how the system evolves across ordered time steps. *Cross-sectional learning survives permutation because observations are independent units. Dynamic learning does not, because the meaning of each observation is tied to what came before it.*

Adapting Conformal Prediction for Forecasting

So far, we have established that forecasting differs fundamentally from regression because the temporal order introduces dependence. A natural question now arises: if forecasting breaks the standard assumptions, how can we apply Conformal Prediction in this setting? We have examined the problem, and understood where classical exchangeability fails. Thus, it is time to shift our focus toward the solution, and explore how conformal methods can be adapted to work effectively for forecasting.

In classical regression, conformal prediction treats residuals as interchangeable. We compute errors on a calibration set, extract a quantile, and construct prediction intervals assuming that future errors behave similarly. In time series, however, residuals evolve over time. Periods of stability may be followed by volatility. Seasonal peaks may carry larger forecast errors than off-season weeks. Structural shifts can suddenly alter the behavior of the series. Treating all past residuals as equally informative about the future ignores this temporal structure.

To handle this, conformal prediction for forecasting modifies how calibration is performed. Instead of assuming full exchangeability across the entire dataset, we rely on structured or localized calibration. Recent residuals may be given more importance than the distant ones. Errors may be computed separately for different forecast horizons. Calibration may be performed in rolling or expanding windows that preserve the time order. In some settings, blocks of observations are used to maintain dependence structure, while still estimating reliable quantiles.

The core idea remains unchanged: we use past forecast errors to quantify the future uncertainty. What changes is how we define the "past", and how we ensure that those errors are relevant to the current temporal context.

Another important adjustment concerns multi-step forecasting. When predicting several steps ahead, uncertainty compounds. The error distribution for one-step-ahead forecasts is not the same as the error distribution five steps ahead. Conformal methods in forecasting therefore often construct horizon-specific intervals, allowing uncertainty to widen naturally as the forecast horizon increases. Instead of forcing a cross-sectional assumption onto sequential data, we redesign the calibration step to respect temporal dependence, while preserving statistical validity as much as possible. In the next section, we will move from intuition to construction. We will examine concrete conformal forecasting algorithms, understand how residuals are computed in a time-aware manner, and build prediction intervals step by step for practical forecasting scenarios.

Building Conformal Intervals for Forecasting

In the previous sections, we discussed why forecasting presents unique challenges for conformal prediction. Unlike regression problems, time series data is inherently sequential, meaning that observations cannot be shuffled and treated as interchangeable. Forecasting models must always learn from the past to predict the future, and any uncertainty estimation method must respect this temporal structure. With this understanding in place, we now turn to a practical question: how do we construct conformal prediction intervals for forecasting problems?

The central idea remains the same as in other conformal settings. We use past forecast errors to estimate how uncertain future predictions might be. However, the way we compute and use these errors must be adapted to the sequential nature of time series data. Forecasts must be generated step by step using only historical information, and residuals must reflect genuine out-of-sample forecasting performance, rather than errors computed from randomly split data.

In this section, we will build conformal forecasting intervals progressively, starting from the simplest case. We begin with one-step-ahead forecasting, where the goal is to construct uncertainty intervals for the next time step. We then extend this framework to rolling calibration methods that allow intervals to adapt to changing volatility in the series. Finally, we examine how conformal prediction can be applied to multi-step forecasting, where uncertainty naturally increases as predictions extend further into the future.

By the end of this section, we will have developed a clear and practical framework for constructing conformal prediction intervals that respect the sequential structure of time series data, while maintaining the model-agnostic flexibility that makes conformal prediction so powerful.

One Step Ahead Split Conformal Forecasting

We begin with the simplest extension of conformal prediction to time series: constructing intervals for one-step-ahead forecasts. While the overall conformal logic remains unchanged, using past errors to quantify future uncertainty, the training and calibration strategy must be modified to respect the temporal structure.

In time series, observations are sequentially dependent. Shuffling the data would destroy the very structure the model is trying to learn. Therefore, the primary modification in forecasting conformal methods is **how we split the data**:

- The split is chronological, not random.
- Training uses only past observations.

- Calibration residuals are computed strictly forward in time.
- No future information is ever used to predict the past.

This seemingly simple adjustment introduces an important conceptual shift. In regression, calibration residuals are interchangeable across the dataset. In forecasting, residuals represent genuine out-of-sample forecasting errors that occur in temporal order. Each residual reflects how the model performed when predicting the next unseen time step using only the historical data.

Thus, while conformal prediction still wraps around a trained model, the training strategy itself becomes time-aware:

- Fit the forecasting model on an initial historical window.
- Generate one-step-ahead forecasts sequentially over a calibration window.
- Compute absolute residuals from these genuine forward predictions.
- Use their empirical quantile to construct an interval for the next time step.

The structure of conformal prediction remains intact. What changes is the discipline with which temporal order is preserved.

With this key distinction from regression established, we now formalize the procedure step by step.

Data Generation and Chronological Split

To illustrate the conformal forecasting procedure, we begin by generating a synthetic time series containing trend, seasonality, and random noise mimicking real-world time series such as demand, energy consumption, or financial prices.

Once the series is generated, we divide it into two sequential parts:

- **Training window:** used to fit the forecasting model
- **Calibration window**: used to compute forecast residuals

Unlike regression problems where data can be randomly shuffled, time series data must always be **split chronologically**. This ensures that the model only learns from past observations, and never has access to future information.

```
# ------------------------
# 1. Data Generation (Trend + Seasonality + Noise)
# ------------------------
n = 200
t = np.arange(n)

trend = 0.1 * t
seasonality = 5 * np.sin(2 * np.pi * t / 20)
```

```
noise = np.random.normal(0, 2, n)

y = trend + seasonality + noise

# ------------------------
# 2. Chronological Train / Calibration Split
# ------------------------

train_size = 100
cal_size = 50

train = y[:train_size]
calibration = y[train_size:train_size + cal_size]
test = y[train_size + cal_size:]
```

For simplicity, we use a naive persistence model where the next value is predicted as the most recent observation. This allows us to focus on the conformal procedure, rather than model complexity.

Model Training

Using only the training portion of the time series, we fit a forecasting model. The model learns how to predict the next observation based solely on past values. The forecasting model can be anything, for example:

- ARIMA
- Exponential smoothing
- Prophet
- Gradient boosting
- LSTM
- Any forecasting architecture

Conformal prediction does not modify the forecasting model itself. Instead, it wraps around the model, and uses its historical forecast errors to construct uncertainty intervals.

```
# ------------------------
# 3. Naive last value forecast model
# ------------------------
# Simple forecasting model (naive persistence)
def forecast(history):
    return history[-1]
```

For simplicity, we use a naive persistence model where the next value is predicted as the most recent observation. This allows us to focus on the conformal procedure, rather than model complexity.

Generate Calibration Forecasts

Next, for each time point in the calibration window, we generate **one-step-ahead forecasts** using only past information.

$$t \cdot \epsilon \cdot \text{calibration} \cdot \text{window}$$

$$\hat{y}_{n+1} = f(y_1, y_2, \ldots\ldots, y_n)$$

We then compute residuals for one step ahead throughout the calibration period.

These residuals represent how wrong the forecasting model was on unseen data. Importantly, these residuals respect time order, and reflect genuine out-of-sample forecasting performance.

```
# -------------------------
# 4. Residuals on Calibration
# -------------------------
history = list(train)

preds = []
residuals = []

for actual in calibration:

    pred = forecast(history)
    preds.append(pred)

    residual = abs(actual - pred)
    residuals.append(residual)

    history.append(actual)

residuals = np.array(residuals)
```

Each prediction uses only past observations, and uses it to forecast the next time, mimicking a real forecasting system operating sequentially through time.

Estimate the Conformal Quantile

Let the calibration residuals be:

$$r_{train+1}, r_{train+2}, \ldots\ldots\ldots r_T$$

For a desired miscoverage level ⟨ (for example 0.1 for 90% intervals), we compute:

```
# -------------------------
# 5. Quantiles based on calibration
# -------------------------

alpha = 0.1
```

```
q = np.quantile(residuals,1-alpha)
print("Conformal quantile:", q)
```

The following is a visualization of full process, including the conformal intervals.

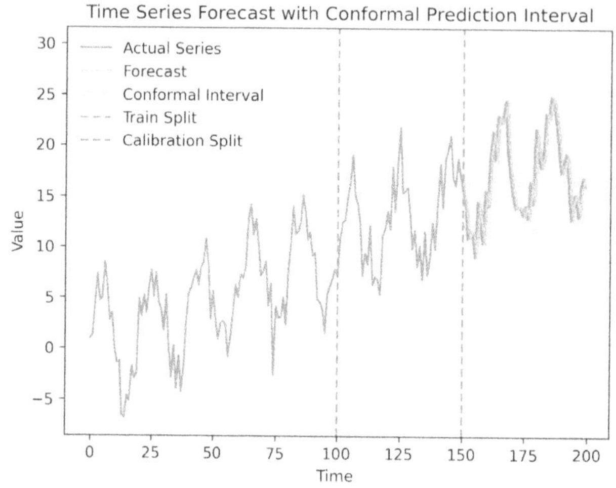

Figure 5.5: *One Step Ahead Conformal Interval*

Rolling Calibration

In the previous subsection, we constructed conformal forecast intervals using a fixed calibration window. Residuals from a predefined portion of the data were used to estimate a quantile that determines the width of the prediction interval. While this approach is simple and effective, it implicitly assumes that the uncertainty observed during the calibration period remains representative of future uncertainty. In many real-world time series, this assumption may not hold.

Time series data often exhibits evolving behavior. Volatility may increase or decrease over time, seasonal patterns may shift, and structural changes may alter the forecasting performance of the model. When such changes occur, residuals from earlier periods may no longer accurately reflect the magnitude of current forecast errors. As a result, prediction intervals constructed from a fixed calibration set may become either too narrow during volatile periods or unnecessarily wide during stable phases.

Rolling calibration addresses this limitation *by continuously updating the residuals used for uncertainty estimation*. Instead of relying on a fixed set of calibration errors, the method maintains a moving window of recent forecast residuals. As new observations arrive, the oldest residuals are removed, and the newest residuals are added to the calibration set. The conformal quantile is then recomputed using this updated window.

This approach allows prediction intervals to adapt to the evolving characteristics of the time series. When the forecasting errors increase, the residual window captures larger deviations, and the intervals widen accordingly. Conversely, during stable periods when forecast errors shrink, the intervals naturally tighten.

Thus, by recalibrating the conformal quantile over time, rolling calibration provides a practical way to maintain reliable uncertainty estimates in non-stationary forecasting environments, while still preserving the core principle of conformal prediction, that is, using past forecast errors to quantify the future uncertainty.

Data Generation

Before introducing rolling conformal calibration, it is useful to revisit the assumptions behind the constant calibration strategy we explored earlier. *Constant calibration relies on the idea that the model's past errors provide a reliable estimate of the uncertainty it will face in the future*. In other words, the distribution of forecasting errors observed during the calibration period is assumed to remain stable over time. When this assumption holds, the historical residuals serve as a dependable guide for constructing prediction intervals.

However, many real-world forecasting environments rarely behave this way. The statistical properties of time series data often evolve over time. Demand patterns may suddenly become more volatile due to market events, promotional campaigns, supply disruptions, or seasonal peaks. When such changes occur, forecasting models may still capture the overall trend or seasonal structure reasonably well, but the magnitude of the prediction errors can change significantly. *This creates a critical limitation for constant calibration. If prediction intervals are constructed using residuals from a period when demand variability was low, those intervals may become too narrow when the system enters a more volatile regime. As a result, the model continues to produce intervals that reflect past stability, rather than current uncertainty*.

Rolling conformal calibration addresses this limitation by allowing the uncertainty estimate to evolve over time. Instead of relying on a fixed set of historical residuals, the calibration window is continuously updated using the most recent forecasting errors. This enables the prediction intervals to adapt as the behavior of the time series changes. To understand why this distinction matters, we will construct a forecasting scenario where the underlying volatility of the data changes over time. This will allow us to compare how constant and rolling calibration strategies behave when the future no longer resembles the past.

Imagine a retail company forecasting the daily sales of a popular product. *Under normal conditions, sales follow predictable patterns driven by a combination of long-term growth and periodic demand cycles. However, external factors such as marketing campaigns, competitor activity, or sudden shifts in customer behavior can cause demand variability to increase sharply. During such periods, forecasting models may still capture the general trend of sales, but the magnitude of forecasting errors can increase substantially*. Our simulated dataset reproduces this exact behavior.

The time series is composed of three main components:

- **Trend:** representing gradual growth in demand as the product becomes more popular over time.
- **Seasonality:** capturing periodic fluctuations in sales, such as weekly or monthly demand cycles.
- **Random noise:** representing unpredictable variations in customer purchases.

However, the key feature of this dataset is that the **variance of the noise changes over time**. For the first part of the series, the random noise is relatively small, representing a stable sales environment where demand fluctuates only mildly around the trend and seasonal pattern. Later in the series, the noise becomes significantly larger, representing a regime shift where sales become much more volatile. This could correspond to situations such as a large marketing campaign, a sudden surge in demand, or increased market competition. **Importantly, this change in volatility occurs after the calibration period used by conformal prediction.** This setup allows us to simulate a very common real-world forecasting challenge: the model's historical errors no longer represent the uncertainty it will face in the future.

If conformal intervals are constructed using only past calibration errors, they may severely underestimate the true uncertainty once the environment changes. Rolling calibration strategies attempt to address this issue by continuously updating the uncertainty estimates based on the most recent forecasting errors.

```
# --------------------------------
# 1 Generate synthetic time series
# --------------------------------

n = 420
t = np.arange(n)

trend = 0.03 * t
season = 3*np.sin(t/8)

noise = np.concatenate([
    np.random.normal(0,1,200),    # train
    np.random.normal(0,1,100),    # calibration
    np.random.normal(0,6,120)     # test regime shift
])

y = trend + season + noise
series = pd.Series(y)
```

Later, just like earlier, we compute one-step ahead forecast residuals during the calibration window, and use this as the basis for rolling errors.

```
# --------------------------------
# 2 Calibration predictions
```

```
# --------------------------------

history = list(train)
pred_calib = []

for i in range(len(calib)):

    pred = forecast_one(pd.Series(history))
    pred_calib.append(pred)

    history.append(calib.iloc[i])

pred_calib = np.array(pred_calib)

calib_resid = np.abs(calib.values - pred_calib)
```

We first compute constant intervals by computing quantiles on the fixed calibration window taken during data splitting, and use this to compute converge for the entire test period.

Rolling versus Constant Interval

```
# --------------------------------
# 3 CONSTANT INTERVAL
# --------------------------------

q_const = np.quantile(calib_resid,0.9)

history = list(series[:calib_end])

pred_test = []
lower_const = []
upper_const = []

for i in range(len(test)):

    pred = forecast_one(pd.Series(history))

    pred_test.append(pred)
    lower_const.append(pred - q_const)
    upper_const.append(pred + q_const)

    history.append(test.iloc[i])

pred_test = np.array(pred_test)
lower_const = np.array(lower_const)
upper_const = np.array(upper_const)
```

Next, we construct a rolling calibration window with a fixed size (40 in this example). *For each test point, we compute the forecast error and append it to the residual list.* The interval width is then recalculated using only the most recent 40 errors, allowing the uncertainty estimate to focus on the latest forecasting behavior, and adapt to the evolving volatility in the series.

```
# -------------------------------
# 4 ROLLING INTERVAL
# -------------------------------

window = 40

history = list(series[:calib_end])
errors = list(calib_resid)

rolling_lower = []
rolling_upper = []

for i in range(len(test)):

    pred = forecast_one(pd.Series(history))

    q_roll = np.quantile(errors[-window:],0.9)

    rolling_lower.append(pred - q_roll)
    rolling_upper.append(pred + q_roll)

    err = abs(test.iloc[i] - pred)

    errors.append(err)
    history.append(test.iloc[i])

rolling_lower = np.array(rolling_lower)
rolling_upper = np.array(rolling_upper)
```

The following is the final comparison of both type of intervals in our dataset with evolving variability.

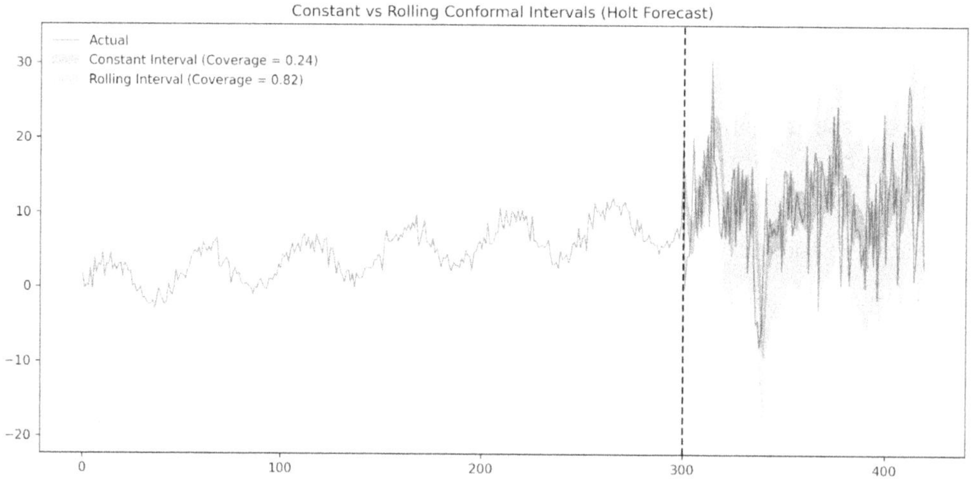

Figure 5.6: *Rolling and Fixed Interval Comparison*

From the plot above, we can observe how the rolling calibration strategy allows the forecasting intervals to evolve over time. *As new observations arrive, the rolling method continuously incorporates the most recent forecasting errors into its calibration window, and updates the interval width accordingly.* When the volatility of the time series increases, the recent errors become larger, and the rolling intervals naturally widen to reflect this change in uncertainty. In contrast, the constant calibration intervals remain fixed because they rely only on residuals computed during the earlier calibration period, which in this example, corresponds to a relatively stable demand environment. As a result, those intervals fail to capture the increased variability observed in the test period. This example highlights an important advantage of rolling conformal calibration in forecasting problems such as: by grounding its uncertainty estimates in the most recent model performance, it can adapt to evolving data dynamics, and maintain more reliable prediction intervals when the future begins to differ from the past.

Conformal Intervals for Multi-Step Forecasting

So far, we have focused on constructing conformal prediction intervals for the **next immediate time step**. In this setting, the model produces a one-step-ahead forecast, and the uncertainty around that prediction is estimated using past forecasting errors. Both constant and rolling calibration strategies operate under this framework, differing only in how the residuals used for calibration are selected. While this approach is useful for understanding the mechanics of conformal forecasting, many real-world forecasting problems require **predicting multiple future time steps simultaneously**. *In practice, organizations rarely forecast just the next observation. Retailers may forecast product demand for the next week, energy providers may estimate electricity consumption for the next 24 hours, and financial institutions often project market indicators several days or months into the future.* These tasks require **multi-step forecasts**, where predictions extend several periods ahead, rather than stopping at the next time point.

Forecasting further into the future introduces an additional challenge: **uncertainty typically grows with the forecast horizon**. Errors made in earlier predictions can propagate forward, and the model becomes increasingly uncertain as it moves further away from the observed data. As a result, the distribution of forecasting errors for the next time step may look very different from the errors observed several steps ahead. Because conformal prediction relies on historical errors to construct prediction intervals, this horizon-dependent uncertainty must be handled carefully. A single residual distribution may not adequately represent the variability associated with different forecast horizons. Instead, we must consider how forecasting errors behave at each step into the future, and adjust the conformal calibration process accordingly.

In the following sections, we will explore how conformal prediction can be extended to multi-step forecasting problems, and how prediction intervals can be constructed in a way that reflects the increasing uncertainty as the forecast horizon grows.

Uncertainty in Multi-Step Forecasting

In the previous examples, we focused on **one-step-ahead forecasting**, where the model predicts only the next observation in the time series. In this setting, the forecasting error depends primarily on how well the model captures the recent structure of the data. Once the next observation becomes available, the model can incorporate that new information, and generate the following prediction. Multi-step forecasting operates under a different dynamic. Instead of predicting just the next value, the model must produce forecasts for several future time points simultaneously, such as the next 5 days, the next 12 months, or the next 24 hours. **As the forecast horizon increases, the model moves further away from the observed data, and must rely increasingly on its own predictions to estimate the future values.**

This introduces a phenomenon known as **error propagation**. A small forecasting error at the first horizon can influence the prediction for the second horizon, which may in turn affect the third horizon, and so on. As a result, forecasting uncertainty tends to grow as we move further into the future. In practical terms, this means that the distribution of errors for a one-step forecast may look very different from the errors observed several steps ahead.

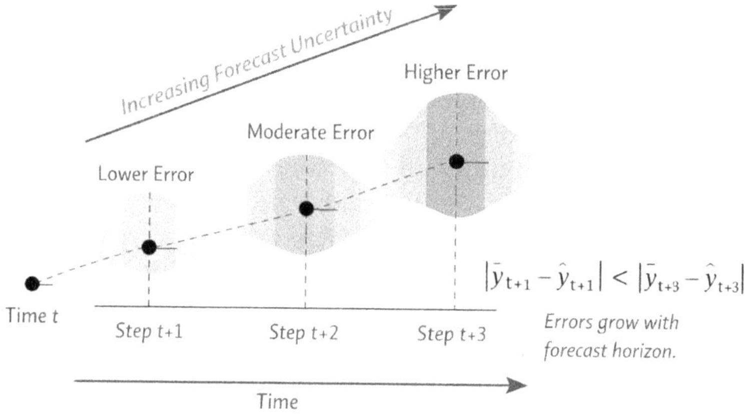

***Figure** 5.7: Rolling and Fixed Interval Comparison*

This pattern reflects the fact that predictions made further into the future carry greater uncertainty. Consequently, if conformal prediction intervals were constructed using a single residual distribution for all forecast horizons, the resulting intervals could underestimate uncertainty for longer horizons. To address this issue, conformal forecasting methods often compute **horizon-specific residual distributions**, allowing each forecast step to have its own uncertainty estimate. This ensures that prediction intervals expand appropriately as the forecast horizon increases. In the next subsection, we will examine how these horizon-specific errors can be computed, and how they can be used to construct conformal prediction intervals for multi-step forecasts.

Horizon Specific Conformal Calibration

Building on the idea of error propagation discussed earlier, the key implication is that **forecast errors are not identically distributed across horizons**. A one-step forecast error reflects only the uncertainty in predicting the immediate next observation, whereas longer-horizon errors incorporate both model uncertainty, and the accumulation of earlier prediction errors. Because of this, using a single pool of residuals to calibrate intervals for all horizons would ignore this structural difference, and typically lead to intervals that are too narrow for distant forecasts.

Horizon-specific conformal calibration addresses this by **computing residual distributions separately for each forecast horizon**. During the calibration phase, the forecasting model is repeatedly asked to generate multi-step predictions from different points in the calibration window. For each starting point t, the model produces predictions for $t+1,t+2,t+3,...t+1,t+2,t+3,...$, and the corresponding errors are recorded by comparing these predictions with the actual observations. These errors are then grouped by their horizon such as: all one-step errors form one set, all two-step errors form another, and so on.

Each of these sets captures the empirical uncertainty associated with predicting that particular distance into the future. Conformal quantiles are then computed independently from these horizon-specific residuals. When generating prediction intervals, the model applies the quantile corresponding to the appropriate horizon, ensuring that the interval width reflects the level of uncertainty observed historically at that forecast distance.

This strategy directly incorporates the **growing uncertainty introduced by error propagation**. Near-term forecasts rely on residuals that are typically smaller and more stable, while longer-horizon forecasts use residuals that naturally account for the compounded variability seen during calibration. As a result, prediction intervals expand in a structured way across horizons, providing uncertainty estimates that remain aligned with the dynamics of the forecasting process, rather than relying on a single, horizon-agnostic error distribution.

Just like in previous sections, let us summarize the whole process step-by-step through a dummy data example.

Data Generation

To illustrate horizon-specific conformal calibration, we begin by constructing a synthetic time series designed to clearly demonstrate how forecasting uncertainty grows with the prediction horizon, and hence, need for horizon-level conformal intervals. The data is generated using a simple autoregressive process, where each observation depends strongly on the previous one plus a random noise component. This structure is useful for understanding how forecasting errors naturally propagate forward: when the model predicts one step ahead, it relies only on observed history, but when predicting two or three steps ahead, those forecasts increasingly depend on earlier predictions, rather than real observations. Any small error in an earlier step therefore carries forward, and amplifies in later horizons. *To make this effect even more visible, the noise term in the simulation gradually increases over time, introducing higher volatility in later periods.* This combination of strong temporal dependence, and the growing noise produces a realistic forecasting environment where short-horizon predictions remain relatively stable while longer-horizon forecasts become progressively more uncertain. By generating data with these properties, we create a controlled setting where readers can clearly observe how forecast errors expand with horizon length, providing a natural motivation for computing conformal calibration separately for each forecast horizon.

```
# -------------------------
# 1. Generate autoregressive time series
# -------------------------

n = 220
series = [10] #starting value
for i in range(1, n):
    noise = np.random.normal(0, 2 + 0.03*i)
    value = 0.9 * series[-1] + noise
    series.append(value)
series = np.array(series)

plt.figure(figsize=(10,4))
plt.plot(series)
plt.title("Synthetic Autoregressive Demand Series")
plt.xlabel("Time")
plt.ylabel("Demand")
plt.show()
```

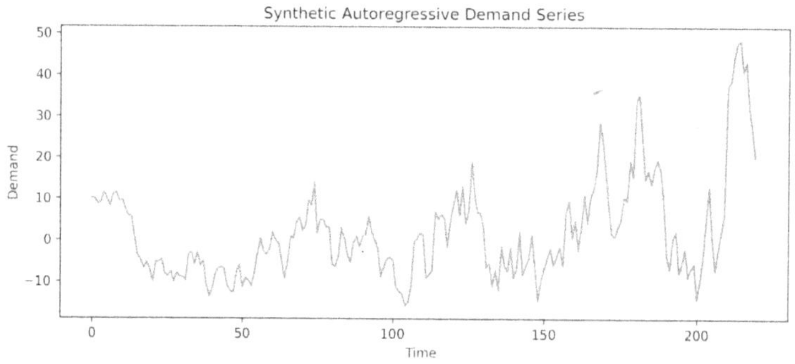

Figure 5.8: *Autoregressive Noise Time Series*

Here, as discussed, each point in the time series depends strongly on the previous observation, while the noise component gradually increases over time. As a result, when a forecasting model learns this structure, and generates multi-step predictions, any uncertainty present in earlier steps tends to propagate forward. In a multi-step setting, later forecasts increasingly rely on earlier predictions, rather than actual observations, causing the accumulated noise to amplify the overall uncertainty as the forecast horizon increases.

Horizon-Level Residuals

Now, we follow the similar train-calibration-split strategy, and post that collect horizon level residuals for next three time steps, instead of a single time step from the calibration period.

```
# -------------------------
# 2. Collect horizon residuals
# -------------------------

max_horizon = 3
residuals = {h: [] for h in range(1, max_horizon+1)}
history = list(train)

for i in range(len(calib)-max_horizon):
    fit = AutoReg(history, lags=1).fit()
    forecast = fit.forecast(steps=max_horizon)
    for h in range(1, max_horizon+1):
        actual = calib[i+h-1]
        pred = forecast[h-1]
        residuals[h].append(abs(actual - pred))
    history.append(calib[i])
```

Later, we compute the bounding quantiles across these horizons to create horizon specific intervals.

```
# -------------------------
# 3. Compute conformal quantiles
# -------------------------
alpha = 0.1
q = {h: np.quantile(residuals[h], 1-alpha) for h in residuals}
```

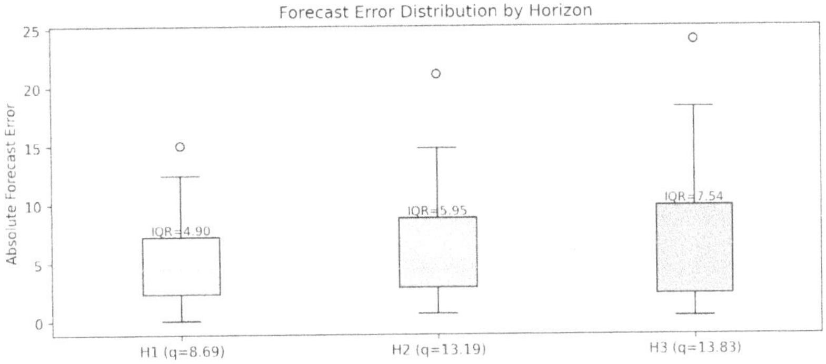

Figure 5.9: *Horizon-wise Errors*

The horizon-wise residual plot clearly illustrates how forecasting errors evolve as we move further into the future. The first box represents the distribution of one-step-ahead errors, which remain relatively small because the model relies directly on observed data. The second and third boxes correspond to two-step and three-step forecasts, where the spread of errors increases noticeably hence the quantile band. This widening distribution reflects the accumulation of uncertainty introduced by earlier predictions, and the growing influence of noise in the system. The conformal quantiles shown alongside each horizon reinforce this observation: the threshold required to achieve the desired coverage increases progressively as the forecast horizon expands.

This behavior highlights the key motivation for horizon-specific conformal calibration. Since the magnitude of forecast errors changes with the prediction horizon, treating all residuals as if they come from the same distribution would underestimate uncertainty for longer-term forecasts. Thus, by computing calibration residuals separately for each horizon, conformal prediction allows interval widths to adjust naturally to the level of uncertainty observed historically. The resulting intervals remain tight for near-term predictions, while expanding appropriately for distant horizons, ensuring that uncertainty estimates remain realistic, and statistically reliable in multi-step forecasting settings.

Conclusion

Forecasting is inherently an exercise in reasoning about an uncertain future. Traditional forecasting systems typically summarize this uncertainty with a single point estimate, offering a concise but incomplete picture of what may lie ahead. While point forecasts provide a useful baseline, they often fail to capture the variability that decision-makers must contend with in real-world environments. Throughout this chapter, we explored how conformal prediction extends forecasting models by transforming these single-value predictions into calibrated prediction intervals that explicitly quantify uncertainty.

We began by examining the limitations of relying solely on point forecasts. In operational settings, a single predicted value rarely provides enough information to guide decisions. Whether forecasting demand, revenue, energy consumption, or system load, organizations must constantly balance competing risks: preparing for higher-than-expected outcomes, while avoiding unnecessary overcommitment of resources. Conformal forecasting addresses this challenge by attaching statistically valid intervals to predictions, providing a clearer picture of the range within which future outcomes are likely to fall.

A central theme of this chapter was understanding why forecasting problems differ from standard prediction tasks. Time series data is inherently sequential, meaning observations cannot be arbitrarily shuffled without breaking the underlying temporal structure. This characteristic challenges the exchangeability assumptions that conventional conformal methods rely on. As a result, applying conformal prediction in forecasting requires adapting the calibration process to respect the temporal order of the data.

To address this, we developed practical approaches for constructing conformal intervals in forecasting settings. We first explored next-step forecasting, where residuals derived from sequential predictions form the basis for calibration. This framework established the foundation for conformal forecasting by ensuring that prediction intervals reflect genuine out-of-sample forecasting errors.

We then extended this idea to rolling calibration, a technique that continuously updates the calibration window as new observations arrive. In many real-world systems, volatility and demand patterns evolve over time. A static calibration window may therefore fail to reflect the current uncertainty. Rolling calibration allows conformal intervals to adapt dynamically by incorporating the most recent forecasting errors, enabling the intervals to remain aligned with the changing system behavior.

Finally, we examined multi-step forecasting and the phenomenon of error propagation. As forecasts extend further into the future, predictions increasingly depend on earlier predicted values rather than observed data. This naturally causes uncertainty to grow with the forecast horizon. Horizon-specific conformal calibration addresses this by estimating residual distributions separately for each forecast step, ensuring that prediction intervals expand appropriately as the forecasting horizon increases.

Taken together, these techniques demonstrate that conformal prediction provides a flexible and model-agnostic framework for uncertainty quantification in time series forecasting. One of the most compelling advantages of conformal forecasting just like in the case of its other two supervised algorithms predecessors is that it does not require redesigning the underlying forecasting model. Instead, it acts as a calibration layer that can be placed on top of the existing forecasting systems. Whether the underlying model is a classical time series method such as ARIMA or exponential smoothing, a machine learning model such as gradient boosting, or a deep learning architecture such as LSTMs or transformers, conformal prediction can be applied to produce statistically calibrated prediction intervals.

This property makes conformal forecasting particularly attractive in real-world systems. In practice, forecasting pipelines already exist in many organizations and are often deeply integrated into planning and operational workflows. Conformal prediction can be plugged into these pipelines with minimal disruption, using the model's historical forecasting errors to calibrate uncertainty estimates. Once deployed, the system can automatically update prediction intervals as new data arrives, ensuring that the uncertainty estimates remain aligned with the model's evolving performance.

The practical impact of this capability can be significant. *In supply chain management, conformal intervals allow planners to determine appropriate safety stock levels by quantifying the range of possible demand outcomes. In energy systems, calibrated uncertainty intervals enable operators to plan for fluctuations in electricity demand or renewable energy supply. In financial forecasting, prediction intervals provide risk-aware projections that help institutions evaluate potential downside scenarios. Across these applications, the key advantage lies in the ability to move from deterministic forecasts toward uncertainty-aware decision frameworks.*

Perhaps, the most important shift introduced by conformal forecasting is conceptual. Instead of asking, "*What will happen?*", decision-makers can begin asking, "*What range of outcomes should we prepare for?*" This subtle change fundamentally alters how forecasts are used. When uncertainty is explicitly quantified and calibrated using historical performance, forecasting models become not just predictive tools but decision-support systems.

As forecasting continues to play a critical role in modern data-driven organizations, methods that provide both accurate predictions and reliable uncertainty estimates will become increasingly important. Conformal prediction offers a principled and practical approach to achieving this balance. Therefore, by combining predictive models with calibrated uncertainty estimates, conformal forecasting allows organizations to make decisions that are not only informed by data but also resilient to the inherent unpredictability of the future.

With this chapter, we now have a complete understanding of how conformal prediction extends across the major machine learning settings: classification, regression, and forecasting. In each case, the core principle remains the same — using a model's past behavior to construct reliable uncertainty estimates around its predictions. *While the way uncertainty is expressed differs across these problems (prediction sets for classification, intervals for regression, and calibrated bands for forecasting), the underlying goal remains consistent: transforming raw predictions into outputs that communicate both outcomes, and their associated uncertainty.*

In the next chapter, we will cover the implementation of conformal systems in real world systems talking about challenges and deployment at scale. In the chapters that follow, we will move beyond individual algorithms, and focus on the broader ecosystem of conformal prediction. We will explore how these methods can be scaled to large datasets and production environments, discuss practical considerations when deploying them in real-world systems, and examine emerging research directions that are shaping the future of uncertainty-aware machine learning.

Points to Remember

- **Forecasting differs from standard prediction problems** because predictions are made sequentially across time, and uncertainty often grows as we move further into the future horizon.

- **Traditional forecasting models typically produce point forecasts**, but these single values hide the variability that naturally exists in time-series systems such as demand, sales, or energy usage.
- **Forecast errors tend to vary across horizons**, meaning predictions one step ahead are usually more reliable than predictions several steps into the future.
- **Conformal forecasting extends the idea of conformal prediction to time-series problems**, constructing prediction intervals around each forecasted value.
- **Calibration errors from past forecasts are used to quantify uncertainty**, allowing the model's historical performance to determine how wide future intervals should be.
- **Prediction intervals can be built horizon-wise**, meaning each forecast horizon receives its own calibrated uncertainty band, based on its historical error behavior.
- **As the forecast horizon increases, interval widths typically expand**, reflecting the natural increase in uncertainty further into the future.
- **Conformal forecasting does not require assumptions about the underlying data distribution**, making it robust across different forecasting models and datasets.
- **These intervals provide planners with a range of plausible outcomes**, allowing decision makers to prepare for both optimistic and pessimistic scenarios.
- **In real-world forecasting systems, conformal intervals transform forecasts from static estimates into risk-aware signals**, enabling more reliable planning and resource allocation.

Multiple Choice Questions

1. What is the main limitation of point forecasts in time-series systems?
    a. They require large training datasets.
    b. They do not capture seasonal patterns.
    c. They hide the uncertainty around future outcomes.
    d. They cannot handle multiple variables.
2. In forecasting, how does prediction uncertainty generally behaves as the forecast horizon increases?
    a. It remains constant.
    b. It decreases steadily.

   c. It increases with the horizon length.
   d. It becomes zero.

3. Conformal forecasting constructs prediction intervals using:
   a. The future unseen data
   b. Parametric distribution assumptions
   c. Historical forecast errors
   d. Neural network gradients

4. What role does the calibration set play in conformal forecasting?
   a. It trains the forecasting model.
   b. It estimates the distribution of prediction errors.
   c. It replaces the training dataset.
   d. It determines model architecture.

5. A 95% conformal prediction interval means:
   a. 95% of predictions will be exactly correct.
   b. The interval will always contain the true value.
   c. Approximately 95% of true outcomes should fall within the interval.
   d. The model accuracy is 95%.

6. Horizon-wise conformal intervals are useful because:
   a. Forecast errors behave differently at different horizons.
   b. They reduce the training time.
   c. They remove the need for calibration.
   d. They guarantee perfect predictions.

7. If forecast intervals become wider as the horizon increases, this typically reflects:
   a. Model instability
   b. Natural growth of uncertainty over time
   c. Incorrect training data
   d. Overfitting

8. What is the key advantage of conformal forecasting compared to traditional statistical intervals?
   a. It assumes normally distributed errors.
   b. It requires deep learning models.

   c. It provides distribution-free validity guarantees.
   d. It eliminates forecasting errors.

9. In conformal forecasting, the interval width primarily depends on:
   a. The model's training accuracy only.
   b. The magnitude of historical prediction errors.
   c. The number of model parameters.
   d. The training dataset size.

10. If a forecasting model consistently produces extremely wide conformal intervals, this suggests:
    a. The model is perfectly calibrated.
    b. The model's predictions are highly certain.
    c. The model has large historical errors or uncertainty.
    d. The dataset is too small to train.

11. In real-world decision systems, conformal forecasting intervals help planners:
    a. Eliminate uncertainty completely
    b. Understand the range of plausible future outcomes
    c. Avoid using forecasting models
    d. Replace the historical data

12. In time-series forecasting, what does a forecast horizon represent?
    a. The length of the training dataset.
    b. The number of variables in the model.
    c. How far into the future the prediction is made.
    d. The model's optimization steps.

13. If a conformal interval fails to contain the true value more often than expected, this indicates:
    a. Overcoverage
    b. Undercoverage
    c. Perfect calibration
    d. No uncertainty

14. What is the primary purpose of adding prediction intervals to forecasts?
    a. To increase the training speed
    b. To quantify the uncertainty surrounding predictions

c. To reduce the dataset size

d. To eliminate the forecast bias

15. In business systems such as demand forecasting, conformal intervals are particularly useful because they:

    a. Allow decisions to consider best-case and worst-case scenarios

    b. Remove the need for forecasting models

    c. Guarantee the exact demand values

    d. Replace the planning systems

Answers

1. c
2. c
3. c
4. b
5. c
6. a
7. b
8. c
9. b
10. c
11. b
12. c
13. b
14. b
15. a

Key Terms

- **Point Forecast:** A single predicted value produced by a forecasting model for a future time step without expressing the uncertainty around that prediction.
- **Forecast Horizon:** The number of time steps into the future for which predictions are made in a forecasting problem.
- **Prediction Interval:** A range around a forecasted value that represents the set of plausible future outcomes with a specified confidence level.

- **Conformal Forecasting:** An extension of conformal prediction applied to time-series forecasting that constructs statistically valid prediction intervals around forecasts.
- **Calibration Set:** A holdout portion of data used to measure historical forecast errors, and determine the width of conformal prediction intervals.
- **Residual (Forecast Error):** The difference between the actual observed value and the predicted value produced by a forecasting model.
- **Marginal Coverage:** A statistical guarantee that the true future value will fall inside the prediction interval with a specified probability on average.
- **Horizon-wise Calibration:** A conformal strategy where prediction intervals are calibrated separately for each forecast horizon to account for varying uncertainty.
- **Error Propagation:** The phenomenon where prediction errors accumulate and amplify, as forecasts extend further into the future.
- **Sequential Data:** Data where observations are ordered in time, and each value may depend on previous observations.
- **Time-Series Dependency:** The property of time-series data where current values are influenced by the past values.
- **Rolling Calibration:** A calibration approach where the most recent forecast errors are continuously used to update conformal intervals as new data arrives.
- **Fixed Calibration Window:** A conformal approach where a fixed set of historical residuals is used to compute prediction interval widths.
- **Forecast Uncertainty Band:** The shaded region around a forecast that visualizes the prediction interval across time.
- **Distribution-Free Guarantee:** A key property of conformal prediction where valid coverage is achieved without assuming any specific probability distribution for the data.

References

1. A Gentle Introduction to Conformal Time Series Forecasting by M. Stocker et al.

CHAPTER 6
Scalable Conformal Prediction

Introduction

In the previous chapters, we focused on the statistical foundations of conformal prediction, and saw how it provides reliable uncertainty estimates using past model errors. The methods we discussed work well in controlled settings where datasets are manageable, predictions are made in batches, and the data distribution remains relatively stable. In such environments, computing residuals, calibrating error distributions, and generating prediction intervals is straightforward and computationally inexpensive. However, real-world machine learning systems rarely operate under such ideal conditions. Modern production systems generate millions of predictions every day, often in real time. Data arrives continuously, rather than in fixed batches, models are retrained frequently, and the underlying data distribution can change over time due to seasonality, user behavior, market conditions, or external events. In these environments, the challenge is no longer just how to construct valid prediction intervals, but how to maintain those guarantees, while operating under constraints such as limited computation time, memory usage, and system latency.

To address these challenges, *conformal prediction must be treated not just as a statistical method, but as a system design problem.* We need strategies for parallelizing residual computation, distributing calibration across multiple machines, maintaining rolling calibration windows for streaming data, and monitoring coverage in real time to detect when recalibration is necessary. *In other words, the problem shifts from "How do we compute conformal intervals?" to "How do we build systems that continuously produce conformal intervals reliably at scale?"*

By the end of this chapter, you will understand that scalable conformal prediction is not a new statistical method, but an engineering framework that allows the theoretical guarantees of conformal prediction to survive in real-world, large-scale machine learning systems.

Structure

In this chapter, we will cover the following topics:

- The Challenge of Scaling Conformal Prediction
- Parallel and Distributed Conformal Prediction
- Streaming Conformal Prediction

The Challenge of Scaling Conformal Prediction

In the earlier chapters, conformal prediction was presented as a post-processing layer on top of a machine learning model. After training the model, we computed nonconformity scores on a calibration dataset, selected a quantile from those scores, and used that quantile to construct prediction intervals or prediction sets. This workflow is simple and effective when working with static datasets and offline predictions. However, *when conformal prediction is deployed inside a real-world machine learning system, this workflow must operate continuously, rather than once. Predictions are generated repeatedly, new data keep arriving, models are retrained periodically, and uncertainty estimates must remain calibrated over time.* As a result, conformal prediction is no longer a one-time statistical procedure; it becomes a continuous system process.

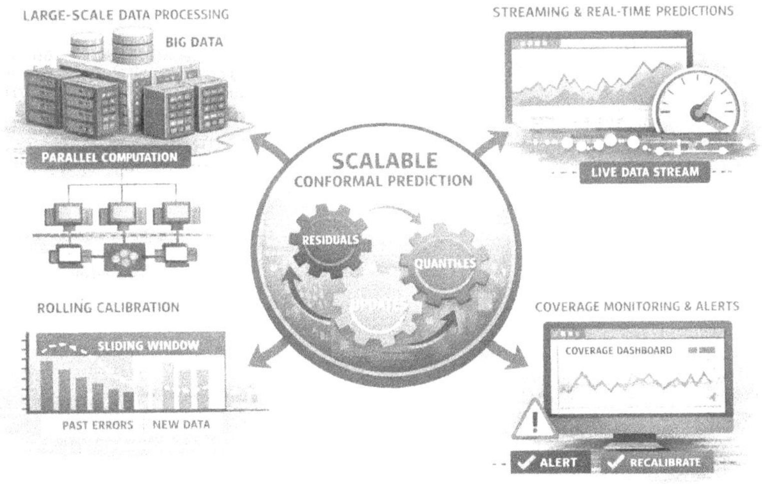

Figure 6.1: *Introduction*

To understand the scalability problem more clearly, it is useful to look at the conformal prediction pipeline from a systems perspective. In practice, a conformal prediction system typically involves the following steps:

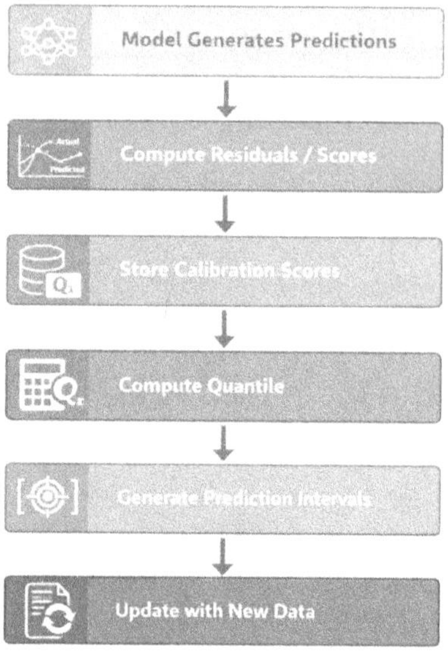

Figure 6.2: CP *Workflow*

When this pipeline runs on a small dataset, it is easy to manage. But at scale, each step introduces engineering challenges.

- The first bottleneck can appear in residual computation. In large systems, predictions may be generated for millions of observations per day, but the actual outcomes may arrive later. The system must therefore compute residuals asynchronously, and store them for calibration. This means conformal prediction requires a feedback loop where predictions and actual outcomes are matched later to compute errors. Designing and maintaining this feedback pipeline is one of the first practical challenges in scalable conformal prediction. This bottleneck is typically addressed by building asynchronous feedback pipelines that log predictions, and later join them with actual outcomes to compute residuals in batch or streaming systems.
- The next bottleneck can appear in storing calibration scores. In theory, conformal prediction assumes access to all past nonconformity scores. In practice, storing all historical residuals quickly becomes impractical due to memory constraints. For example, a system generating one million predictions per day would accumulate hundreds of millions of residuals in a year. Storing and querying such large calibration datasets efficiently requires database design decisions, sampling strategies, or rolling calibration windows. Scalable conformal systems address this by using rolling calibration windows, sampling strategies, or compressed data structures to limit how many residuals must be stored.
- Another problem can be during quantile computation. Conformal prediction relies on quantiles of the calibration scores, but computing quantiles over very

large datasets repeatedly can be computationally expensive. In distributed environments, residuals may be stored across multiple machines, and computing a global quantile requires aggregation across partitions. This introduces the need for approximate quantile algorithms or distributed aggregation methods. This is typically solved using approximate quantile algorithms and distributed quantile computation frameworks that avoid recomputing exact quantiles on the full dataset.

- Finally, latency constraints introduce another layer of complexity. In many applications, prediction intervals must be generated in real time. This means the conformal system cannot compute quantiles or residuals at prediction time. All heavy computations must be done offline, and the prediction service should only apply a precomputed quantile to generate intervals instantly. This is handled by separating offline calibration from online prediction, where precomputed quantiles are stored, and applied in real time with minimal computation.

These challenges show that scaling conformal prediction is not just about handling more data. It requires designing systems that can:

- Continuously collect model errors
- Efficiently store and update calibration data
- Compute quantiles on large or distributed datasets
- Recalibrate under changing data distributions
- Serve prediction intervals in real time

At this point, conformal prediction starts to look less like a statistical formula, and more like a data system with multiple moving components. *The problem shifts from "How do we compute conformal intervals?" to "How do we build a system that continuously computes and updates conformal intervals efficiently?"*

This system perspective will guide the rest of this chapter. In the next sections, we will see how parallel computing helps with residual computation, how distributed systems help with quantile estimation, how streaming methods help with recalibration, and how production monitoring ensures that coverage guarantees continue to hold over time.

Parallel and Distributed Conformal Prediction

In the previous section, we examined the main bottlenecks that arise when conformal prediction is deployed in large-scale systems. We saw that the challenges are not purely statistical, but computational and architectural. Residuals must be computed for massive datasets, calibration scores must be stored and updated efficiently, and quantiles must be estimated over potentially millions of non-conformity scores. When these operations are performed on small datasets, they are straightforward. When performed at scale, they require distributed computation.

This is where parallel and distributed computing become essential. **The key observation is that many steps in conformal prediction are naturally parallelizable.** *Residuals for different observations can be computed independently. Non-conformity scores can be calculated across multiple machines at the same time. Even quantile estimation can be performed using distributed aggregation methods.* By recognizing this structure, we can redesign conformal prediction pipelines so that they scale to large datasets and high-throughput systems.

In modern Machine Learning (ML) systems, data is rarely stored or processed on a single machine. Instead, data is distributed across clusters, and computations are performed using distributed frameworks such as **Spark [1], Dask [2], or cloud-based data processing systems.** To make conformal prediction work in such environments, we must rethink the calibration process in a distributed setting. Instead of computing residuals on a single calibration dataset, we compute residuals across partitions. Instead of storing calibration scores in a single file, we store them in distributed storage. Instead of computing exact quantiles on a single machine, we compute approximate or aggregated quantiles across the cluster.

From a systems perspective, scalable conformal prediction can be viewed as a distributed data processing pipeline with three main parallel components:

- Parallel prediction and residual computation
- Distributed storage of calibration scores
- Distributed or approximate quantile computation

Once these components are designed properly, conformal prediction can operate at the same scale as the underlying machine learning system, adding uncertainty estimates without becoming a computational bottleneck.

The goal of this section is to understand how conformal prediction can be parallelized and distributed in practice. We will see how residual computation can be parallelized across data partitions, how calibration scores can be aggregated across machines, and how quantiles can be computed efficiently in distributed environments. By the end of this section, conformal prediction should no longer look like a small statistical procedure, but like a scalable system that can run alongside large-scale machine learning pipelines.

When conformal prediction is deployed in real-world systems, as discussed, one of the biggest computational challenges is scale. Predictions may be generated for millions of observations per day, residuals must be computed once actual outcomes arrive, and calibration quantiles must be updated regularly. To make this feasible, conformal prediction pipelines are designed to run in parallel. However, parallelization in such systems is not done in just one way; it can happen at multiple levels depending on the structure of the data, the model architecture, and the latency requirements of the system.

This section explains the different levels at which parallelization is performed, how the appropriate level is chosen, and how the entire distributed pipeline is implemented in practice.

Levels of Parallelization

Parallelization in conformal prediction systems typically happens at three main levels of granularity: prediction-level parallelization, entity-level parallelization, and time-level parallelization (especially in forecasting systems). Each level corresponds to a different way of dividing the workload.

Prediction-Level Parallelization

This is the most common form of parallelization. Here, the dataset is divided into multiple batches, and each batch is processed independently by different worker machines.

Each worker (*think of it as an independent computation unit that performs a small chunk of the whole task*):

- Receives a batch of input data
- Generates predictions using the trained model
- Computes residuals once actuals arrive
- Stores residuals in a central calibration store

This approach works because prediction and residual computation for one observation do not depend on another observation in regression or classification problems. From a distributed systems perspective, this step behaves like a **map operation:**

Input → Model Prediction → Residual → Store Residual

This approach can be commonly used in different business scenarios:

- **Credit risk scoring:** A bank may generate credit risk scores for millions of customers every day. Each customer's risk score is independent of other customers, so that predictions and residuals can be computed in parallel across customer batches.

- **Fraud detection:** A payment system evaluates each transaction independently to determine whether it is fraudulent. Since each transaction is scored independently, predictions and residuals can be computed in parallel across transactions.

- **Recommendation systems:** Platforms such as e-commerce or streaming services generate recommendations for millions of users. Predictions for each user can be computed independently, allowing parallel computation across users.
- **Customer churn prediction:** Telecom and subscription companies predict whether each customer is likely to leave the service. Each customer's prediction is independent, so that predictions and residuals can be computed in parallel across customers.

In all these cases, each prediction can be computed independently, making prediction-level parallelization highly scalable.

Entity-Level Parallelization

In many business problems, predictions are made for independent entities such as:

- Products
- Stores
- Customers
- Warehouses
- Routes
- Regions

In such cases, the entire conformal pipeline (prediction → residual → calibration) can be parallelized across entities. For example:

- Each store can have its own demand model and residual distribution.
- Each product category can have its own calibration residuals.
- Each customer segment can have its own uncertainty distribution.

Here, residuals are independent **across entities**, even though they may not be independent **within an entity** (especially in forecasting). This allows the system to distribute computation across entities, instead of across individual rows.

This type of parallelization is commonly used in:

- **Retail demand forecasting (per SKU or per store):** Large retailers forecast demand for thousands of products across many stores. The demand pattern of each SKU-store combination is mostly independent, so that forecasts and residuals can be computed separately for each series using individual models. This allows conformal intervals to adapt to each product's variability, while computation runs in parallel across thousands of SKUs or stores.
- **Energy load forecasting (per region):** Electricity demand varies by region due to weather, population, and industrial activity. Forecasts and residuals are

therefore computed separately for each grid or region. Parallelizing across regions allows energy companies to forecast load and uncertainty for multiple regions at the same time.

- **Manufacturing yield prediction (per production line):** Each production line has different machines, operators, and conditions, leading to different error patterns and uncertainty levels. Yield predictions and residual calibration are done per production line. Since lines operate independently, computations can run in parallel across all production lines for real-time monitoring.

In the preceding scenarios, there is a common pattern where we run different models at a given granularity, and this gives us an opportunity to make computations faster by parallelizing them.

The level at which parallelization is applied can be chosen based on how the data can be divided into chunks so that the available compute resources (worker nodes) can be utilized as efficiently as possible.

Therefore, the goal of parallelization is not just to split the work, but to split the work into the **largest number of independent chunks that can fully utilize the available compute. If the number of chunks is too small, some worker nodes will remain idle. If the number of chunks is too large, the system may spend more time managing tasks than actually computing**. So the objective is to find the right level where the data can be divided into many independent chunks that keep all workers busy without creating excessive overhead, and keep each data point in each chunk such that it can be independently computed.

We can think of this as a simple relationship:

Efficient Parallelization = Largest number of independent chunks that can efficiently utilize the available compute resources.

Technical Implementation

Prediction and residual computation are typically **implemented using distributed batch processing systems.** The goal is to ensure that predictions and residuals are computed close to where the data is stored, rather than moving large volumes of data to a single machine for processing. In large-scale systems, data is often stored across multiple machines in distributed storage systems. If all this data had to be moved to one central machine to compute predictions and residuals, the time required to transfer the data would become a major bottleneck, often larger than the computation time itself. This problem is commonly referred to as data movement cost, and in large systems, moving data is often more expensive than computing on it.

To avoid this problem, modern distributed systems follow a different approach: instead of moving data to the model, the model is sent to the data. *Each machine processes the data stored locally, generates predictions, and computes residuals on that machine itself. Only the much smaller outputs – such as residuals or summary statistics – are then sent to a central system for aggregation and quantile computation.*

This approach significantly reduces network usage, improves computation speed, and allows the system to scale horizontally, which simply means that instead of making a single machine more powerful, we increase the number of machines, and process more data in parallel. As the dataset grows, more machines can be added to the system, and each machine handles a portion of the data. Because residual computation is performed locally on each machine, the system can handle very large datasets without a proportional increase in computation time.

From a system design perspective, this principle – *computing near the data and only moving small results – is one of the key ideas that makes scalable conformal prediction feasible in real-world machine learning systems*. The process typically works as follows:

- **Data Partitioning:** The dataset is first divided into multiple partitions or batches. In distributed storage systems such as data lakes or distributed databases, this partitioning often already exists. Data may be partitioned by date, region, customer segment, product category, or simply by row ranges. Each partition represents a subset of the full dataset.
- **Distributed Prediction:** The trained machine learning model is then deployed to worker nodes in the cluster. Instead of moving all data to a single machine, each worker loads the model and generates predictions for its local data partition. This step is often called batch inference or batch scoring.
- **Local Residual Computation:** Once predictions are generated and actual outcomes are available, each worker computes residuals or nonconformity scores locally within its partition. For regression problems, this may be the absolute error or squared error. For classification problems, this may be a probability-based non-conformity score.
- **Writing to Calibration Store:** The computed residuals are then written to a calibration store. This store may be:
    - A distributed file system
    - A database table
    - A data warehouse table
    - A streaming data store
- **Aggregation and Quantile Estimation:** A separate process reads residuals from the calibration store, and computes quantiles. This step may also be distributed, depending on the size of the calibration data. The following figure summarizes the full process of how the parallelization stream works to create scalable systems.

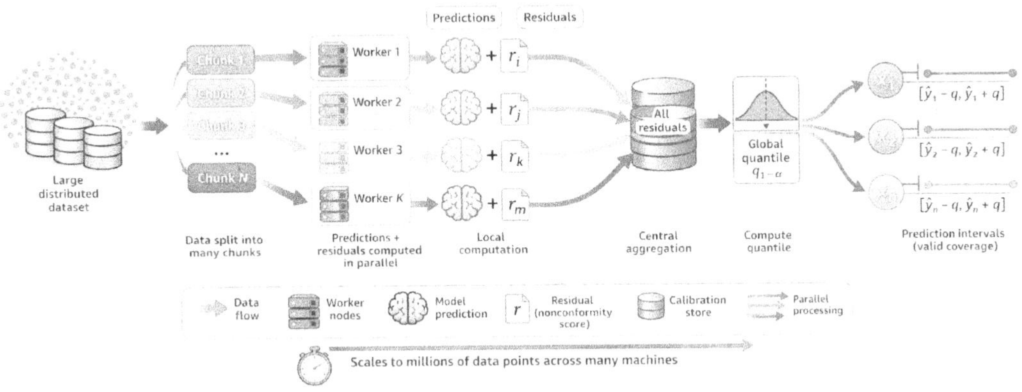

Figure 6.3: *Parallelization*

Streaming Conformal Prediction

In the earlier sections of this chapter, we examined why conformal prediction becomes difficult to implement in large-scale environments. The main computational challenge came from three places: residual computation, storing calibration scores, and computing quantiles repeatedly over large datasets. We then saw how parallelization helps address the first part of this problem. Residuals and nonconformity scores can be computed across multiple machines or across multiple entities such as products, users, or regions, allowing calibration data to be generated efficiently even when the dataset is very large. Parallelization, therefore, solves the problem of **how to compute calibration scores at scale**.

However, computing residuals at scale is only one part of the problem. Once residuals are computed, the conformal prediction system must still store calibration scores, compute quantiles, and ensure that the calibration distribution remains relevant as new data arrives. This is where the second scalability challenge appears. In many real-world systems, data does not arrive once in a large batch but continuously over time. Predictions are made every minute, every hour, or every day, and actual outcomes become available later. This means the calibration distribution must be continuously updated, rather than computed once and reused forever.

This is where streaming conformal prediction becomes important. While parallelization helps us compute residuals across large datasets, streaming conformal prediction helps us **update calibration efficiently over time**. Instead of recomputing calibration from scratch every time new data arrives, the system updates its calibration distribution incrementally by adding new residuals, and removing the old ones. In this way, parallelization and streaming solve two different parts of the scalability problem. **Parallelization allows us to handle large volumes of data, while streaming allows us to handle continuously the arriving data.**

When these two ideas are combined, conformal prediction becomes scalable in a practical sense. Residuals can be computed in parallel across distributed systems, and the calibration distribution can be updated incrementally using a sliding window. The quantile used for prediction intervals or prediction sets is therefore based on recent residuals computed at scale, rather than on a fixed dataset computed once in the past. This combination allows conformal prediction to operate in environments where both the **data volume is large** and the **data distribution changes over time**.

From a system design perspective, this means conformal prediction is implemented as a continuous pipeline. Residuals are computed in parallel wherever predictions and actual outcomes are processed. These residuals are then sent to a central calibration store that maintains a moving window of recent nonconformity scores. A quantile is computed from this calibration store and is used by the prediction service to generate intervals or prediction sets for new predictions. As new residuals arrive, the calibration store and quantile are updated, and future prediction intervals automatically adjust. The system, therefore, continuously learns from recent errors, while still being able to process large amounts of data through distributed computation.

This leads to an important way to think about scalable conformal prediction. Scalability is not achieved through a single technique, but through a combination of system design choices. Parallelization handles computation across large datasets, distributed storage handles large calibration data, and streaming calibration ensures that the uncertainty estimates remain valid as the environment changes. Together, these components transform conformal prediction from a static statistical procedure into a scalable system that can operate in real-world machine learning pipelines.

In other words, scalable conformal prediction is not just about computing quantiles faster. It is about designing a system where residual computation, calibration storage, and quantile estimation are all structured in a way that can handle large data volumes, distributed infrastructure, and continuously arriving data. Once implemented in this way, conformal prediction becomes a practical tool that can provide reliable uncertainty estimates even in large-scale, real-time machine learning systems.

The key step in a streaming conformal prediction system is generating predictions, and storing them so that residuals can be computed later. When a new input arrives, the machine learning model generates a prediction. The conformal layer immediately uses the current quantile to generate a prediction interval or prediction set. This step must be fast because it often runs in real time.

At the same time, the system stores the prediction in a prediction log, so that it can later be matched with the actual outcome. This prediction log typically stores the prediction value, timestamp, prediction ID, and sometimes, the model version. This storage step is important because, in many real-world systems, the actual outcome is observed later, and residuals cannot be computed unless predictions are stored and matched correctly.

Technically, this step is usually implemented using model serving systems and prediction logging infrastructure.

- Predictions are typically generated through **model serving APIs** or **batch scoring pipelines**. If the system requires real-time predictions, models are deployed as APIs using tools such as FastAPI, Flask, or cloud model serving platforms. APIs are used because they allow other applications to request predictions on demand with very low latency. This is common in systems such as fraud detection and recommendation systems, where predictions must be generated instantly. On the other hand, if predictions are generated in bulk, such as daily demand forecasts for thousands of products, batch scoring systems using Spark, Databricks, or scheduled pipelines are used instead of real-time APIs.
- At the same time, every prediction must be stored in a **prediction log** so that it can later be matched with the actual outcome. This prediction log is a critical component of streaming conformal prediction because it enables residual computation. The choice of storage depends on the scale and latency requirements of the system. For high-throughput systems where predictions are generated continuously, prediction logs are often written to streaming systems such as Kafka, which can handle large volumes of events and allow downstream systems to process predictions and actual outcomes asynchronously. For batch systems, prediction logs are usually stored in data lakes or warehouse tables such as S3, Azure Data Lake, Delta Lake, BigQuery, or Snowflake, because these systems are designed for large-scale storage and batch processing.

In the following figure, we see a summary of the streaming process workflow.

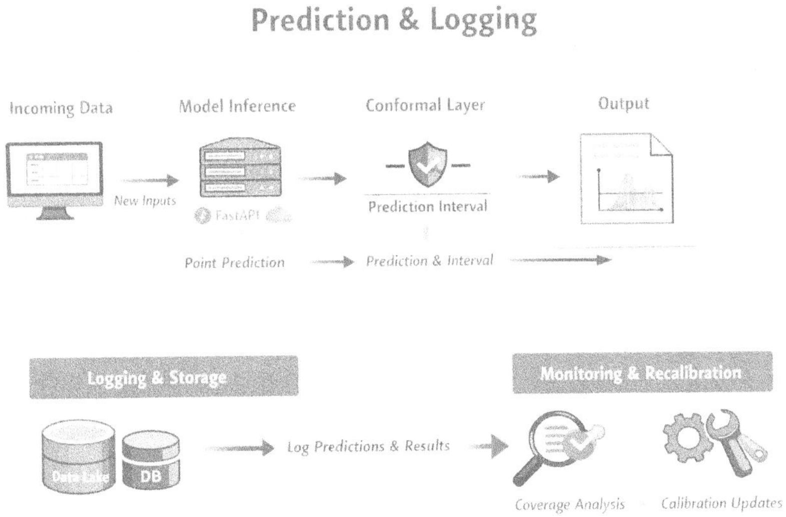

Figure 6.4: *Streaming CP*

The architectural idea here is important. Prediction generation is an **online process**, meaning it must be fast and responsive, while prediction logging is part of the **data pipeline**, meaning it must be reliable and scalable. The prediction service focuses on low latency, while the logging system focuses on durability, and the ability to join predictions with actual outcomes later. Separating these two concerns allows the system to scale, while still maintaining the feedback loop required for conformal calibration.

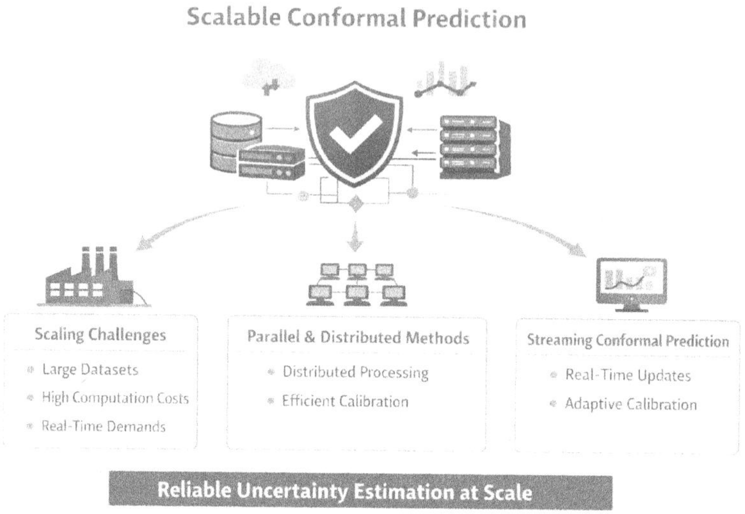

Figure 6.5: *Conclusion*

Conclusion

In this chapter, we explored how conformal prediction can be adapted to modern large-scale machine learning systems, where the volume of data, computational constraints, and real-time requirements introduce significant practical challenges. While conformal prediction provides strong statistical guarantees and reliable uncertainty estimates, applying it directly in such environments is not straightforward, as the calibration step requires storing and processing large numbers of non-conformity scores and repeatedly computing quantiles. This makes scalability not just an optimization problem, but a system design challenge. To address this, we examined how parallel and distributed conformal prediction allow residual computation, calibration, and aggregation to be spread across multiple machines, enabling the framework to integrate seamlessly with modern distributed data processing systems and cloud-based pipelines.

The key idea is that conformal prediction aligns naturally with distributed computation because non-conformity scores can often be computed independently and combined later without affecting validity. We then extended this idea to streaming conformal prediction, where calibration is no longer treated as a one-time step but as a continuous process. In such systems, predictions are generated in real time, residuals are computed as actual outcomes arrive, and calibration distributions are updated dynamically using the recent data. This allows prediction intervals and prediction sets to adapt to changing data patterns and maintain valid coverage even under distribution shifts. Together, these approaches show that conformal prediction can move beyond static, small-scale settings, and become a practical, scalable component of real-world machine learning systems, enabling models to not only make accurate predictions but also communicate reliable uncertainty at scale.

The main takeaway from this chapter is that conformal prediction is not limited to small datasets or offline experiments. With the right design, it can be scaled to distributed systems, large datasets, and real-time prediction environments, while still preserving its most important property such as: reliable uncertainty quantification with statistical guarantees. As machine learning systems continue to operate in increasingly large and dynamic environments, scalable conformal prediction becomes a critical tool for building systems that are not only accurate but also reliable and trustworthy at scale.

Points to Remember

- Conformal prediction provides valid uncertainty estimates, but naive implementations can become **computationally expensive when datasets are very large**, requiring scalable approaches to remain practical.
- The main computational bottleneck in conformal prediction is the calibration step, especially when prediction sets, or intervals, must be recomputed for large volumes of data.
- Parallel conformal prediction **distributes model training, calibration, and interval computation across multiple processors or machines**, significantly reducing the computation time, while maintaining validity guarantees.
- Distributed conformal prediction allows conformal methods to be applied in big data environments using distributed computing frameworks, where calibration scores can be computed across data partitions and aggregated.
- Streaming conformal prediction is designed for real-time or sequential data, where new observations arrive continuously, and uncertainty estimates must adapt over time, without retraining from scratch.
- In streaming settings, the **recent data is often more relevant than older data, so rolling calibration windows are used to maintain approximate exchangeability** and valid uncertainty estimates.
- There is always a **trade-off between computational efficiency and statistical efficiency:** using smaller calibration sets or distributed approximations improves speed but may slightly affect interval sharpness.

- Scalability techniques do not change the core idea of conformal prediction – they only change how calibration scores are computed and updated efficiently.
- The goal of scalable conformal prediction is to make reliable uncertainty estimation possible in real-world systems such as large-scale forecasting, online recommendation systems, fraud detection, and real-time monitoring.
- As machine learning systems move from research environments to production systems, scalable conformal prediction becomes essential for deploying uncertainty-aware models in practice.

Multiple Choice Questions

1. What is the main goal of scalable machine learning?
   a. To improve model accuracy
   b. To handle large datasets and high computation efficiently
   c. To reduce the number of features
   d. To avoid using the training data
2. Which of the following is a common challenge in scalable machine learning?
   a. Too little data
   b. Too many simple models
   c. Memory and computation limits
   d. Lack of algorithms
3. What is distributed computing in machine learning?
   a. Running a model on a single CPU
   b. Splitting computation across multiple machines
   c. Using only the GPU
   d. Using only cloud storage
4. Which framework is commonly used for large-scale distributed data processing?
   a. NumPy
   b. Pandas
   c. Apache Spark
   d. Matplotlib

5. What does data parallelism mean?
    a. Different models trained on the same data.
    b. Same model trained on different parts of the data.
    c. One model trained on one machine only.
    d. Training without splitting the data.
6. What best defines model parallelism?
    a. Splitting data across machines
    b. Splitting the model across multiple machines
    c. Training multiple models independently
    d. Using only one CPU
7. Why is batch processing used in scalable ML?
    a. To reduce model accuracy
    b. To process data in smaller, manageable chunks
    c. To avoid training
    d. To remove noise
8. What is online learning in scalable systems?
    a. Training model only once
    b. Training model without data
    c. Updating the model continuously as new data arrives
    d. Training model only on weekends
9. What is a major benefit of using cloud platforms for scalable ML?
    a. Unlimited local storage
    b. Manual model training
    c. On-demand compute resources
    d. No need for data
10. Which of the following helps in scaling conformal prediction?
    a. Using smaller datasets
    b. Using calibration on the full dataset repeatedly
    c. Using approximate or split conformal methods
    d. Avoiding calibration

11. Why is retraining expensive in large-scale systems?
    a. Models are too small.
    b. Data and computation are large.
    c. Features are less.
    d. Algorithms are simple.
12. What is a data pipeline in machine learning systems?
    a. A visualization tool
    b. A sequence of data processing steps
    c. A model evaluation metric
    d. A database
13. Which of the following is important for scalable ML systems in production?
    a. Only model accuracy
    b. Only model complexity
    c. Monitoring, retraining, and data pipelines
    d. Only the training data
14. What is the main idea behind scalable conformal prediction?
    a. Apply CP only on small datasets
    b. Avoid uncertainty estimation
    c. Make conformal prediction work efficiently on large datasets
    d. Use CP only for classification
15. What is the main challenge when applying conformal prediction in large-scale machine learning systems?
    a. Choosing the machine learning model
    b. Computing calibration scores on very large datasets
    c. Selecting input features
    d. Visualizing prediction intervals

Answers

1. b
2. c
3. b
4. c

5. b
6. b
7. b
8. c
9. c
10. c
11. c
12. b
13. b
14. c
15. b

Key Terms

- **Scalable Conformal Prediction:** An implementation of conformal prediction designed to work efficiently on large datasets, distributed systems, and real-time machine learning pipelines, while maintaining valid uncertainty guarantees.
- **Calibration Bottleneck:** The computational challenge in conformal prediction is caused by the need to compute, store, and process large numbers of non-conformity scores for calibration.
- **Parallel Conformal Prediction:** A scalable approach where residuals or nonconformity scores are computed across multiple machines, data partitions, or entities simultaneously to reduce the computation time.
- **Distributed Calibration:** A system design where calibration scores are stored and processed across distributed storage and computing systems, rather than on a single machine.
- **Prediction Log:** A storage system that records model predictions, timestamps, and identifiers, so that predictions can later be matched with actual outcomes to compute the residuals.
- **Sliding Calibration Window:** A calibration approach where only the most recent residuals are stored and used for quantile computation, allowing the system to adapt to the recent model performance.
- **Streaming Conformal Prediction:** A conformal prediction setup where calibration scores and quantiles are updated continuously as new data arrives, instead of being computed once on a fixed dataset.

- **Incremental Quantile Update:** A method for updating conformal quantiles as new residuals are added and old residuals are removed, without recomputing the quantile from scratch.
- **Prediction Service:** The component of a machine learning system that generates predictions, and applies conformal intervals or prediction sets in real time.
- **Calibration Service:** The component of the system responsible for computing residuals, maintaining calibration scores, and updating quantiles used by the prediction service.

References

1. Apache Software Foundation. *Apache Spark: Unified Analytics Engine for Large Scale Processing.*
2. Dask Development Team. Dask: *Parallel Computing with Python.*

CHAPTER 7

Real-World Applications of Conformal Prediction

Introduction

So far in this book, we have explored conformal prediction from multiple angles and across different machine learning settings. We began by identifying a fundamental limitation of traditional models: they produce point predictions without communicating uncertainty, creating a gap between prediction and confidence that can lead to risky decisions in real-world environments. We then built the foundation of conformal prediction as a model-agnostic framework that uses past errors to quantify uncertainty in a statistically valid way. These ideas were extended across regression, classification, and forecasting, where conformal prediction enabled prediction intervals, prediction sets, and time-evolving uncertainty estimates respectively. We also examined how conformal prediction can be scaled to large datasets and production systems, making it practical for real-world deployment. Throughout, real-world examples across domains such as demand forecasting, credit risk, healthcare, and manufacturing helped build intuition and highlight why uncertainty-aware predictions are more useful than point estimates alone.

In this final chapter, we shift our focus from methods to applications, moving from understanding how conformal prediction works to how it is used in practice. Instead of introducing new algorithms, we explore how prediction intervals and prediction sets influence real-world decision-making across domains. We will examine how organizations use conformal outputs to design decision rules, allocate resources, and manage risk in environments where uncertainty is unavoidable. The chapter covers applications in finance, retail and supply chain, healthcare, and manufacturing, each illustrated through intuitive case-study-style scenarios. The goal is to connect the theory developed throughout the book to practical systems, showing how conformal prediction becomes a tool not just for better predictions, but for better decisions under uncertainty.

Structure

In this chapter, we will cover the following topics:

- Applications of Conformal Prediction in Finance
- Applications of Conformal Prediction in Retail

Applications of Conformal Prediction in Finance

Finance is one of the most decision-sensitive industries when it comes to machine learning. Many financial decisions, such as approving a loan, setting a credit limit, pricing insurance, detecting fraud, or managing investment risk, are not just prediction problems. They are **risk management problems**. A wrong decision does not just reduce accuracy; it directly translates into financial loss, regulatory issues, or customer dissatisfaction.

Traditional machine learning models are already widely used in finance for tasks like credit scoring, default prediction, fraud detection, and risk modeling. However, most of these models still produce **point estimates or single probabilities**, and business decisions are made directly based on those numbers. The problem is that a single number does not tell us how reliable that prediction is. Two customers may both receive a default probability of 20%, but the model might be very confident about one prediction, and very uncertain about the other. From a risk perspective, these two cases should not be treated the same, but traditional ML systems treat them identically because they do not quantify uncertainty explicitly.

This is where conformal prediction changes the workflow. Instead of giving only a single probability of default, conformal prediction can provide a **prediction interval for risk** or a **prediction set for risk category**, which allows financial institutions to make **different decisions for confident cases and uncertain cases**. In practice, this leads to better risk management policies, such as approving low-risk applicants automatically, rejecting high-risk applicants, and sending uncertain cases for manual review.

Problem Setting - Loan Decision Engine

Imagine a lending company, **Company X**, that is planning to expand its loan business into new customer segments. **Traditionally, the company has been providing loans to customers with stable income, strong credit history, and well-documented financial records**. In this segment, the company has several years of historical data, and its credit risk models perform reasonably well. Encouraged by this success, the company now wants to grow its business by offering loans to a broader set of customers, including self-employed individuals, gig workers, and customers from regions where the company has not operated before.

However, expanding into new customer segments introduces new challenges. In the traditional segment, the model has seen many similar customers in the past, so that its predictions are relatively reliable. In the new segment, many applicants may have profiles that are different from the historical data. Some customers may have irregular income, limited credit history, or non-traditional financial profiles. In such cases, even if the model produces a probability of default, the reliability of that prediction may vary significantly from one applicant to another.

To manage loan approvals, Company X uses a machine learning model that predicts the **Probability of Default (PD)** for each applicant. Based on this predicted probability, the company follows a decision policy after multiple trials and errors. The following is what the decision system looks like.

Current Decision Policy
(Without Conformal Prediction)

Predicted Probability of Default	Decision
PD < 10%	✓ Approve
10% ≤ PD < 25%	Manual Review
PD ≥ 25%	× Reject

Figure 7.1: *Loan Decision Engine*

This policy allows the company to automate clear cases and send borderline cases to human credit officers. However, as the company expands into new segments, several practical problems begin to appear.

Where This Policy Fails: The Uncertainty Problem

At first glance, the decision policy looks reasonable. The model estimates the Probability of Default (PD), and based on that number, the system decides whether to approve, reject, or send the application for manual review. This approach assumes that the PD number is reliable and comparable across all applicants.

But in practice, this assumption often fails.

Imagine two loan applicants:

- Applicant A → Predicted PD = 8%
- Applicant B → Predicted PD = 8%

Under the current policy, both applicants will be automatically approved because their PD is below 10%. However, the model may not be equally confident about both predictions.

- Applicant A may belong to a customer segment the model has seen thousands of times (salaried employees with stable income, strong credit history).
- Applicant B may belong to a segment with very little historical data (self-employed, new to credit, irregular income).

Even though both have the same predicted PD, the **uncertainty around these predictions may be very different**. This leads to a hidden problem in the current system: **The decision policy is based only on the prediction, not on the uncertainty of the prediction**.

This creates several business risks:

- Some risky customers may be approved because the model was uncertain, but still produced a low PD.
- Some good customers may be rejected because the model was uncertain, and produced a high PD.
- Manual review may be triggered for cases where the model was actually very confident, wasting operational resources.
- The system treats all predictions as equally reliable, which is rarely true in real-world data.

This problem is not due to the model being bad; it is due to the system **not knowing when the model is unsure**. As discussed earlier in the book, machine learning models often produce precise-looking predictions even when uncertainty is high, which can lead to risky decisions if that uncertainty is ignored.

So the real problem is not just predicting PD. The real problem is:

**How confident are we in this PD prediction,
and should the decision depend on that confidence?**

This is exactly where conformal prediction changes the system, not by replacing the model, but by changing how decisions are made using the model's uncertainty.

Introducing Conformal Prediction into the Decision System

In the previous section, we identified a critical weakness in the existing decision system: decisions are being made using only the predicted Probability of Default (PD), without considering how reliable that prediction actually is. The model produces a number, and the system assumes that number is equally trustworthy for every applicant. But in reality, machine learning models are not equally confident across all predictions.

For some applicants, the model has seen many similar examples in the past, and can make stable predictions. For others, the model may be operating in unfamiliar regions of the data, where predictions are much more uncertain. The problem is that this uncertainty is invisible in a traditional machine learning setup, and as a result, the decision policy treats confident and uncertain predictions in exactly the same way.

This is where conformal prediction changes the system — not by changing the model, but by changing how we use the model's output. Conformal prediction sits on top of the existing model and uses the model's historical prediction errors to quantify how wrong the model has been in the past on similar data points. It then uses this historical error behavior to construct a range around the model's prediction, representing the set of values that are statistically consistent with the model's past performance. Instead of producing just a single PD value, the system now produces a prediction along with an uncertainty range. This range reflects how confident the system is about that particular prediction.

So instead of the system saying:

"The probability of default is 12%."

The system now says:

"The probability of default is 12%, but based on past model errors, the true risk is likely to lie between 6% and 22%."

This additional range completely changes how we interpret the prediction. The single number is no longer treated as a precise truth, but as the center of a range of plausible outcomes. Narrow ranges indicate that the model has historically been accurate for similar cases and the prediction is reliable. Wide ranges indicate that the model has historically made larger errors for similar cases, and the prediction is less reliable. In other words, the system now not only predicts risk, but also communicates how much that risk estimate can be trusted.

This allows the organization to move from a **prediction-based decision system** to a **risk-aware decision system**. Earlier, the decision policy depended only on the predicted PD. Now, the decision policy can depend on the entire interval of possible risk values. This is a much more realistic way to make decisions in finance, because financial decisions are always made under uncertainty, and what matters is not just the expected outcome, but also the worst-case and best-case scenarios.

The New Decision System (With Conformal Prediction)

This leads to a new decision framework where decisions are based not just on the predicted PD, but on the **conformal prediction interval**. The key idea is simple: instead of asking "*What is the predicted risk?*", the system now asks "*What is the range* *of possible risk, and what is the worst-case scenario within that range?"* This makes the decision process more aligned with how risk is managed in real financial systems.

Under this new system, decisions are made by comparing the conformal interval with the business risk thresholds. Rather than placing a customer into a decision category based on a single PD value, we look at where the entire interval lies relative to the approval and rejection thresholds.

The new decision logic works as follows:

- **Approve** → If the entire conformal interval lies below the approval threshold
- **Reject** → If the entire conformal interval lies above the rejection threshold
- **Manual Review** → If the conformal interval overlaps the middle or crosses thresholds

This system behaves very differently from the traditional system. Earlier, a customer with PD = 9% would always be approved. But now, if that 9% comes with a wide interval like [4%, 18%], the system recognizes that the true risk could actually be much higher, and the application may be sent for manual review instead of automatic approval. On the other hand, a customer with PD = 12% might previously have gone to manual review, but if the conformal interval is narrow like [11%, 13%], the system may decide that the risk is well understood, and make a faster decision.

So the new system is no longer making decisions based only on predicted risk – it is making decisions based on **certainty about the risk**.

This creates a much more structured automation strategy:

- Low risk and high confidence → Automate approval
- High risk and high confidence → Automate rejection
- Any case with high uncertainty → Send to manual review

This is a very important operational improvement because manual review is expensive and slow, so it should be used only where the model is uncertain – not simply where the prediction falls in a fixed PD band. Conformal prediction helps route only the **uncertain cases** to humans, while allowing confident cases to be automated safely.

From a business point of view, this new system achieves three things simultaneously:

- Reduces risky approvals
- Reduces unnecessary manual reviews
- Makes the decision system more transparent and risk-aware

This is why in many real-world applications, conformal prediction is not just a modeling improvement – it becomes a **decision system design tool**. The biggest value comes not from the interval itself, but from how that interval is used to redesign policies, automation rules, and risk management strategies. One practical way a company could arrive at this new system is by **analyzing historical loan decisions and model errors, and observing that most financial losses occurred in cases where the model was uncertain but the system still made fully automated decisions**. This insight naturally leads to a policy where automation is allowed only when the model is confident, and uncertain cases are handled differently with the defined bands for room of errors based on the losses (*For example, they may find that when the upper bound of predicted risk is below a certain level, defaults are extremely rare, and when the lower bound is above another level, defaults are very frequent, while the region in between contains mixed outcomes and higher uncertainty.*) The updated decision rule system can be defined as follows:

***Figure* 7.2:** *Updated Decision Engine*

Business Impact

In real-world business settings, the performance of a machine learning system is not measured only by model accuracy, but by its impact on revenue, losses, and operational costs. A prediction model may be statistically accurate, but if the decisions made using that model lead to higher defaults, lost customers, or inefficient use of resources, the overall business outcome may still be poor. Therefore, when evaluating decision systems, the correct comparison is not just between models, but between the **financial outcomes produced by different decision strategies**.

To understand the business value of uncertainty-aware decision systems, we need to compare how a traditional prediction-based decision system and an uncertainty-aware decision system perform in terms of approvals, defaults, operational costs, and overall profit. The key difference between these two systems is not necessarily in how well they predict risk, but in how they **act on that risk**. Traditional systems make decisions directly from predicted values, while uncertainty-aware systems make decisions based on the range of possible outcomes and the associated risk. This difference in decision strategy leads to different approval patterns, different default rates, different operational costs, and ultimately different revenue outcomes.

In the following comparison, we will evaluate both approaches from a business perspective by analyzing how many customers are approved, how many default, what costs are incurred during the decision process, and what the final profit looks like under each system under a simple scenario. Let us again consider a loan system processing **10,000 applications per month**:

- Profit per good loan = ₹10,000
- Loss per default = ₹50,000
- Manual review cost per case = ₹500

Traditional System (Point Prediction Based)

The traditional system uses a single probability threshold. The following is the split for those 10k applications:

- **Auto Approve:** 5,500
- **Auto Reject:** 3,500
- **Manual Review:** 1,000 (borderline cases based on score near threshold)

The manual team approves 600, and rejects 400.

The following were the Default rates observed for the approved cohorts:

- **Auto-approved default rate:** 4% → 220 defaults
- **Manual approved default rate:** 6% → 36 defaults

So:

- **Total approved:** 5,500 + 600 = 6,100
- **Total defaults:** 220 + 36 = 256
- **Good customers:** 5,844

The following is the profit calculation:

Profit from good customers = 5,844 × 10,000 = ₹5.844 Cr

Loss from defaults = 256 × 50,000 = ₹1.28 Cr

Manual review cost = 1,000 × 500 = ₹0.05 Cr

Net Profit = 5.844 – 1.28 – 0.05 = ₹4.514 Cr

Uncertainty-Aware System (Conformal Prediction Based)

Now the system uses prediction intervals to decide which cases go to manual review.

- **Auto Approve:** 5,000 (very safe cases)
- **Auto Reject:** 3,000 (very risky cases)

- **Manual Review:** 2,000 (uncertain cases)

The manual team approves 1,200, and rejects 800.

- **Auto-approved default rate**: 2% → 100 defaults (post-capturing uncertainty, we see improvement in default rate as expected at the cost of more manual review)
- **Manual approved default rate**: 6% → 72 defaults (assuming manual efficiency remains the same)

So:

- Total approved = 5,000 + 1,200 = 6,200
- Total defaults = 100 + 72 = 172
- Good customers = 6,028

Profit Calculation:

Profit from good customers = 6,028 × 10,000 = ₹6.028 Cr

Loss from defaults = 172 × 50,000 = ₹0.86 Cr

Manual review cost = 2,000 × 500 = ₹0.10 Cr

Net Profit = 6.028 – 0.86 – 0.10 = ₹5.068 Cr

The following is the overall summary of the two processes.

	Traditional System	Uncertainty-Aware System
Applications	10,000	10,000
Total Approved	6,100	6,200
Defaults	256	172
Good Customers	5,844	6,028
Manual Review Cost	₹0.05 Cr	₹0.10 Cr
Profit	₹4.51 Cr	₹5.068 Cr

***Figure* 7.3:** *Business Impact Comparison*

By introducing an uncertainty-aware decision system, we can clearly see that automated decision quality improves, even though it introduces some additional manual review effort. However, the key insight is that not all errors have the same cost. In lending, the cost of approving a bad loan is significantly higher than the cost of manually reviewing a borderline application. By identifying uncertain cases, and routing them for manual review, the system reduces costly defaults, while allowing confident approvals to remain automated. The result is a net financial gain for the business, even after accounting for the additional operational cost.

In this example, we used a simple decision rule based on prediction intervals – approve when the risk is clearly low, reject when the risk is clearly high, and send uncertain cases for manual review. In practice, this decision layer can be made more sophisticated. For example, the review threshold can be adjusted dynamically based on current default rates, economic conditions, or portfolio risk appetite. Different customer segments could have different uncertainty thresholds, high-value loans could require tighter confidence bounds, and low-value loans could be approved with wider intervals. The system could even incorporate optimization logic to minimize the expected cost rather than using fixed rules.

Applications of Conformal Prediction in Retail

Retail is one of the most operationally sensitive areas where machine learning forecasts directly drive business decisions. **Unlike many other domains, retail decisions such as how much inventory to order, how much safety stock to maintain, how to price products, and how to plan promotions are made every week or even every day**. These decisions are not just forecasting problems; they are inventory risk management problems. Ordering too much leads to wastage, storage costs, and heavy discounting, while ordering too little leads to stockouts, lost sales, and poor customer experience.

Traditional machine learning models are widely used in retail for **demand forecasting, price optimization, promotion planning, and replenishment planning.** However, most forecasting systems still produce a single number: the expected demand for next week or next month, and inventory decisions are made directly based on that number. The problem is that demand is inherently uncertain. Two products may both have a forecast of 1,000 units for next week, *but the model may be very confident about one forecast, and very uncertain about the other*. From an inventory planning perspective, these two situations should be handled differently, but traditional systems treat them the same because they do not quantify uncertainty explicitly.

This is where conformal prediction changes the workflow. Instead of providing just a single demand forecast, conformal prediction provides a prediction interval, a range within which the actual demand is likely to fall with a certain level of confidence. This allows retailers to make different inventory decisions for stable products versus uncertain products. *For example, products with very stable demand and narrow intervals can be replenished using automated ordering, while products with highly uncertain demand and wide intervals may require safety stock adjustments, manual planner intervention, or more conservative ordering strategies.*

In other words, conformal prediction allows retail companies to move from a forecast-based planning system to a risk-aware inventory planning system, where decisions are not based only on expected demand, but also on how uncertain that demand is.

Problem Setting: Retail Inventory Decision Engine

Imagine a large retail company, Company R, that sells thousands of products across multiple stores and online platforms. *Every week, the company must decide how much inventory to order for each product. If the company orders too much, unsold inventory leads to storage costs, heavy discounting, and wastage. If the company orders too little, products go out of stock, resulting in lost sales and poor customer experience.* So the core business problem is not just predicting demand: it is deciding how much inventory to order under uncertainty.

To solve this problem, Company R uses a machine learning forecasting model that predicts next week's demand for each product. Based on this forecast, the company follows a simple replenishment policy developed over time through operational experience.

The decision policy works roughly like this:

- If forecasted demand is very high → Increase stock to avoid stockouts
- If forecasted demand is very low → Reduce replenishment to avoid overstock

This decision is made using a demand forecasting model that predicts next week's demand for every **product–store combination**.

To make this discussion concrete, let us focus on one specific **product**. Suppose, the company is trying to decide weekly replenishment for a **volatile product** (for example, a snack item or seasonal item) at a **mid-sized store**, where weekly demand typically ranges between **400 and 1,600 units**, depending on promotions, weekends, and local demand fluctuations.

Based on historical sales for this product–store combination, the company has designed a simple data-driven replenishment rule that converts the forecast into an order quantity. For the said product x store combination, it looks something like this.

Inventory Decision Rules

Forecasted Weekly Demand	Order Decision
Forecast < 500 units	Order = 90% of Forecast
500 ≤ Forecast < 1500	Order = 100% of Forecast
Forecast ≥ 1500 units	Order = 110% of Forecast

Figure 7.4: *Replenishment Rule Engine*

Whenever we see a low expected demand with respect to historical patterns, we stock up less, and when we see a high future demand, we stock up more to avoid out-of-stock problems.

As seen in previous examples, this system originally looks like a logical way to go about replenishments. The model forecasts demand, and the replenishment system uses that forecast to decide how much to order. But this system assumes that the forecasted number is equally reliable for all products.

This assumption is where the real problem begins.

Consider two products:

- Product A → Forecasted demand = 1,000 units
- Product B → Forecasted demand = 1,000 units

Under the current system, both products will be replenished with similar quantities because the forecast is the same. However, the model may not be equally confident about both forecasts.

- Product A may be a **fast-moving staple product** with years of stable historical data. Demand is predictable, and the model has seen similar patterns many times.
- Product B may be a new product, a seasonal product, or a promotion-driven product where **demand fluctuates heavily and historical data is limited**. (our example product belongs to this category).

Even though both products have the same forecast, the uncertainty around these forecasts may be very different. But the current system treats both forecasts as equally reliable because it only uses the point forecast, and does not account for uncertainty.

This leads to several business problems:

- Some products are overstocked because the forecast was uncertain, but the system still ordered large quantities.
- Some products go out of stock because the forecast was uncertain, but the system trusted it too much.
- Manual planners spend time reviewing products where the forecast was actually very reliable.
- The system cannot distinguish between predictable products and unpredictable products.

So the real problem is not just forecasting demand. The real problem is:

**How confident are we in this demand forecast,
and should inventory decisions depend on that confidence?**

We can see the pattern here, while the domain changes, but the core problem fundamentally remains the same.

Uncertainty Aware System

In the previous subsection, we built a simple rule engine that converts a demand forecast into an order quantity. The system was straightforward, transparent, and easy to implement. Given a forecast, the system simply applied a rule: reduce orders when demand is low, order exactly the forecast in the mid-range, and increase orders when demand is high. This kind of rule-based replenishment system is actually very common in retail and supply chain planning because it is easy to operationalize, and easy for planners to understand.

The model predicts that demand next week will be 1,000 units, and the system blindly applies the rule associated with 1,000 units. But in reality, not all forecasts are equally reliable.

Consider two product-store combinations where the forecast for both is 1,000 units.

- For Product A, historical demand has been very stable: most weeks, demand falls between 950 and 1,050 units.
- For Product B, demand has been highly volatile: demand has ranged between 600 and 1,400 units in the recent weeks.

Even though the forecast is the same (1,000 units), the risk associated with the decision is completely different.

- For Product A, ordering 1,000 units is relatively safe.
- For Product B, ordering 1,000 units is risky — we may stock out if demand spikes to 1,400, or overstock if demand drops to 600.

But the traditional system treats both cases exactly the same because it only sees the point forecast. The uncertainty, the variability, the risk, and the possible range of outcomes are completely hidden behind that single number. This is the core problem with point forecasts: **they look precise, but they do not tell us how wrong they might be.**

This is where uncertainty-aware forecasting using Conformal Prediction changes the decision process, not by replacing the forecast, but by adding a reliable range around it. Instead of predicting only demand, we now predict an interval through the techniques, we studied in earlier chapters:

Demand Interval = [Lower Bound, Upper Bound]

This interval represents a realistic range in which demand is expected to fall, based on the model's historical errors on similar data. If the model has been very accurate in the past, this interval will be narrow. If the model has struggled, and made large errors, the interval will be wider. In other words, the interval automatically adjusts to how uncertain the model is for that particular product-store combination.

So now, instead of making decisions using only the forecast, the decision engine uses the interval.

This changes the nature of the decision:

- The **forecast** tells us the most likely demand.
- The **lower bound** tells us a realistic worst-case (low demand scenario).
- The **upper bound** tells us a realistic best-case (high demand scenario).

So the decision is no longer based on a single guess, but on a **range of plausible outcomes**. And this is a much more natural way to make business decisions, because in real life, planners are always thinking in terms of best case, worst case, and most likely case. Conformal Prediction simply makes the model think the same way.

The important thing to notice here is that we did not change the forecasting model, we did not redesign the supply chain system, and we did not introduce a complicated optimization algorithm. We simply added one extra piece of information: **how uncertain the forecast is.**

And that small change is enough to build a much smarter decision system. Hence, here is how the updated system looks like:

Updated Inventory Decision Rules

Demand Interval (CP)	Order Decision
Upper Bound < 500	Order = 90% of Forecast
500 ≤ Interval ≤ 1500	Order = Forecast
Lower Bound ≥ 1500	Order = 110% of Forecast

***Figure* 7.5:** *Updated Replenishment Rule Engine*

The updated rule system changes **what the decision is based on**. Earlier, the system made decisions using only a single forecast value. Now, the system makes decisions using the **prediction interval** — specifically, the lower bound and upper bound of demand. This small change makes the system uncertainty-aware, without making it complicated.

In the updated rule engine, the decision logic becomes more realistic:

- If the **upper bound is still low (< 500)** → demand is very likely low → order conservatively (90% of the forecast).
- If the **lower bound itself is high (≥ 1500)** → demand is very likely high → increase order (110% of the forecast).

This is powerful because the system is no longer reacting to just the forecast number, but to the **risk around the forecast**. Two products may both have a forecast of 1,000 units, but if one has an interval [950, 1050] and another has [400, 1600], the decisions should not be the same, and now they will not be. The system only orders high inventory when it is sure about the high demand, and vice versa.

Business Impact

To understand the business impact of uncertainty-aware decision-making, let us put some numbers to make things clear. Let us assume we are selling a product with a selling price of ₹500 and a cost price of ₹300. For simplicity, **we assume a contribution profit of ₹200 per unit sold.** This is not the final company profit, but the profit contribution per unit after covering the product cost. This is the number that matters when making inventory decisions, because each additional unit sold contributes this much toward the overall profit.

However, inventory decisions are not just about profit; they are about **risk**. If we order too much and the product does not sell, we do not lose the full ₹300 cost *because unsold inventory is usually discounted, and sold later through promotions, bundles, and so on*. Suppose, we are able to recover ₹220 from unsold inventory. That means the loss per unsold unit is **₹300 – ₹220 = ₹80**.

On the other hand, if we order too little, and the demand is higher than expected, we lose the opportunity to sell the product. In this case, we lose the full profit we could have made, **which is ₹200 per unit.**

Let us summarize all of these associated costs together:

- **Overstock cost: ₹80**
- **Stockout losses: ₹200**

This tells us something very important: **stockouts are much more expensive than overstock**. This is true for many retail businesses because losing a sale also means losing customer trust, potential repeat purchases, and market share.

Now, let us evaluate both the systems over a period of **100 weeks** (roughly 2 years of weekly ordering decisions for a product-store combination). The following is a dummy example of how the numbers can look.

Operational Outcomes Over 100 Weeks

Metric	Traditional System	Uncertainty-Aware System
Units Sold	90,000	94,000
Overstock Units	12,000	8,000
Stockout Units	10,000	6,000

Figure 7.6: Comparison Analysis

In an ideal scenario, after introducing the uncertainty-aware system, *we would expect both stockouts and overstock situations to reduce*. This happens because the system no longer reacts to a single forecast number, but instead, adjusts decisions based on how uncertain the demand is. When the interval indicates that demand could be higher than the forecast, the system orders slightly more, reducing stockouts. When the interval indicates that demand could be lower, the system orders more conservatively, reducing overstock. In other words, inventory decisions become more aligned with the actual demand behavior, rather than a single estimate.

This is the key reason behind the numbers observed in the table. The uncertainty-aware system does not necessarily increase inventory overall; instead, it reallocates inventory more intelligently across weeks. Some weeks we stock a little more to avoid lost sales, and some weeks we stock a little less to avoid excess inventory. **Over time, this balancing effect leads to fewer missed sales, fewer unsold units, and higher overall units sold.** The improvement does not come from predicting demand perfectly, but from making better decisions under uncertainty, which is exactly what conformal prediction enables.

Note: One *small trade-off of the uncertainty-aware system is that more decisions start falling into the middle bucket. In the traditional system, decisions are made using a single forecast number, so the system tends to make more extreme decisions, either ordering much less or much more, depending on which side of the threshold the forecast falls. However, once we introduce uncertainty intervals, some forecasts that looked clearly low or high now appear uncertain because their intervals overlap with the middle range. As a result, the system chooses the middle rule more often, instead of making aggressive high or low inventory decisions. While this may make the system appear less decisive, this can actually be a beneficial behavior: the system is avoiding extreme decisions when uncertainty is high, which reduces the chances of large overstock or large stockouts, leading to more stable and profitable outcomes over time.*

The following is how the overall monetary impact looks.

Component	Formula	Traditional	Uncertainty-Aware
Profit from Sales	Sold × ₹200	90,000 × 200 = **₹1.80 Cr**	94,000 × 200 = **₹1.88 Cr**
Loss from Overstock	*Overstock × ₹80*	12,000 × 80 = **₹0.096 Cr**	8,000 × 80 = **₹0.064 Cr**
Loss from Stockouts	*Stockout × ₹200*	10,000 × 200 = **₹0.20 Cr**	6,000 × 200 = **₹0.12 Cr**
Net Profit		**₹1.504 Cr**	**₹1.696 Cr**

***Figure* 7.7:** *Revenue Impact*

When we compare the traditional forecast-only system with the uncertainty-aware decision system, we observe a meaningful improvement in the overall profitability. In our simulated business scenario, **the uncertainty-aware system resulted in**

approximately 12% higher net profit. This improvement does not come from increasing prices or reducing costs, but purely from making better inventory decisions. By using demand intervals instead of single forecasts, the system was able to reduce both overstock and stockout situations. Overstock reduces because we avoid over-ordering when demand is uncertain, and stockouts reduce because we increase inventory when the demand range indicates potential upside. In other words, the system does not try to predict demand more accurately — it tries to make better decisions given uncertainty. This is a very important distinction. The goal of uncertainty-aware systems is not just better predictions, but better decisions. Even if two models have the same average forecast accuracy, the one that understands uncertainty will almost always make more profitable decisions because it manages risk more intelligently. This is the true business value of conformal prediction — it transforms machine learning from a prediction tool into a decision-support system.

This example is a simplified simulation designed to build intuition. Real-world business outcomes depend on many additional factors such as pricing, supply constraints, lead times, and market conditions. The purpose here is not to estimate exact profit, but to demonstrate how uncertainty-aware decision systems can reduce overstock and stockouts, leading to better business outcomes.

Conclusion

In this chapter, we moved from prediction to decision-making and saw an important shift in how machine learning systems should be used in real-world environments. Through the case studies discussed in this chapter, we further reinforce the key takeaway that we have been talking about throughout this book such as: conformal prediction does not replace machine learning models; it enhances them by adding a reliable measure of uncertainty. This additional layer of information allows decision systems to behave differently when the model is confident versus when the model is uncertain. This is something traditional machine learning systems are not designed to do.

Across the case studies, we observed a common pattern. When decisions were made using only point predictions, the system treated all predictions equally, regardless of how uncertain the model was. **This often led to extreme outcomes such as over-allocation, under-allocation, missed opportunities, or unnecessary risk.** However, once conformal prediction intervals or prediction sets were introduced, the system became uncertainty-aware. Instead of making a single rigid decision, the system could adjust its actions based on the level of uncertainty, becoming more conservative in uncertain situations and more aggressive when the model was confident. This led to more stable operations, better resource utilization, and improved overall outcomes.

Another important observation from this chapter is that the value of conformal prediction comes not from improving the model's accuracy, but from **improving**

the decision-making process built on top of the model. This is a very important distinction. In many real-world systems, the biggest losses do not come from small prediction errors, but from bad decisions made with overconfident predictions. Conformal prediction addresses this problem by making the uncertainty visible and measurable, allowing systems to manage risk more intelligently.

In summary, this chapter demonstrated that conformal prediction is not just a theoretical framework, but a practical tool for building safer and more reliable machine learning systems. Its real-world value lies in transforming machine learning from a **prediction engine into a decision-support system**, one that understands not only what might happen, but also how uncertain that prediction is, and adjusts decisions accordingly.

Points to Remember

- Conformal Prediction does not replace machine learning models — it wraps around them to quantify uncertainty.
- Point predictions are not enough for decision-making; decisions require understanding risk and uncertainty.
- Prediction intervals and prediction sets convert model outputs into decision-ready information.
- The biggest benefit of conformal prediction appears in uncertain or borderline cases.
- In automated decision systems, uncertainty can be used to decide whether to automate, review, or delay a decision.
- The true value of conformal prediction is not just better predictions, but better decisions.

Multiple Choice Questions

1. What is the main purpose of conformal prediction in real-world systems?
    a. To improve model training speed
    b. To replace machine learning models
    c. To quantify uncertainty in predictions
    d. To reduce data collection requirements
2. Why can point predictions be risky in business decision systems?
    a. Because they are always inaccurate
    b. Because they hide the uncertainty behind the prediction

   c. Because they require large datasets
   d. Because they cannot be automated

3. The prediction interval represents the following in conformal prediction:
   a. The exact value the model will predict.
   b. The range where the true value is expected to lie with a certain confidence.
   c. The range of training data.
   d. The model's loss function.

4. How does uncertainty-aware decision-making improve business outcomes?
   a. By increasing model complexity
   b. By reducing both overstock and stockout decisions
   c. By eliminating demand variability
   d. By making predictions deterministic

5. In an uncertainty-aware system, what should happen when uncertainty is very high?
   a. Automatically take the decision
   b. Ignore the prediction
   c. Defer the decision or send for human review
   d. Reduce the dataset size

6. What is the main advantage of conformal prediction compared to model probability scores?
   a. It makes models faster.
   b. It provides statistically valid uncertainty estimates.
   c. It reduces the need for training data.
   d. It removes model errors.

7. How does conformal prediction help in automated decision systems?
   a. By removing uncertainty
   b. By converting predictions into decision rules based on uncertainty
   c. By replacing business rules
   d. By eliminating the need for human intervention

8. In classification problems, conformal prediction outputs:
    a. A single class label.
    b. A prediction set of possible labels.
    c. Only probabilities.
    d. Only errors.
9. In LLM-based systems, conformal prediction can be used to:
    a. Make the model generate longer text
    b. Measure the reliability of generated answers
    c. Train the language model faster
    d. Replace the language model
10. The biggest impact of conformal prediction in real-world systems is:
    a. Better hardware utilization
    b. Better user interface design
    c. Better decision-making under uncertainty
    d. Faster model training

Answers

1. c
2. b
3. b
4. b
5. c
6. b
7. b
8. b
9. b
10. c

Key Terms

- **Uncertainty-Aware System:** A decision system that uses both predictions and their uncertainty to make better decisions.

- **Overstock:** A situation where more inventory is ordered than actual demand, leading to holding or wastage costs.
- **Stockout:** A situation where demand exceeds the available inventory, leading to lost sales and revenue.
- **Decision Rule Engine:** A system that converts model predictions (and uncertainty) into business actions such as order quantity, approve/reject, or review.
- **Model-Agnostic:** A method that can be applied on top of any machine learning model without changing the model itself.
- **Uncertainty-Aware Automation:** A system design where decisions are automated only when the model is confident, and deferred when uncertainty is high.
- **Reliability Layer:** A layer added on top of machine learning models (like conformal prediction) that measures and communicates uncertainty before decisions are made.

Index

www.ingramcontent.com/pod-product-compliance
Lightning Source LLC
LaVergne TN
LVHW060449061126
851857LV00016B/1773
* 9 7 8 8 1 6 9 6 4 6 4 1 3 *